A Million Little
Bricks

A Million Little
Bricks

THE UNOFFICIAL ILLUSTRATED HISTORY OF THE **LEGO** PHENOMENON

Sarah Herman

SKYHORSE PUBLISHING

First published under the title *Building a History* in Great Britain in 2012
by Remember When, an imprint of Pen & Sword Books Ltd

Skyhorse Publishing books may be purchased in bulk at special discounts
for sales promotion, corporate gifts, fund-raising, or educational purposes. Special editions can also be created to specifications. For details, contact the Special Sales Department, Skyhorse Publishing, 307 West 36th Street, 11th Floor, New York, NY 10018 or info@skyhorsepublishing.com.

Skyhorse® and Skyhorse Publishing® are registered trademarks
of Skyhorse Publishing, Inc.®, a Delaware corporation.

Visit our website at www.skyhorsepublishing.com.

10 9 8 7 6 5 4 3 2 1

Library of Congress Cataloging-in-Publication Data
Herman, Sarah.
 A million little bricks : the unofficial illustrated history of the LEGO phenomenon / Sarah Herman.
     p. cm.
 Includes bibliographical references and index.
 ISBN 978-1-62087-054-9 (hardcover : alk. paper)
 1. LEGO koncernen (Denmark) 2. Toy industry--Denmark. 3. Toy industry--United States. 4. LEGO toys. I. Title.
 HD9993.T694L444 2012
 338.7'68872--dc23
                            2012018220
 Printed in China

For Ian—because you love me enough to let me build your Unitron Monorail (set 6991).

Contents

Acknowledgments

While writing a book often feels like a solo voyage, there are many people who have helped me along on my LEGO adventure. Thank you to Jens Nygaard Knudsen, Nathan Sawaya, Kenneth Brown, and Joe Meno for sharing your thoughts; Wayne Hussey and everyone at BrickCon 2009 for making me feel so welcome; Troels Witter for helping me out and speaking Danish; Jordan "Sir Nadroj" Schwartz for the building tips and general all-around awesomeness; Dad (OBE)—your nautical wisdom knows no bounds; Fiona Shoop for your initial guidance and ideas; Doctor Lee Jones for the LEGO gifts and being a true gentleman; Alex Eylar for all the amazing MOCs you built for the cover—shame we couldn't use them all; Isabel Atherton for being the loveliest agent *ever*; and all my wonderful friends and family who put up with me droning on about LEGO stuff.

NOTE FROM THE AUTHOR

In this book, LEGO sets are usually referred to by name and set number. The set number often follows the name of the set, or a reference to it, in parentheses. As sets sold in different parts of the world sometimes have completely different names, I have endeavored, where possible, to include the set number to avoid any confusion and to make clear which sets are being referred to. Predominantly names featured in U.K. catalog are used for more recent LEGO sets, but some U.S. names also appear. The main references used to clarify set names and numbers were *LEGO Collector: Collector's Guide* (Fantasia Verlag GmbH, 2008), and the websites www.brickset.com, www.peeron.com, and www.worldbricks.com.

In the Beginning...

A company made a brick and the rest, as they say, is history. But this company didn't just make any brick—it made one that went on to define play time for generations of children around the world. A brick that over sixty years later still inspires and enthralls children of all ages to create, to build, and to play; a brick that still goes missing under the sofa, probably ends up in the vacuum cleaner, and definitely hurts to accidentally step on as much as it ever did. A commonly cited fact is that there are sixty-two LEGO bricks for every human living on Earth. This

Life, replicating toys, replicating life: A LEGO minifigure gets to work shipping out the latest LEGO sets in 2010's City Truck (3221). © Ruben Saldana

unfathomable number exists because every hour of every day of the year for over fifty years, the LEGO Group has been churning them out, along with plastic people, monkeys, windows, palm trees, horses, swords, and just about every other conceivable thing you could imagine in miniature. Possibly more shocking, however, is that you can take a LEGO brick built in 1958 and snap it together with a brick from 2012 as if more than fifty years had never happened.

But they did happen, of course. In fact, the LEGO Group's history started long before January 28, 1958, when the famous LEGO brick was patented.

The privately owned company may now sell its products in 130 countries, but toy manufacturing was never what LEGO Group founder Ole Kirk Christiansen intended to spend his life doing. This generational family company has progressed from carpentry workshop and wooden toy maker to plastic pioneer and household name with many highs and some lows in between.

The development of a play system based around LEGO bricks in the late 1950s, which was unrivaled by other toy makers at the time, led to rapid expansion and a growing collection of sets and parts. Over the next twenty years, ideas were developed and pushed, with new systems for advanced building, the infant market, and moving sets with wheels, gears, and motors. By the 1980s the minifigure had populated this LEGO world and new, exciting play themes began to emerge. As the toys pushed boundaries, so did the LEGO Group, opening theme parks and developing a recognizable brand through various avenues including video games, stores, clothing, and the LEGO website. As the century progressed, the company continued to challenge itself with the development of robotics, story-based themes, and licensed toys. But with management spread thin, the LEGO Group faced serious financial problems and the future of LEGO bricks hung in the balance.

But just as LEGO toys are suitable for children, so is this story—it does have a happy ending. According to the LEGO Group, children spend five billion hours a year playing with LEGO bricks, and those little studded building blocks that continue to sell year after year were the key to the biggest comeback in recent toy-making history. The company fought its way out of financial ruin to become a more profitable producer of better toys, focusing on the development of diverse and delightful play themes made from LEGO bricks. Gone are the superfluous products created in uncertain times and the unusual licensing decisions. In their place are toys kids want, no, *need* to have, supported by digital and online media they love to explore.

But the LEGO world is bigger than its design and manufacturing processes, the LEGOLAND parks, building systems, play themes, and all its success and (few) failures, all of which are explored here. The LEGO world is made up of millions of fans, most young, many not, who see LEGO bricks as more than a toy; as an artistic medium, a way to learn, or a window to an entire subculture of like-minded individuals who attend LEGO conventions, enter building competitions, and spend their spare time playing with bricks and accessing the online fan community. And this part of the company's history is explored here, too.

As the LEGO Group has passed from one generation to the next, so have its toys. Plastic boxes filled with bricks stored away for years are dug out for children, grand-children, nieces, and nephews or for oneself—as if instinctively we know never to throw them away. And why would we? The quality of LEGO toys is clear; any child no matter his age or abilities can enjoy them, and they're as relevant today as ever—no matter what crazes kids are into, the LEGO brick never goes out of fashion.

LEGO Certified Professional and artist Nathan Sawaya summed up the classic toy's charm when he said, "Playing with LEGO toys growing up let me build anything I wanted to build. It let my imagination control the playtime. If I wanted to be a rock star that day, I could build myself a guitar. If I wanted to be an astronaut, I could build myself a rocket. . . . It was Christmas 1978 when I received my first box of LEGO bricks from my grandparents. I remember ripping into the package and building a LEGO house right then, oblivious to the rest of Christmas morning. It seems like I have been creating with LEGO ever since that day."

A company made a brick. And the rest, as they say, is history. But it wasn't just any company. It was the LEGO Group.

A Million Little
Bricks

CHAPTER 1

1891–1953: Bricks and Mortar

odtfred Kirk Christiansen (1920–1995) may have been the person to develop and patent the famous LEGO brick design in 1958, but the LEGO story began with a different man some years before he was born. A few miles outside of Billund, Denmark—a town famous for its connection to the LEGO name and the original LEGOLAND theme park—in the Grene Church cemetery, is the final resting place of Ole Kirk Christiansen, Godtfred's father and the father of the LEGO Group.

Ole Kirk (OKC) was born into poverty in the farming community of Filskov, near Billund, in 1891 and went on to work as a carpenter, honing the skills which would lead to the creation of wooden toys and, later, plastic building blocks. These intersecting bricks would inspire the development of a system of play synonymous with the LEGO name and the most popular toy of the last 100 years, according to a 2004 survey carried out by the V&A Museum of Childhood.

When the young Danish carpenter opened his wood-working shop in Billund in 1916, a year before the town received electricity, he never expected to make his fortune in the toy business. It's also likely that he never imagined Billund, once a town described in Henry Wiencek's book *The World of LEGO Toys* as a backwater home to only a few hundred people, becoming one of Denmark's most visited destinations. Today, Billund is home to over 6,000 people, as well as LEGO headquarters, LEGOLAND Billund, and the country's second busiest airport, which was built by the LEGO Group in 1964.

OLE KIRK CHRISTIANSEN (1891–1958)

From the age of six, Ole Kirk worked as a farmhand tending to the family's sheep while also attending school for two days each week to learn to read and while. While out in the fields, the young boy would whittle wood, and so began his love for shaping and creating objects. In 1905, when he was fourteen years old, he became an apprentice carpenter to one of his older brothers, Kristian Bonde Christiansen. After his training was complete, he practiced his trade working in Germany and Norway between 1911 and 1916. It was in Norway that he met Kirstine Sörensen, who became his wife after he returned to central Jutland in 1916. The twenty-five-year-old carpenter used his savings from working abroad to buy the local woodworking shop and set up his own carpentry business in Billund. He had four sons with Kirstine—Johannes, Karl Georg, Godtfred, and Gerhardt—before she died in 1932. Two years later he married Sofie Jörgensen, with whom he had one daughter, Ulla. Ole Kirk instilled a solid work ethic in his sons, all of whom were involved in the company from young ages, and focused on the importance of manufacturing high-quality products and harvesting a good reputation over making a quick profit. Arguably, without the foundation of Ole Kirk's teachings, which have passed on down the generations, the LEGO brand would not be the international success story it is.

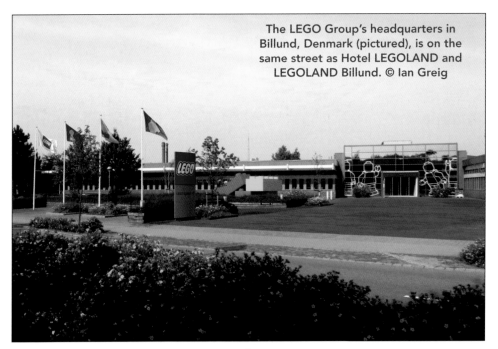

The LEGO Group's headquarters in Billund, Denmark (pictured), is on the same street as Hotel LEGOLAND and LEGOLAND Billund. © Ian Greig

Throughout the late 1920s, Ole Kirk's growing business restored old buildings, developed new structures, and created goods such as ladders and ironing boards for his small community—mainly local farmers and their families. By the end of the decade he no longer worked alone but employed a small workforce. But this new business venture was not without its setbacks. And Ole Kirk demonstrated unshakeable strength of character when, in 1924, two of his sons (Godtfred and Karl Georg) accidentally set light to wood shavings in the workshop, which quickly resulted in the whole premises and the family home being destroyed by fire. This tragic accident was looked at as a reason to expand the business, and Ole Kirk had the plans drawn up for a large building that would house his new workshop and a small flat for his family. The rest of the building's space would be rented out to provide an additional income.

By the 1930s the Great Depression had begun to affect farming prices in Europe (dropping in some areas by 60 percent), meaning Ole Kirk's customers could no longer afford his services or products. In early 1931 Ole Kirk was forced to lay off some employees, reducing his workforce to just seven people by 1932. The business in decline, this was the year Ole Kirk started making affordable wooden toys—brightly colored animals, piggy banks, and racing cars he hoped to sell to the farming families in the area. But by the end of 1932 he faced bankruptcy and turned to his siblings for help. They loaned him money but asked that he stop producing toys, something they saw as unprofitable. Ole Kirk continued, however, and in 1934 named the company LEGO, a contraction of the Danish phrase *leg godt*, meaning "play well."

Despite being famed for producing the plastic LEGO brick and the LEGO System, Ole Kirk's company started out producing toys out of wood. Some reports indicate that it was the production of scaled models (for his other carpentry projects) that got him thinking about making toys, while others claim the idea was suggested to him by a social worker. Either way, soon enough, miniature vehicles—cars, trains, planes, and buses—began to appear among the ironing boards, step-ladders, and wooden stools. These simple-looking toys may seem bulky and plain, especially by today's standards, but they were built with the same level of skill and craftsmanship that Ole Kirk had been putting into his furniture and carpentry for years. Believing that "only the best was good enough" (the company motto), even for a child's toy, Ole Kirk's toy manufacturing process was as meticulous as all his other work, if not more so. The birchwood used to build the toys was cut from the forest, dried outside for two years, and then dried in a kiln for three weeks before it was considered suitable for the workshop. After the toys were assembled, they were sealed, sanded, primed, and finally painted three times over to produce a top-quality finish. Once, when Ole Kirk's son Godtfred skipped a layer of painting to save money, his father ordered him to return the shipment and repaint all the toys himself, reminding his son of the importance of product quality over profiteering.

Known locally as "The Lion House" because of the two statues guarding the door, Ole Kirk's new home and workshop, built in 1924, still stands in Billund today and forms part of the LEGO Museum. © Ian Greig

A price list from 1932 shows twenty-eight different toys listed, including a six-wheeled school bus, a tramcar, and a lorry. It also shows that Ole Kirk continued to manufacture practical furniture and household items alongside the colorful new additions to his product line—not that the people of Billund could really afford either. While his first toy range enjoyed some success, the families in the area were poor, and would sometimes exchange food for toys rather than money. In 1932 a wholesaler went bankrupt, leaving Ole Kirk with a surplus of toys. Selling them door-to-door, he even traded some toys for a sack of almonds.

These trains, planes, and automobiles were soon joined by a menagerie of animal creatures in 1935. From bejeweled elephants and jolly green mallards to ladybirds, squirrels, and puffed-up cockerels, the animal kingdom had arrived. Some of these new designs were more complicated than their transportation predecessors, especially the pull-toys, which incorporated moving parts and noise mechanisms, the patterns for which Ole Kirk carefully drew up himself. They included a man riding on a goat, which would move up and down as you pulled it along—it was based on the Hans Christian Andersen story *Clumsy Hans*—a monkey riding a car and a pony towing a brightly colored cart. One of the most recognizable and most popular LEGO pull-toys was also one of the first. The wooden duck was sold in various incarnations for twenty-two years (1935–1957) and is typical of the wooden designs the LEGO Group produced during the thirties and forties. As it moves along on wheels, its beak opens and closes, while the base includes a mechanism that "quacks" at the same time. Because of the expanding workload, the painting of early LEGO ducks was contracted out to locals. In the 1940s, TLG started stenciling the ducks instead to save time and labor costs. Because of this and its longevity, the LEGO wooden duck is available in hundreds of variations.

Over the next twenty-eight years, TLG manufactured not only wooden toys but also a variety of other wood-based products. In one 1950's LEGO catalog there are 120 products listed (over 200 designs were produced in total), and while there are the expected wooden animals, trains, and trucks, there's also an abacus, a skipping rope, and a dustpan and brush. The company also made doll buggies, wheelbarrows, chalkboards, and coat hangers designed by Dagny Holm (Ole Kirk's cousin, who would go on to be one of the chief designers of LEGOLAND Billund). These toys may have been a diver-

THE LEGO NAME

In 1934 Ole Kirk held a competition to name the toy company with a bottle of his homemade wine for the winner. None of the entrants' choices impressed him more than his own, though, so he stuck with "LEGO." Ole Kirk didn't know it at the time, but *LEGO* is also the Latin word for "I put together" or "I assemble," a definition that would come to be more than appropriate in the years to come.

One of the original wooden ducks is proudly displayed at the
LEGO Museum in Billund. © Alex Howe

This manual wood-working machine, on display at the LEGO Museum, enabled Ole Kirk to mass-produce parts for his wooden toys. Later, these were replaced by electric machines. © Alex Howe

sion from the carpentry work Ole Kirk had trained for, but they were not that unusual when compared to the toys being produced by other European toy makers at the time. Prior to the twentieth century, Germany had been the epicenter of toy manufacturing, and one particular village, Seiffen in the Ore Mountains region of Saxony, was renowned for its production of detailed wooden toys and traditional Christmas figures and decorations, which were, and still are, exported all over the world.

As a small company with just ten employees in 1939, the LEGO Group had tough competition from these and other imported toys. Despite the fact that LEGO wooden toys were never sold outside of Denmark (with the exception of some sales in Norway), the company wasn't immune to the trends and crazes of the toy industry. A popular and well-known LEGO story is that of Ole Kirk's brush with the yo-yo. In the mid-1930s, the demand for yo-yos was at an all-time high in America after Duncan Toys took over a Californian yo-yo manufacturing company and began promoting yo-yo contests. The craze soon found its way to European shores, especially after the first World Yo-Yo Competition was held in London in 1932. Fully equipped to deal with the demand for the little wooden toys, Ole Kirk set about producing a large supply for Danish children, but as all crazes soon do, this one died out, leaving Ole Kirk with a huge surplus of yo-yos he was unable to sell. He struck on a great idea—turn the yo-yo discs into wheels for his toys including a brand-new toy truck, and his thinking paid off—the truck was a success. This was an important lesson for the toymaker, and for the company, which avoided following popular trends and toy crazes for many years to come. He learned the importance of innovation and originality over following in the footsteps of other manufacturers, and perhaps the most important point of all: If you want to have longevity, and customers who keep coming back for more, you have to sell them a toy that has endless possibilities.

Despite a factory fire in 1942, the LEGO Group continued to grow and to produce wooden toys even after the introduction of plastic toys in 1949. In fact, plastic and metal were incorporated into some of the designs—see *Monypoli* below. Unfortunately, as the company's plastic toy line developed and aligned itself with the large-scale manufacturing of the future of toys, the sales of the wooden line peaked in 1952, and remained slow thereafter.

As Bill Hanlon explains in his 1993 book *Plastic Toys: Dimestore Dreams of the '40s and '50s*, it's hard to imagine the world around us without plastic. Over sixty years of development and manufacturing has resulted in the abundance of the safe plastic-based toys we know today, and the LEGO Group is an important part of that history. There was a surge in the use of plastic injection-molding during World War II because of the increase in demand for mass-produced and affordable items. Unlike wood or metal toy production, where fine details were costly to include and uniformed precision was harder to achieve, injection-molding provided the toy industry with a cheaper product that was faster to produce. As Hanlon explains, the advantages were many. Color could be added to the cellulose acetate granules (the type of plastic originally used by the LEGO Group), rather than painting the toys after molding, meaning the color could not chip or peel; plastic was relatively strong and did not splinter like wood; transparent parts, such as car windshields, could be added in plastic; and they were also far more hygienic than their wooden counter-

MONYPOLI

Monypoli might sound similar to the Parker Brothers/Hasbro property game *Monopoly*, but there were no Scottie dogs, fake money, and definitely no jail to be found on this board. This road safety game was the first board game produced by the LEGO Group and, until fairly recently remained the only one. Released in 1947, it included a game board, a traffic sign instruction poster, game cards, a die and cup, small metal cars, and wooden circular tokens. Although TLG did not revisit board game manufacturing—with the exception of licensed products—for many years to come, the motifs of road safety and traffic police were incorporated into the construction system that was developed a few years later.

parts. Perhaps one of the most fundamental differences between the two types of manufacturing was the fact that they were usually lighter and therefore cheaper to ship on a large scale. This cost difference was passed on to the consumer, meaning children were able to save whatever small amount of money they had to buy cheap plastic toys.

The LEGO Group joined the world of plastic toys in 1947, when it became one of the first companies in Denmark to own an injection molding machine. Ole Kirk saw a real future in plastic toys, and had wanted to buy three machines, but at DKK 30,000 (approximately $65,000 in 2012 dollars) each, his family managed to persuade him to wait until they were certain the investment would pay off. But Ole Kirk had been keeping his eye on the industry and saw how plastic toys were beginning to become more available across Europe—and the reaction was positive. The company spent two years creating designs and molds and in 1949 released the first of their plastic toys. These included a plastic rattle shaped like a bloated fish designed by Godtfred Kirk Christiansen. The toy was made by fusing two mirror-image pieces together. Many different colored plastic granules were mixed before heating, so the rattle was available in a huge variety of color patterns. The details (eyes, fins, lips) were hand-painted afterward with the same level of quality and precision already associated with LEGO toys.

As TLG became more comfortable with the material and the equipment, toys became more detailed. The 1951 *Teddyflyver*—a small teddy bear flying a brightly colored plane, consisted of five separately molded parts, and was available in a variety of color combinations. In the same year, TLG released its first Ferguson farm vehi-

One of the earliest injection-molding machines with teddy mold on display at the LEGO Museum.
© Ian Greig

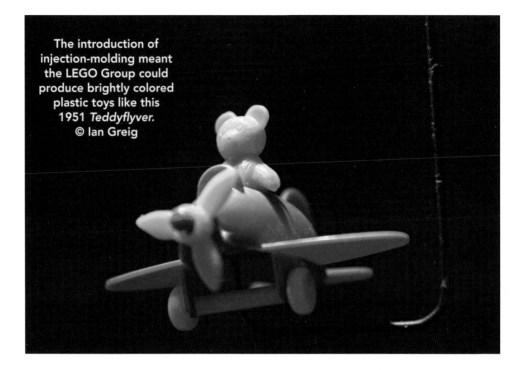

The introduction of injection-molding meant the LEGO Group could produce brightly colored plastic toys like this 1951 *Teddyflyver.*
© Ian Greig

cles—its most complex plastic creations at the time. The Ferguson *Trackto*, modeled on the popular British tractor designed by Harry Ferguson, consisted of between ten and fifteen separate parts and was mainly available in gray and red, although there were also rare colors, such as a limited number of transparent tractors. The tools and molds required to produce the *Tracktor* cost DKK 30,000—more than the price of a real Ferguson TE 20 at the time. But the expense paid off because the model, either bought and assembled as a set or as individual pieces, was a big hit for the company. There were also a number of farming tools and additional vehicles available—some accessories were made in association with another manufacturer called Triton. Not only did this toy introduce the idea of "added play value"—giving children the opportunity to build as well as play with the finished product—but it was the first time the LEGO Group had employed the sales method of stocking toy stores with sets as well as boxes of individual parts, something it would continue to do with the Automatic Binding Brick and LEGO bricks.

The introduction of plastic toys also marked the first LEGO creation that the company felt warranted a patent. Somewhat surprisingly, the first LEGO patent was for a toy gun. Today, the LEGO Group is careful not to produce "war toys"—although weapons relevant to particular themes and characters are included, they are not the focus of any LEGO toy. In 1945 TLG produced a wooden pistol and then reproduced it in plastic four years later. Available in black, green, and blue, this toy pistol had a clever self-loading mechanism that meant it could rapidly fire the

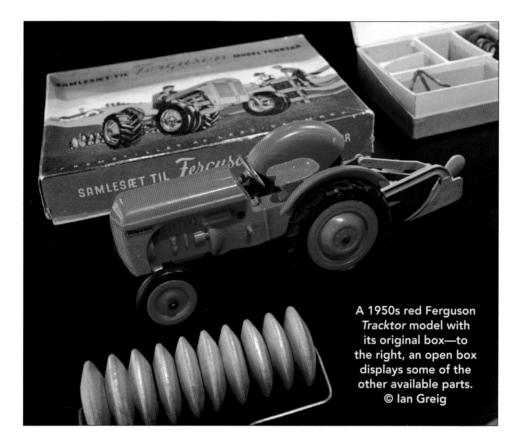

A 1950s red Ferguson *Tracktor* model with its original box—to the right, an open box displays some of the other available parts.
© Ian Greig

plastic projectiles that were also available. When you pressed the trigger, it would load a projectile from the magazine into the back of the barrel where a main spring would release it before pushing the trigger forward, ready for the next shot. So unique was the gun that Godtfred, who was now regularly designing toys for the company, patented it.

The evolution of the first plastic LEGO brick was as logical as that of the wooden gun to plastic gun or the wooden truck to the plastic Ferguson farm vehicles. TLG had made traditional wooden building blocks for years. The first ones, released in the 1940s, were painted in different colors and hollowed out to include a rattle inside. Later versions, such as the LEGO *Klodser*, was a set of thirty-six bricks that measured four centimeters (about 1.6 inches) and featured letters and numbers painted on the sides. Other bricks varied in size and some had pictures of animals painted on. With the introduction of plastic, there was more opportunity for creativity when it came to the simple idea of building bricks.

Of course, Ole Kirk and Godtfred were not the only people to have considered the possibilities of plastic building bricks. Wooden construction toys such as Lincoln Logs (first released in 1916), created by Frank Lloyd Wright's son, John, had been growing in popularity throughout the 1930s and '40s, as well as A. C. Gilbert's steel Erector sets in America and Frank Hornby's earlier Meccano construction kits in Britain. Some companies had begun to develop the idea of turning traditional building blocks into a more sturdy brick-building system such as the 1934 Bild-O-Brik and 1935 British-made Minibrix. Both toys were made from hard rubber rather than plastic. Minibrix kits consisted of a number of parts to create building structures (bricks, roof tiles, doors, windows, etc.). Most parts connected together with the use of lugs, or "pips" as they were known in the company, protruding from the bottom on the brick which connected into small holes in the top of another brick. One man, however, is known for laying the foundations for the brick TLG would go on to develop—British toymaker Hilary Page and his Kiddicraft Company.

Toy historian Kenneth Brown describes Hilary Fisher Page as a pioneer of plastic toys based largely on his observations of children and how they play. While other toy manufacturers were busy producing the toys parents thought their little ones should be playing with, Hilary Page was spending one day a week attending different nurseries, gaining a deeper understanding of child psychology and ascertaining the suitability of plastic as a moldable, colorful, non-toxic, and hygienic material.

In 1937 Hilary Page produced a line of plastic "Sensible Toys" mainly modeled on Russian toys he had previously imported as well as building bricks, which he named Interlocking Building Cubes and patented in 1940. Unlike the earlier Minibrix cubes, these small 2 × 2 bricks were hollow on one side. Four small studs on the top side of each brick prevented lateral movement when another brick was stacked on top of it. The marketing emphasis of these bricks were on their practicality and indestructibility—the packaging claiming it would be impossible for a child to remove any trace or color or damage the material itself, and that the bricks could be washed indefinitely—rather than the creativity associated with later LEGO bricks. Illustrations and photographs on packaging showed children simply stacking bricks in towers, rather than building anything in particular. Despite the initial success of Page's plastic toys (sold initially under the name Bri-Plax, due

British toymaker Hilary Fisher Page in the 1950s. © Geraldine and Vivienne Page

Hilary Page's large
Interlocking Building Cubes
were patented in 1940.
© www. hilarypagetoys.com

to his investors' uncertainty about the success of plastic) production ceased during World War II. Kiddicraft picked up in the postwar years and when the plastic industry boomed, Hilary Page was ahead of the game in terms of development.

He pushed the design of the Building Cubes and made a couple of significant changes in the late 1940s, resulting in the release of the Self-Locking Building Bricks. Patents granted in 1947 and 1949 respectively were for a smaller 2 × 4 studded brick (alongside 2 × 2 bricks) and bricks with slits on the ends into which window/door/roof components could be connected. This was a significantly advanced building system from the Interlocking Building Cubes, as it encouraged children to build structures using an overlapping building method that replicated real-life construction. A patent was also granted in 1952 for a supporting sheet onto which children's creations could be built and then transported. A 1948 advertisement for the bricks states that they are an absorbing and instructive hobby, suitable for chil-

dren over the age of seven. This new toy was a big leap from the nursery building blocks the market was familiar with. A box of Self-Locking Building Bricks, known as "No.1 Set" included a selection of 2 × 2 and 2 × 4 bricks in red, yellow, blue, green, and white, as a number of matching window and door pieces and illustrations of possible models children could re-create using the set. But while Kiddicraft's development of the plastic brick was innovative, it failed to ignite the same level of interest from consumers as construction toy giant Meccano—by 1951, a Meccano factory in Bobigny, France, was producing more than 500,000 sets every day. The Self-Locking Bricks continued to be part of the Kiddicraft catalog and Hilary Page soon turned his attention to the development of other toys including the Kiddicraft Miniatures—a line of licensed replicas of everyday products including Heinz soups, Quaker Oats, Persil laundry powder, and a full range of spirits, beers, and even cigarettes!

While the Interlocking Building Cubes and Self-Locking Building Bricks may not be household names today, as Tim Walsh explains in his book *Timeless Toy*, they influenced Ole Kirk and Godtfred's creation of the original LEGO bricks. The production

The contents of the original
Kiddicraft No.1 Set of Self-Locking
Building Cubes.
© www.hilarypagetoys.com

of plastic building blocks at TLG came hand in hand with the introduction of plastic in the late 1940s. In a 1950s retailers' catalog LEGO *Plastic Kubus* were advertised alongside plastic dolls, vehicles, and toy pistols. These were simple plastic alphabet blocks with letters and images painted on the sides. The plastic injection molding machine Ole Kirk had purchased from the U.K. in 1947 came with sample toys to show its capabilities. One such product was Kiddicraft's brick.

In a 1988 Privy Council ruling (*InterLEGO AG* v. *Tyco Industries Inc.*), Lord Oliver of Aylmerton explained how for all practical purposes the original building bricks created by the LEGO Group, known as Automatic Binding Bricks, were precise copies of Hilary Page's design. The Kiddicraft brick had no patent protecting it in Denmark and Godtfred had admitted in court that he and his father took the samples of Kiddicraft's bricks and used them as a model. Small changes were made to create molds for the LEGO bricks—the rounded corners were straightened, the size of the brick was converted from inches to centimeters and millimeters (the metric system was in use in Denmark from 1908), altering the size of the brick by one-tenth of a millimeter. Another design change was to the studs themselves, which were had rounded tops on the Kiddicraft bricks and were flattened for the LEGO bricks. There is also a noticeable difference in the shape of the slits on the side of the bricks, which are slightly curved on the Self-Locking Building Bricks and straight in LEGO's new design.

Released in 1949, initially, LEGO's Automatic Binding Bricks had no identifiable markings—later, molds would include "LEGO" on the under-side of the brick. They were known as Automatic Binding Bricks in Denmark rather than having a Danish name. After World War II all LEGO toys would take on English names as had become the common practice among Danish companies.

In comparison with the Kiddicraft bricks, the Automatic Binding Bricks were not particularly well made—excess plastic often filled the side slits of early versions. LEGO was not used to the precision required for creating such small parts, and the equipment was still relatively new to them. Despite having molding machines, a lot of the work was still done by hand and was still fairly labor-intensive. The bricks themselves had no real fastening mechanism and their hollow shells were prone to problems such as cracking and shrinking, meaning when the plastic was cooled the bricks did not always fit together with the precision LEGO bricks are known for today. The first bricks made were 2 × 2 and 2 × 4 bricks with the slits, and an assortment of various-size windows and a door panel. Bricks were available in red, green, white, and a sandy

"Hundreds of hours of worth-while play," declared the box of Kiddicraft's No. 1 Set. This original box lid shows just some of the possible creations children could build using the plastic bricks. © www.hilarypagetoys.com

yellow. They were sold as a part of gift sets, similar to the Kiddicraft boxes—four different sets were released in 1949 and then a further three in 1950 (these sets were the first of the 700 series—the prefix product number used for gift boxes and basic sets until the mid-1960s). The elements were arranged in a zig-zagged pattern in a shallow box—the covers of which featured illustrations of children happily building houses, factories, and walls from the new bricks.

Despite the rising popularity of its plastic toys, the bricks were not an immediate success. As LEGO moved into the 1950s, the sales of plastic toys were increasing, and between 1952 and 1953 they accounted for around half of LEGO's income. The Automatic Binding Bricks, however, weren't faring so well and accounted for only 5 to 7 percent of LEGO's sales. Deciding the name might be putting buyers off, in 1953 Godtfred, now Junior Managing Director, changed it to LEGO *Mursten* (LEGO bricks), which illustrates the growing importance of the construction toy within the company and a dedication to developing it into a popular brand. Evidently, many of LEGO's other wooden and plastic toys such as cars, trucks, and tractors complemented the large, colorful sets of bricks which children could use to create their own houses, farms, and shops. LEGO *Mursten* tried to find its feet on the toy market through what appeared to be a rather unplanned and chaotic marketing strategy. Between 1951 and 1955, LEGO gift sets of house-style buildings emerged, as well as supplementary sets, such as a collection including just windows and doors—LEGO *Mursten* was also available as individual brick items which could be bought for as little as six-hundredths of a Danish Krone (about nine U.S. cents in 2012) for a 1 × 2 brick. Although the LEGO name was molded onto every brick from 1953 onward, rather than brand the product with one cohesive packaging style, three different box types were used, their availability overlapping each other. Furthermore, before 1955 each individual LEGO product that was released featured a completely different design on the box, although the name LEGO *Mursten* was always present, meaning the brand failed to secure a memorable and firm place in the minds of consumers.

In the early 1950s, LEGO introduced a number of different parts to help develop the building capabilities of its new line. Initially bricks were only available as 2 × 2 and 2 × 4 studded bricks, but they soon brought out 1 × 2 bricks, 2 × 3 bricks, round bricks, corner pieces, and different size thin base plates that allowed larger, more elaborate creations to be built. The slotted Kiddicraft bricks may have been the starting point for LEGO *Mursten*, but in 1954 a new brick-compatible window/door system was developed that meant the slots were soon to be made redundant— instead, window pieces were clipped onto brick studs with wings. The bricks did not change immediately, though, and the old slot-in window pieces were sold up until 1956. Through these innovations the LEGO Group was developing a recognizable building system of its own and a company more heavily associated with building bricks than other toys. Following on from the success of the Ferguson Tractor model, it continued to produce other popular metal and plastic toys including a number of

These toys were made with zinc metal bases and plastic chassis and were the inspiration for the Town Plan 1:87 scale vehicles of the late 1950s and early 1960s. © Ian Greig

1:43 and 1:38 scale-model vehicles based on other real car and truck manufacturers'. Models of Chevrolet trucks and VW Beetles were some of the most popular LEGO toys until the introduction of the System of Play.

The 1950s was a crucial decade for the LEGO Group, as the company saw changes in management, production, and a new manufacturing focus brought about by Godtfred's determination to develop a toy system all children wanted to play with. He had helped to introduce plastic toys to their customers and brought about the production of LEGO *Mursten* with his father, but building bricks were not yet the company's core product, or its best-selling one. Plastic toys were becoming more widely available and acceptable across Europe, despite critics blasting them as second-rate to traditional wooden toys, claiming they would not stand the test of time. Although he may not have known it, Godtfred had created a product that had the ability to resonate with generations to come—he just had to find a way to make sure it would. And that's exactly what he did.

FROM FATHER TO SON

It was in 1951, when Ole Kirk's health began to deteriorate after a stroke, that his son Godtfred, who had been named junior vice president one year earlier, began to assume more of his father's responsibilities—he was just thirty years old. Despite not having the academic qualifications readily associated with someone in his position, Godtfred (or GKC as he was known) had spent ten years working for his father, designing toys and watching the company develop. Despite Godtfred's brothers and uncle working in the factory, he was the one Ole Kirk decided would be best qualified (he was the operations manager at the time) to take up this important position, which would prepare him to eventually take over from his father completely.

Ole Kirk may not have been in good health, but that didn't stop him trying to force his hand and insist on the building of a new factory in 1952—something his son thought was quite unnecessary, especially as they'd only just finished paying off the cost of the current factory—Ole Kirk had his way, however, and it was up to GKC to find the money. Despite their differences, and GKC threatening to leave LEGO for good, the driven son persevered with his father's business and was integral in the production of the first LEGO bricks and even more so in the development of the System of Play in the mid-1950s. Despite only speaking Danish, GKC made business trips abroad to Norway and Sweden to show off the LEGO bricks to possible partners—these trips would be key in LEGO's success in years to come. In 1957, when his brothers Karl George and Gerdhart were named heads of plastic production and wood production, respectively, the position of managing director went to GKC. Sadly, a year later, months shy of the production of the "real" LEGO brick, Ole Kirk died. The directorship of LEGO and its 450 employees passed to GKC, and it was therefore his decision to discontinue the production of wooden toys when the factory where they were made burned down in 1960—the third LEGO factory fire in its short history. By 1962 Karl George, Gerhardt, and Johannes had all left the company, leaving GKC in charge of the LEGO name. It would be his son, Kjeld Kirk Kristiansen (the family name was spelled differently on Kjeld's birth certificate, hence the change in spelling of the Christiansen name), who would then take over from him as chairman of the board in 1986, when he resigned his position from the company. Godtfred died nine years later, a few days after his seventy-fifth birthday.

CHAPTER 2

1954–1977: Systematic Success

The name "LEGO" was officially trademarked by the company in 1954, as if in preparation for the success that lay ahead. The word, invented by Ole Kirk Christiansen, was soon to be synonymous with wholesome childhood play across the world. But before the LEGO Group became a formidable competitor (and champion) in the international toy industry ring, a few things needed to happen.

Despite having developed a good-quality, reliable product, LEGO bricks had not taken off in the way Ole Kirk and Godtfred would have liked. When traveling to a toy fair in the U.K. in 1954, Junior Vice President Godtfred got talking to a Danish department store buyer from Copenhagen. The man commented on how it was such a shame there was no toy currently available that functioned as part of a really good system—which would encourage consumers to keep coming back to that product. Back in Billund, it was as if Godtfred had taken the man's words as a challenge, and he set about re-examining the company's current toy output. At the time, the LEGO Group was producing about 200 different toy items, so Godtfred drew up a list of ten basic qualities that a good LEGO product should possess, to help him determine which product might lend itself well to this new "system." These qualities included some of the things LEGO toys are most revered for today: unlimited play potential, suitable for girls and boys of any age, quality and attention to detail, and long hours of play that encourage development, imagination, and creativity. It soon became clear to Godtfred that LEGO bricks offered the most potential to be at the heart of the company's new venture.

A year of development followed during which Godtfred centered the existing LEGO gift sets and components around a single building theme. Since the majority of LEGO models used to promote the product were scaled-down building structures a "town plan" theme was decided upon and the company set about developing new town-related sets and accessories. Godtfred combined the best of the bricks' design and creativity—a construction system with windows and doors that was already ideally suited to building houses, shops, town halls, and factories—with trees, cars, and traffic signs to enable children to build up a more complete "world" for their LEGO models.

The additional accessories built in the popular model railway HO building scale (1:87) were not made from compatible LEGO brick components but rather from a mixture of metal and plastic parts. The introduction of scale model vehicles, trees, and signs brought the brick models to life, making LEGO bricks no longer something you simply built with, but a toy that could be used to create your own play environment—a basis for a fictional world that you controlled. It was also hoped that the street environment would be educational, encouraging children to learn about road safety, similar to the 1947 Monypoly board game.

Initially, eight lorries were designed and sold alongside the LEGO Town Plan sets and pieces—they were based on the British Bedford lorry (later replaced by Mercedes trucks under a new licensing agreement), and had metal frames and wheels and a plastic body. These moving parts helped bring the Town Plan to life, and they were soon joined by a VW bus in 1956 and a Beetle in 1958. Jaguar, Ford,

Plastic bricks were combined with these metal trees and 1:87 scale vehicles to create a more recognizable world in miniature. © Ian Greig

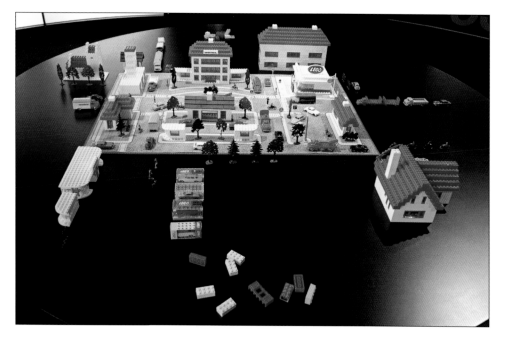

A Town Plan layout on display at the LEGO Museum shows some of the earliest Town building designs in red, white, and blue LEGO elements. © Ian Greig

Citroen, Fiat, Vauxhall, and Morris all got in on the LEGO 1:87 model car market, ensuring their vehicle designs made it onto living room floors around Europe. These miniature vehicles reigned over LEGO towns everywhere until 1969 when they were discontinued. The introduction of a LEGO System wheel in the early 1960s saw the gradual phasing out of the 1:87 scale models, replaced by cars, trucks, trains, and other vehicles built from LEGO bricks.

Originally consisting of the *Mursten* series of basic "giftbox" sets, (known as the 700 series because of their product numbers), these new vehicles, and other accessories, the Town Plan was tied together with a vinyl play mat for children to build on—the building of a town was encouraged by the street layout of roads and green lawn areas. The Town Plan *System I Leg* (System of Play) was unveiled at the Nuremberg Toy Fair in 1955, and despite receiving some rather uninterested responses from the German market, the Danish people had begun to catch on to what the LEGO Group was creating, so much so that Danish sales of LEGO *Mursten* products had nearly doubled as 1956 drew to a close. With Godtfred's list of principles in mind, new designs were rolled out each year, keeping the brand fresh and exciting and giving consumers the opportunity to develop and add to their own collection.

From 1957, products were branded "LEGO System" and boxes of LEGO bricks and sets featured the Town Plan design on the front, often with two or three children

(including Godtfred's own children) playing happily. Designs became more adventurous and soon LEGO towns could include a fire station, a petrol station complete
with Esso petrol pumps, a VW garage, and a church, as well as traffic police to keep
their eyes out for speeding 1:87 scale cars. The LEGO Group sold a few sets designed for children to build specific models such as the VW Garage (306—shown
below) and Car Showroom (307) but the majority of sales were still through the larger
700 "gift boxes"—wooden compartmentalized boxes with a variety of bricks and
specialty pieces. Although a lot of the basic parts packs could be used to build
anything, the image of children building a townscape adorned the boxes, steering
children toward this building theme, encouraging them to build up their own Town
Plan collection. Most significantly, the LEGO Group introduced a play space to en-
compass your own LEGO town—initially in 1955 there was a flexible plastic rollaway

Some of the earliest 700 System sets were available in metal canisters such as these.
On the right are some of the "200" series of smaller sets of LEGO *Mursten*; the
numbers indicate the size of brick available in each box. © Alex Howe

Set 700/5 was one of the 1958 LEGO System gift boxes available across Europe. The side of the box reads "*Du système dans le jeu*" and "*Systeem in het Spe*"—System of Play for French, Suisse, Belgian, and Dutch customers. © Maxx Kroes

play mat (1200/200) with seven areas designated for building, but the following year a Masonite fiberboard alternative was released (1200A/200A). LG also molded new trees, sign posts, and petrol pumps to support the new theme.

A 1955 Danish catalog printed an illustration of a metropolitan town built from LEGO bricks: A skyscraper looms over people walking the streets while a lorry trundles by and a plane swoops overhead. While the LEGO bricks themselves were very basic—TLG had yet to develop the stud and tube bricks—and there were only a limited number of parts available, this picture truly demonstrates the important part a child's imagination played in the sale of the earliest Town sets.

The LEGO System of Play was one of the most important developments in the company's history. Other toy companies had been producing construction toys for years, some longer than LEGO, and none had been able to develop a system with the potential of the LEGO Town Plan. In the 1950s, Meccano, for example, were producing sets which, while updated, were not that dissimilar to those they had released in the 1930s: boxes of parts designed to construct various creations, which could be larger and more detailed the more parts you owned. But where these other building systems concentrated on the technical potential of the toy and the creation of individual structures, LEGO was encouraging children to build from their imagination, and create a world from LEGO bricks to play with. LG was beginning to set themselves apart.

In 1957 GKC was appointed managing director one year before the death of his father, and the next fundamental development in the LEGO Group's history. While the System of Play had begun to sell in other European countries (the first foreign sales office was set up in Hohenwestedt, Germany, in 1956), the bricks themselves did not have the interlocking capabilities required to build complex structures, or even a simple stack of bricks that would not fall apart if knocked over. So Godtfred set about designing a better brick, producing a number of different designs which were tested with focus groups of children, and the most successful design was selected to become the LEGO brick we know today. This new design widened the divide between the LEGO System and other brick systems that had come before it, especially Hilary Page's Kiddicraft bricks. This was further cemented by the 1958 patent the company obtained to prevent its new bricks from being copied (all of the new designs were patented, in case the LEGO Group had any reason to use them in the future). To increase the brick's "clutch" power, TLG introduced a tubing element underneath each brick which four studs would fit tightly around—the slots at the sides were removed. A 2 × 2 brick now included one tube in the center of its hollow underside, a 2 × 4 brick included three tubes, etc. The bricks could still be

This original Volkswagen garage (306) included two VW Beetles and traffic signs. © Alex Howe

This Esso Filling Station (310) came with an Esso truck (right), signage, and gas pumps. © Thorskegga Thorn

pulled apart with relative ease, but now there was more flexibility with how bricks could fit together and sides of structures could be smooth, without the aesthetic irregularity of the empty slots. When the new brick became available, the LEGO Group also brought out a range of sloping bricks to improve LEGO buildings' roofs, which meant both LEGO toy designers and consumers were able to produce more elaborate designs. New molds were created immediately for all the new tube bricks, but some of the older bricks, especially the 1× bricks (e.g., 1 × 1, 1 × 2, 1 × 6, etc.), were not replaced right away—even today these bricks don't have the same tubes inside as the larger bricks; they have smaller tubes that fit in between rows of studs, rather than in the center of four studs—so it was decided to wait until the old molds wore out before they would be updated.

After the introduction of the new stud-and-tube bricks, Godtfred pushed the LEGO System further, developing bricks and components to enhance this new world. The invention of the LEGO wheel in 1961 revolutionised the System—now cars and trucks could be built *from* LEGO, meaning the System no longer needed to rely on metal and plastic scale models to inject life and movement into the Town Plan. The wheel was one of the first important designs developed by LEGO Futura—a five-person division established in 1959 to come up with creative and original ideas for the LEGO System. The work of LEGO Futura was an extension of Godtfred's informal testing methodology—watching his own children play with LEGO. With the expansion of the company and the brand, the Futura team not only introduced new, innovative elements to the LEGO world, but explored the possibility of introducing computerized parts as well. By 1987 around 150 people worked in this department, and 240 by 1995.

The LEGO wheel was a breakthrough and the wheel-bearing design was unique enough to warrant a patent of its own. Originally available in 2 × 2 or 4 × 4 sizes, the plastic wheels had a small axle attached and a groove around the edge to hold a rubber tire. The axles were slotted in to reciprocal hollowed-out parts of a special 2 × 4 LEGO brick, and were then free to rotate. The design was first available in the 1962 wheel set collection (400), which included eleven pieces, to make up 2 × 2 wheel sets—these would be followed in 1964 by larger wheel sets (401) and white turntables (402) and sets that incorporated the wheels and turntables such as the European Taxi (315) and the Warehouse and Mill set (318). The wheel revolutionized LEGO toys and became an intrinsic part of the LEGO System. By the end of the

This rare box, which contained just two 2 × 4 bricks (either yellow and blue or red and white) was distributed to retailers between 1958 and 1960 to help promote the new stud-and-tube bricks. © Maxx Kroes

Set 314, released in 1963, included the new large and small LEGO wheels and a turntable. © Alex Howe

1990s, LEGO was producing more than three million tires every year for its little toy wheels. In terms of number produced, that made it the largest manufacturer of tires in the world. Futura also developed gears (large round plates with studs and tubes that could be rotated by attaching them to LEGO wheels) and battery-powered motors to make these models move independently. While patented in a number of countries, these sets were only available in the American market from licensee Samsonite, although LEGO System motors and batteries were introduced to Europe with the release of motorized LEGO train sets in 1966.

As well as being the year the wheel made LEGO bricks mobile, 1962 also saw a significant change in the material used to make LEGO. Previously, TLG had been using cellulose acetate to make all its plastic products, but it was decided under the advice of Swiss engineer Hans Schiess who had been employed to lead LEGO's process development lab in Billund that switching to acrylonitrile butadiene styrene (ABS) would provide the company with the reliable, quality product they were trying to produce. The change came when it was discovered that ABS was relatively inexpensive, easy to mold accurately in small measures, and was much more colorfast and durable than its predecessor. In 1963 the change began, phasing out cellulose acetate (at least in the European LEGO market) over the next few years. LEGO has been made from ABS ever since. German company Bayer has been the exclusive

An example of some of the unusual marbled effects found on these rare test bricks. © Maxx Kroes

supplier of LEGO plastics for most of the company's history. Interestingly, TLG supplied Bayer with molds for 2 × 4 bricks with which to test the plastics they were supplying LEGO with, resulting in a number of bricks produced by Bayer as samples. These bricks, while never sold, are highly sought after by some collectors as they are available in a variety of unusual colors (some bricks are translucent, transparent, or have a marbled effect).

In 1959, a year after the first stud-and-tube bricks had been released, a new Town Plan card board (200) that folded out and had metal heels to protect the corners replaced the earlier plastic and fiberboard layouts. This new board would be sold in Europe until 1968, and was the first style to be sold in the U.K. after LEGO began official sales there in 1960 (the U.K. board had a cloth section to support the folding midsection). The company's interest in promoting road safety to children was strengthened by the realistic road signs and road markings on the town plan boards—different countries sold left- or right-hand drive versions depending on the real driving conventions that existed there.

In 1961 the U.K. was one of the first countries to receive a new series of 700 sets—each with a different picture on the box. Rather than radically change the contents of the gift boxes, they were simply updated with the new LEGO bricks. This was the same year TLG released the first Town Plan sets that came complete with a board. (The earlier wooden box town plan sets (700) had included parts to build a town plan scene, but only German sets came with a board on the lid.) A photograph on the box of the 712-piece Town Plan Set (725), available only in North America in 1961, depicted a red and white LEGO town not too dissimilar from the Danish catalog illustration seen six years before, and the use of more photographic images was soon commonplace across the brand, presenting a bright, modern image and replacing the more illustrative style of printing. This can be clearly seen in the supplementary System sets released in the early 1960s where a number of different box sleeves—each featuring a photograph of children playing with LEGO bricks—were used to sell a variety of parts. The contents of each packet were shown on the inner tray.

Godtfred was keen to modernize the image of LEGO toys so he hired a marketing manager and opened a photography department to handle the packaging and marketing materials for the company. In 1960 the cartoon mascot from the 1950s was scrapped and replaced with a robotic-looking figure built from LEGO Bricks. The packaging of the new 700 gift sets released in 1961 featured a gray LEGO baseplate

This impressive collection of 2 × 4 test bricks produced by Bayer shows the wide variety of colors they were produced in, some not available as LEGO bricks until much later. Letters (A–D) on the bricks indicate their clutch strength. © Maxx Kroes

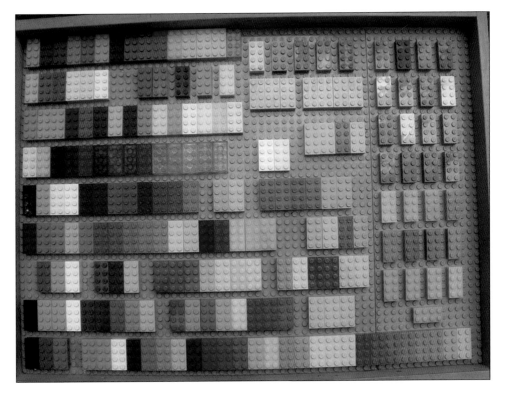

1964 NEW YORK WORLD FAIR

By 1964 LEGO was gaining worldwide recognition, and had become a huge brand in Denmark. The 1964 World Fair in New York was the ideal stage to exhibit LEGO toys on a universal scale, so it was only fitting that the LEGO Group played a key role in the public image of Denmark presented there. The pavilion was targeting children with its Tivoli Gardens theme, and LEGO toys were available both in the exhibit's shops (two exclusive sets were brought from Billund for the event) and to play with in the children's park.

as the backdrop with photographs of children happily playing with LEGO. These photographs were used not only on LEGO's boxes, but across its marketing materials to help develop a recognizable brand across the various international markets LEGO was being sold in.

After nearly ten years of the original Town Plan sets, 1964 saw the release of a new series of basic sets (040 and 050) to incorporate the new building scale brought about by the introduction of LEGO 2 × 2 wheels and other components.

The new metallic edges can be seen on the inside of the System play board, which encouraged children to build a town of their own. © Alex Howe

An original 200 cardboard Town Plan board released in the late 1950s—a young Kjeld Kirk Kristiansen (future CEO and president of the LEGO Group, and Godtfred's son) appeared on the outside. © Alex Howe

As mentioned previously, these sets were packaged differently from their predecessors, with bright photographs showing children happily playing and building houses, planes, and windmills. The 1964 sets were also the first sets to feature proper building instructions. Prior to this, some basic instructions were sometimes printed on the inside of the box lid, but they were incomplete and for younger children incomprehensible. In the U.K., LEGO fans could pick up two different series of blueprints from toy shops for one penny each (one series consisted of blueprints to build a windmill, a boathouse, a London bus, and an astronaut). These blueprints had written instructions that included a shading code to decipher which color brick should be used and built the model up layer by layer, showing an illustration per row.

Originally, it hadn't occurred to LEGO to include detailed instructions with its sets, but as its toys became more focused on the models you could build with them, rather than being just a box of bricks, LEGO Futura and the graphics department teamed up to produce instructions that, at the time, were unique to the toy industry. By showing an illustration of the growing model from an elevated angle, builders could see which elements had been added to from the previous picture, and position the correct bricks accordingly. With no words used at all, the instructions were universal and revolutionary—since then, most other construction toy brands have employed this instruction method.

The LEGO Group brought further clarity to its toys when it began to include a picture of a set's contents on the box. Supplementary sets released in 1966, such as 432 (eight road signs) and 433 (Street Lamps), were the first to show buyers what they were getting with an illustration of the parts included, instead of just showing children building and playing with LEGO—this proved even more useful the larger and more complex the sets became. Today LEGO boxes detail all the pieces included and the number of each in an accessible parts index on the side of each box.

The popularity of the Town Plan reached its peak during the early 1960s. As the decade began to wind down, so did production of Town Plan sets and boards. The 1:87 model cars and trucks were being replaced by the LEGO wheel and all the building possibilities it presented—with that the scale of Town Plan became somewhat obsolete. New supplementary parts sets no longer featured Town Plan

PROMOTIONAL SETS

As production of Town Plan sets in the U.K. stopped toward the end of the 1960s, a promotional deal struck with Kellogg's saw left over Town Plan boards and parts given away in cereal competitions. The 1967 "Win a Town" competition gave children the chance to win a set containing their own Town Plan board and an interesting mixture of parts including Esso gas pumps with Shell signage. Three years later, another competition appeared to "Win your own LEGOLAND." The set available to entrants was similar to the 1971 Village Set with its fire station, two small houses, and an assortment of vehicles and trees. Kellogg's was not the only company helping to use up surplus parts. Despite Town Plan sets being discontinued in North America by licensee Samsonite in 1966, once TLG began proceedings to revoke the Samsonite LEGO license in 1970, the company began producing a few large sets to clear out its inventory. Sears department store's catalog was a regular retailer of Samsonite LEGO products, and exclusively sold an 842-piece Town Plan with an unusual dark gray board.

The LEGO wheel made the building of vehicles easier, such as this London Bus (313), and introduced a new, larger scale to the LEGO System. © Thorskegga Thorn

Street lamps were just some of the accessories available in the new supplementary sets of 1966; others included lettered bricks and road signs. These illustrated boxes were gradually replaced with cellophane-fronted boxes. © Thorskegga Thorn

A group of three LEGO-branded trucks released in 1967 included this blue "truck with flatbed"—
the impact of these designs can still be seen in LEGO trucks today. © Jordan Schwartz

These two cowboys (210) released in 1976 were just some of the variety of figures
the LEGO Group introduced in the 1970s. © Pieter Stok

pictures, but came packaged in simple blue boxes with the LEGO logo and cellophane box fronts revealing the contents. Medium-size sets included pieces to produce a specific model such as a delivery truck (333) or a fire engine (336), while larger basic building sets such as those released in 1968 encouraged children to build anything from a rocket to the Taj Mahal. The focus on the Town System had shifted to a more general building creative aesthetic that incorporated new technology and ideas.

The 1970s saw the Town System evolve from the rigid setting of the Town Plan boards, with 1:87 vehicles and free-standing signs and trees, to a more integrated building system incorporating Homemaker sets for dollhouse-style interiors, LEGO trains and the 1971 release of a selection of large base plates available in different colors encouraging imaginative building. There were some further attempts made at a larger town set, such as LEGOLAND Town Centre (355) and 1975's Harbour Scene and Wild West Scene (364 and 365) that included some of the earliest LEGO figures, which all came with cardboard layouts. The introduction of these simple figures into sets brought new life to LEGO and with it some new settings such as a hospital (363), a station (148), and even a fuel refinery (149). The figures themselves varied in size and shape a couple of times through the mid-1970s, as LEGO designers tried to

Other figures, sometimes referred to as "stiffs" because they had no arms or legs, also started to appear, such as these rescue workers in a 1976 set. © Jordan Schwartz

Prior to 1976's police station, small emergency service vehicles such as this 1973 police car (611) were released. © David Martin

develop a scale and a suitable figure to populate the LEGO world. In the meantime, set designs became more detailed, and the true fun of LEGO building could be seen in sets such as 1976's Police Headquarters (370), followed a year later by Texas Rangers (372) complete with cowboy hats and a cactus. The foundations were set for the contemporary minifigure that appeared for the first time in 1978, and with its arrival came a precise scale for all the houses, castles, and spaceships that followed.

With the company focusing more of its energies on the development of the LEGO bricks and the System toys, it made sense to market the wooden toys under a different name. In July of 1959 the BILOfix brand name was registered and belonged to all non-LEGO System products. A clear distinction had been made—the future of LEGO was in plastic building bricks. The department was overseen by Godtfred's brother Gerhardt who had been made head of the wooden toy division in 1957. With only slight modifications made, the only noticeable difference to the remaining wooden toys was a new BILOfix logo. Some new toys were produced under BILOfix at this time, including the BILOfix Transport truck. Gerhardt also developed a wooden beams and bolts connecting product during 1959, which the BILOfix name is now most associated with. Gerhardt's big promotion didn't last long, though, when another factory fire in 1960 brought wooden toy production at LEGO to an abrupt end. After this incident, the decision was made not to rebuild or reinvest in the product line, and instead to focus solely on the LEGO System of Play. There were some disagreements between the brothers as to whether wooden toy production should end, with Gerhardt feeling strongly that this was the wrong decision. The LEGO System of Play toys were not yet best-sellers, and it was a big risk on Godtfred's part to insist that they were the way forward. In April 1961, Gerhardt and Karl Georg left their jobs to start their own businesses, and Godtfred bought out all three of his brothers, making himself the majority shareholder.

Despite their quality and appeal, the LEGO Group hardly sold its wooden toys outside of Denmark, except some limited exportation to Norway. It's likely their simplicity and similarity to other push-pull toys on the market, being produced by larger, more established manufacturers, prevented them from traveling far beyond Danish borders.

The 1960s saw LEGO sets grow in size, moving away from the 1:87 model scale, and toward a larger scale more in line with the minifigure scale used today. One of the first larger scale sets was the 1964 Train (323), which also hinted at the start of the LEGO Train theme (arriving more completely two years later)—the first distinct theme to emerge after the release of the LEGO System town sets. Toy trains were nothing new, and had already enjoyed phenomenal success for over fifty years when the LEGO Group decided to take them on. From as early as 1891, with the emer-

BILOFIX AFTER LEGO

The name BILOfix is from the Danish "Billions of toys," so it would have been a sad irony for the optimistically named company to have ended after less than a year when its factory burned down. Taking notes from his determined father, Gerhardt Kirk Christiansen decided to leave the LEGO company and set up on his own with the BILOfix brand. In 1962 the new BILOfix company was established in Kolding, Denmark, a seaport town situated approximately twenty-five miles southeast of Billund. A new factory was built and Gerhardt began producing the BILOfix Ingeniørsæts he'd designed and began manufacturing in 1959. This popular toy was made from wooden beams, rods, and bricks which were connected by plastic bolts and screws, initially made at the Billund LEGO factory with the original molds. Exported widely in Europe (including Scandinavia and the U.K.), Canada, and Japan, this award-winning toy enjoyed years of success. After being sold to a Danish toy distributor in the 1970s, the products were made more cheaply, and soon went out of production.

gence of German-made clockwork trains, model train sets had captured the imagination of children all over the world, and as the toys progressed from basic brick-built playthings to scaled-down electric models of real locomotives, they became popular with adult hobbyists, too.

The LEGO Group's early attempts to bring little bricks to the railroad appear amateur compared to the realistic sets available today, but they were working with a smaller selection of LEGO parts, and colors, and the electric technology was still being developed by Futura. Known as the "blue era" trains, because of the bright blue tracks they ran on, these first incarnations were released in Europe in 1966. Some sets such as 111 (1966) and 080 (1967) were push trains without motors, but with the release of 115 (1966)—a starter train set that included a motor—and component sets allowing push trains to be upgraded to motorized sets, the moving LEGO Train was born. Motors were built into the locomotives and battery boxes functioned as a railcar which could be connected behind it to supply the power. The first motorized trains included 4.5 volt batteries and were fairly successful, but in an effort to improve the realism of the train system, LEGO launched a new 12 volt system alongside it in 1969, which was targeted at older children. Rather than trains carrying a battery, the

DUPLO bricks have always been compatible with LEGO bricks, although they're larger, and have hollow studs and bigger play figures. © Harlan Chen

rails were electrified and were controlled by a transformer. The 4.5 and 12 volt trains were sold until 1980 and became increasingly realistic and design-conscious with additions that included a diesel locomotive (723), passenger coaches (131), and a Shell tanker wagon (136).

But it wasn't only older builders who LEGO wanted to attract to its building system. American licensee Samsonite had produced Jumbo bricks in 1964 to target children whom LEGO parts were too small to cater to, and its sales had highlighted the value of the preschool market. There was a European release of two "Jumbo"-style brick sets in 1968, before LEGO set about developing a new type of brick more suitable for the little hands and developing minds they hoped would play with it. Three years after LEGO Train had been launched, the company surged forward with another innovation—the release of the DUPLO brick in 1969. The name "DUPLO" was born out of the fact that the bricks are double the size (in all dimensions) of a regular LEGO brick. The DUPLO brick has seen a few changes—notably to the height of the studs on top (they've grown taller) and the precise shape of the tubes underneath—but in essence its suitability hasn't changed since its conception. Despite having hollowed-out studs, the DUPLO brick is completely compatible with the stud-and-tube system of the regular bricks, so much so that the first DUPLO basic sets (510, 511) included both types of bricks (in 2 × 4 sizes). Available initially in just

One of the earliest DUPLO sets (513) included base plates with wheels for little hands to build mobile creations. © Alex Howe

four colors, red, blue, white, and yellow, LEGO soon saw its new venture take off and it was quick to add to the variety of pieces in the sets including 2 × 2 bricks, large wheeled base plates, and the double concave arches, first featured in 1972, ideal for small hands to hold onto in the middle when trying to connect the studs.

Initially, the target age for the DUPLO bricks was a bit ambiguous—a 1970 catalog did not advise customers with an age, and the 1971 U.K. catalog suggested the bricks were for one- to two-year olds, despite sets still including regular bricks at this time, which are targeted at three- and four- to twelve-year olds. But by 1975, DUPLO had been embraced as an independent arm of the LEGO family, and sets no longer included regular LEGO bricks. Six sets launched that year were sold for "toddlers from 1½ years," and parents were encouraged to help their children make the transition to smaller LEGO bricks around the age of three. As the name DUPLO is not obviously related to toddlers, LEGO varied in its approach and marketing toward the bricks in the 1970s. One 1975 catalog refers to the bricks as "LEGO Nursery Bricks," despite the name "DUPLO" appearing on the boxes (LEGO Nursery Bricks was the name used in Australia), while another 1976 catalog drops the DUPLO tag altogether and sells them as "LEGO Preschool Blocks." By 1977, LEGO had reverted back to DUPLO, and had introduced the red rabbit logo still used today.

DUPLO sets progressed dramatically over these few years, with the introduction of eye bricks, doors, and windows, and DUPLO people together with an entire farmyard of animals in 1979. The DUPLO figures were armless and made up of a chunky body, large head, and occasionally a hat or hair-piece. With fewer smaller parts, they were a lot safer for young children to play with.

While LEGO continued with the production of basic building sets for DUPLO, LEGO had learned from developing the System of Play that providing a framework or theme for children to build in was a successful way to encourage play and to increase sales. This can be seen with some DUPLO sets that are clearly junior versions of the regular LEGO sets. By the end of the 1970s there were DUPLO farm sets (033, 045), a DUPLO police station (522), and even a DUPLO town (524). Sets became more animated with painted details and interesting new parts adding to the play value of the DUPLO world and encouraging children to keep playing with these bricks as they get older.

Going Global: How LEGO Began to Conquer the World

World War II changed the face of European industry. Compared to the atrocities and destruction that occurred across much of Europe, Denmark suffered few casualties during the war, and having surrendered to Germany early on in 1940 in exchange for control over their domestic political affairs, things in Denmark continued relatively unchanged—although food was rationed and some materials were harder to come by. If anything, the LEGO Group flourished during wartime and managed to expand. During the 1930s Germany had been the largest exporter of toys to other European countries, especially Denmark, but soon these manufacturers were forced to contribute to the war effort, which opened up the market for Danish manufacturers to sell more products to the Danish people.

This left TLG in a stronger position financially, after the war ended in 1945, and allowed it to continue with the development of its plastic toy lines, and then the LEGO brick. After the war ended, the Marshall Plan saw European economies grow at an unprecedented rate. Denmark received U.S. $385 million in aid, and across Europe there was a 35 percent rise in industrial production. By 1952 most European countries were better off than they had been before the war and so was the LEGO Group. But it was clear to GKC that to keep a foothold on the toy market they would have to risk expansion, and his Scandinavian business trips in the early 1950s would prove extremely useful—as these were the easiest and most obvious countries to work with first.

Perhaps due to Sweden's close proximity, and the fact that there were no import restrictions there (unlike in Norway, where TLG's only option was to license out molds to a third-party manufacturer), Godtfred went into business with a couple he had met on his earlier business trips—Axel and Greta Thompson. The Danish husband and wife had set up a business producing dollhouses and the accompanying furniture in Lerum, Sweden, and were the exclusive Swedish distributor of LEGO throughout the 1950s until a foreign sales office, LEGO Sweden, was set up there in 1959. This same year LEGO made waves in France, Britain, Belgium, and Sweden by setting up a variety of distribution deals, and sales offices, or arranging licensing agreements, depending on the country's current market. Godtfred also licensed out the molds to an Icelandic rehabilitation center for Tuberculosis patients—where as part of their occupational therapy, patients were involved in the production of LEGO toys from 1956 until 1977. Although Godtfred had to rely on licensing for these initial export agreements, he soon realized that setting up individual sales offices in each country would be the only way to retain control and ensure the quality and consistency of the LEGO brand around the world.

The first foreign sales office, however, appeared in 1956 in the largest toy market in Europe—Germany. The Hohenwestedt office was a result of good fortune and the connections Godtfred had made in Scandinavia. By 1954 Axel Thompson was living in Germany running a toy factory there as well as in Sweden. Excited by the prospect of bringing LEGO to the German market, which had steadily rejuvenated its toy business empire since World War II, Thompson sold his Swedish business to his son and in 1956 became the general manager of LEGO *Spielwaren* GmbH (LEGO Toys) and prepared to go into battle with Godtfred against Deutschland and its critics. After a slow start, a few clever marketing tactics, and the developments of the LEGO brick itself into a better plastic product, sales in Germany steadily rose—by the 1960s Germany was the LEGO Group's largest foreign market, and remains the largest LEGO customer base in Europe today.

By 1960 LEGO was being exported across Europe and distributors were being established, usually replaced later by sales offices, every year. New partners were based in Switzerland, Finland, the Netherlands, and Italy. With so many languages to consider, LEGO stopped producing packaging with language-specific text to avoid having to produce multiple designs. All countries received the same packaging with "LEGO System" as the product's name.

British LEGO Ltd. was established in the U.K. in 1959. Unlike in other territories, such as Germany, where a sales office had been set up, Godtfred decided to license out LEGO to a British manufacturer who was already familiar with the market. Given that Frank Hornby's well-loved Meccano already had such a big share of the market there, it would have been presumptuous to assume a Billund-controlled sales office would have been able to do enough to take a slice of the pie. Courtaulds, a successful plastics and textiles producer, were the company to win the license and set about importing parts from Billund to sell to the U.K. market (and associated territories including Australia and Ireland). A factory in Wrexham, Wales, would manufacturer sets from 1963 until the license agreement ended in the early 1990s and the LEGO Group established its own sales office in the U.K., now based in Slough near the headquarters of the U.K.'s major toy retailers.

British toy historian Kenneth Brown explained how U.K. buyers would have seen LEGO bricks as a British toy, given that it was largely made in the U.K. Of the company's introduction to the U.K. as a toy manufacturer he said, "Where LEGO had the advantage was in presentation and continuous product development, two areas in which Meccano, by contrast, lagged well behind." This innovation can be seen in a popular 1970s LEGO TV commercial featuring the voice of British comedian Tommy Cooper. It features stop-motion animation of a LEGO mouse who must keep transforming into various other LEGO models so as not to be eaten by a LEGO cat (who is also transforming). The commercial demonstrates the versatility and possibilities of LEGO bricks—if you have enough of them—and closes with the statement "LEGO— It's a new toy every day."

By the 1960s it was clear that the LEGO Group was becoming an international affair (from 1962, sales were also taking place in Singapore, Hong Kong, Morocco, and Japan) and without an airport in Billund, around-the-world-travel was proving more time-consuming and costly than necessary. Godtfred purchased a small plane, but was still having to fly it from Esbjerg airport nearly forty miles away from Billund. In 1961 a larger aircraft was purchased and a landing strip and aircraft hangar were built in the field near to the factory. By 1964 the airport was opened to the public and a new passenger terminal was unveiled in 1966 and again in 2002. Today, Billund Airport is the second busiest in Denmark, behind Copenhagen Airport. The airport would prove extremely useful, firstly for the international relationships the company developed during the '60s and '70s, and secondly, but perhaps more surprisingly, for the influx of tourists soon to be making their way to Billund to visit LEGOLAND.

One country that faced import restrictions as late as the 1970s was Italy. LEGO Italy was established in 1961, but ten years later, largely due to an economic recession in the country, the Italian government banned the importation of LEGO toys into the country. In response to this, the LEGO Group established a manufacturing subsidiary in Italy where products would be made and sold. The result of this agreement was LEGO Minitalia: exclusive Italian sets released between 1971 and 1977. Minitalia stands apart from regular sets from the period as they were produced from different molds to regular LEGO bricks. Although some more complex parts (such as boat hulls) were imported, Minitalia created most of its bricks and other parts under license, resulting in bricks having hollow rather than solid studs on top, and either slitted tubes or "x"-shaped interlocking parts underneath. Minitalia sets also included its own range of window and door pieces. The first sets in 1971 consisted largely of red, green, and white bricks, and packaging saw a young boy building different-size houses. Later sets included other colored bricks and featured models of trains, trucks, and boats on the packaging. Unlike the sets being released in the rest of Europe, which were more heavily geared toward the models themselves, these sets were more reminiscent of earlier LEGO, with the photo of a wholesome young boy (girls were not featured on the Minitalia set boxes) playing with the bricks always featuring prominently on the box. While some collectors do not consider these official LEGO sets, due to the irregularity of the bricks, they are very much a part of the company's history. Minitalia shows how important it was for LEGO to get a foothold in as many countries as possible, even if some sacrifices had to be made. This same school of thought was applied to LEGO's first attempt to make waves in the United States.

The European toy-making heritage may have been suppressed during wartime, especially in Germany, but across the Atlantic the toy industry had never been as prolific as it was after World War II ended. While the European manufacturers were getting back on their feet, a booming young population in the United States was hungry for consumer goods, especially new plastic toys to entertain its growing numbers of children. The year 1945 was when toy giant Mattel first opened its doors for business and it wouldn't be long before it was producing Barbie dolls and Matchbox cars for a worldwide audience. By the end of the 1950s, the kids of America were the largest toy market out there—so it's no surprise that the LEGO Group wanted a slice of the pie.

At this time LEGO was still establishing the System of Play and had only launched the modified new LEGO brick in 1958. Having little experience of taking on such a large market and with the wooden toys factory fire in 1960, Godtfred knew the company was not in a position to set up an American sales office. As in Britain, he would need a licensing partner to help TLG break the United States as well. After meeting with King Shwayder, the president of the Colorado-based Shwayder Bros. Trunk Company, Godtfred signed a 99-year licensing deal, giving the company exclusive rights to sell LEGO toys in North America.

Shwayder Bros. set up a separate LEGO sales division and began producing LEGO bricks out of one of its existing plants in Ontario and selling them in the United States from 1961 and Canada from 1962. Taking the name of their famous range

SAMSONITE

Set up by the four Shwayder brothers in 1910, the "Trunk Company" was a suitcase manufacturer that would later become known as the Samsonite Corporation—after a successful range of luggage marketed under that name. In the 1960s, its retail and plastics manufacturing experience encouraged the company to expand, and drew it to the LEGO Group where it bid on and won the license. After over 10 years of LEGO manufacturing, the license was withdrawn in 1972 and Samsonite's association with the LEGO brand remained only in its marketing and distribution of sets in Canada until the late 1980s. The company was sold in 1973, and the Samsonite name has changed hands many times since. Samsonite is now exclusively a luggage manufacturer owned by private equity firm CVC Capital Partners.

By 1963, North American sets no longer included the "by Samsonite" branding, like this wheel set (021). © Jordan Schwartz

of luggage (and later the company's name), products were marketed as "LEGO by Samsonite." In 1965 Samsonite built a new facility in Colorado, exclusively for LEGO products, to cope with the growing demand in the United States. Initially it offered sets that were very similar to those available in Europe—such as a Town Plan set, and supplementary gift sets, but when the new plant opened up, Samsonite began to produce its own LEGO creations, and sets far larger than TLG was making. LEGO Futura even developed exclusive pieces for the American market.

Samsonite produced its own version of what would later be the LEGO Group's DUPLO bricks. Trying to widen the appeal of the LEGO brand, in 1964 Samsonite produced larger bricks (measuring 1 × 2 × 4 inches) known as Jumbo Bricks in the 2 × 4 stud format, as well as toys made from the bricks, such as 1963's Jumbo Brick Pull Toy, which came with its own Jumbo Brick wheels. Unlike the later DUPLO bricks, these were not compatible with LEGO bricks, and can easily be identified by their size and larger flat-topped studs. American consumers were also the first to be able to purchase gears and motors from as early as 1963 when the first sets incorporating this technology were available (001, 002, 003). The gears allowed builders to mechanize their designs with geared transmissions or rotating parts by connecting the simple gear discs to a wheel or wheel brick. Later an electric motor was designed by Futura, which could be incorporated. Despite the gears being physically compatible with LEGO bricks, their design and usage was not fully integrated into the System

This Adventure Set was one of the basic building sets offered by Samsonite in the late 1960s. © Jordan Schwartz

of Play—something the LEGO Group did not achieve until three years later with the introduction of the motorized train in 1966.

Although the North American sets were exclusive to this territory, the choice available was consistently less than the range in Europe. The workmanship is also considered to be of a lower quality—Samsonite LEGO toys continued to be produced in celluloid acetate even when Billund had switched to the more durable and colorfast ABS, presumably to keep costs down. By 1970, the Samsonite catalog included just forty-one available items in comparison with the European catalog from the same year which listed over 100 different products. Perhaps due to the staggering size of the American market, Samsonite was forced to rely on catalog retailers to bring in sales. To these customers it offered some exclusive sets, and in an effort to bring in business, increased the number of pieces per set far beyond anything TLG had produced—one of the last sets produced by Samsonite featured in a 1973 JC Penney catalog. For just $13.99, customers could order a 1,241-piece set, which Samsonite had proudly displayed as a frontier town. This quantity over quality strategy was not common LEGO practice, and reduced profits considerably.

LEGO toys were not deemed a priority for the Samsonite Corporation, however, and it continued to expand, producing other toys, games, children's furniture, and even ice skates, along with the luggage arm of the company. The resources allocated to generating LEGO sales and marketing the product were considerably less than U.S. toy rivals Hasbro and Mattel (Hasbro had been the first to advertise a children's toy on television with Mr. Potato Head in 1952). That's not to say Samsonite didn't understand the ingenuity of the LEGO brand: One of its print adverts from 1967 described it as a toy children wouldn't be tired of by December 26 and refers to it as "the thoughtful toy." This seems in keeping with the creativity and play-longevity associated with the product in Denmark, but the company's attention was split. By the late 1960s it was clear that Samsonite's core experience in marketing and selling luggage was not specific enough to the delicate nature of the toy industry. The LEGO Group moved to withdraw the license from Samsonite in 1972 and soon regained control of the brand in North America, establishing LEGO USA in Enfield, Connecticut.

LEGOLAND: 1968–present

The whole concept of LEGOLAND is the stuff of dreams. For any child who's ever spread out his entire brick collection on the living room floor and marveled at the size and scale of his latest creation, visiting a place where everything he sees has been carefully reduced and reconstructed using that same toy is magical. Beyond that, it's impossible. How can that many LEGO bricks exist in one place? How does one even contemplate producing LEGO models on such a scale and how could anyone have ever envisioned it? A land made from LEGO bricks really was the stuff of dreams, but not anymore. Now, it's a tourist institution, a collection of internationally renowned theme parks teeming with adults and children alike, who arrive in droves to witness the engineering feats of professional LEGO designers and builders.

The original LEGOLAND, opened in 1968, still remains in the birthplace of the brick—Billund, Denmark—but its arms are far-reaching with parks now in England, California, Germany, and Florida. While the parks do serve as a glossy advertisement and retail space for the wide range of LEGO products, they're much more than that. A place where LEGO models are built on a scale like no other, where remarkable designs can inspire intrepid young builders, and iconic landmarks of the world can be visited by strolling through a park. They may not have the real White House, Eiffel Tower, or Mount Rushmore, but what they do have is close enough.

GKC toyed with the idea of building a LEGO park for some years before anything was put on paper. LEGO models intended for trade shows and department stores were frequently being visited by the public, drawing school groups and families to the factory. By the mid-1960s an average of 20,000 people a year made the visit to Billund. GKC noticed the way people marveled at their studio's simple arrangements, but was desperate to keep the factory space clear for the growing workload, so he set about creating an outdoor exhibition instead. Despite the models' popularity over the years, Godtfred's original idea for the park was realistic but modest—an open-air show to fill a garden or possibly a soccer field. But by the time Copenhagen window designer Arnold Boutroup was hired as the park's general director, charged with the task of visualizing their ideas and turning the designs into reality, the company had developed a theme park plan that was as vibrant and varied as LEGO bricks themselves. Although most of these ideas were considered too big, too difficult, and too unrealistic, one of Boutroup's sketches showed a simple, circular, open-air enclosure with a few LEGO towns on display, and this was the model for the park when it opened on June 7, 1968.

Denmark had long been home to both Dyrehavsbakken (opened in 1583) and the Tivoli Gardens (1843), the world's oldest amusement parks, the latter an undeniable inspiration for Walt Disney's original Californian theme park, Disneyland, where he turned children's playthings and cartoons into money-making family fun over a decade before the LEGO Group decided to give it a go. This was all great reference material for GKC and Boutroup when it came to determining how best to sell LEGO as an amusement park experience, but it wasn't until the two men visited the Netherlands' very own miniature city, Madurodam in the Hague, that their vision for LEGOLAND became clear. Opened in 1952, the Dutch miniature town built on the same 1:25 scale used for many of LEGOLAND's structures has been visited by tens of millions of people. Having witnessed the charm and popularity of Madurodam's minute reality first-hand—real Dutch buildings and landmarks shrunk down to give the visitor a true Lilliputian experience—the Danes knew that the same idea could work with LEGO.

Arthur Boutroup may have been influential in designing the park, but it was Dagny Holm, a chief designer in the model shop in Billund, who can be credited with supervising most of the original building work. A clay sculptor by trade, Godtfred's cousin, Holm, initially found it difficult to work in the medium of LEGO bricks, but she soon learned that building a LEGO model was not a case of molding and shaping, as with clay, but rather creating a pattern, similar to embroidery. After years of hard work, Holm, together with her small team, had successfully reproduced hundreds of European buildings including a Dutch town, and Swedish fishing village, as well as many famous Danish landmarks. In total they had used nearly six million bricks. Although some older models have been updated, refreshed, or removed, some of her team's work still stands in Billund today, giving the original park a sense of history not yet associated with the newer incarnations around the world.

With the model building well under way, the plot of land near Billund's airport and the LEGO factory began to be carved out of the Jutland moors in 1966 in preparation for the tiny world that would soon be ready to call it home. The Billund Park that exists today is a far cry from the modest park that was originally built—it now covers an area of nearly 35 acres. Far more than a simple collection of LEGO models, the park was developed to include the main Miniland attraction, Fort LEGOREDO—a Wild West–themed area where you can pan for gold and play in an Indian camp; a driving school where children (aged six to thirteen) can drive electric cars around a realistic course, learning to obey the rules of the road; a life-size LEGO train; a chil-

Taken from LEGOLAND Billund's impressive LEGOTOP viewing platform, this photograph shows part of the park today, including the Peugeot Traffic School, LEGO Studios, and the Knight's Table castle. © Eileen Sandá

Even waterways to represent Europe's rivers and harbors were re-created, as can be seen in this Miniland model of Bergen, Norway. © Eileen Sandá

Miniland's models are made to last, like this re-creation of the Nyhavn district in Copenhagen, which was constructed in the 1980s. © Eileen Sandá

dren's puppet theater; a LEGO building area; and the Christiansen family's prized antique doll collection. The extensive doll collection, not connected to the modern LEGO aesthetic of the rest of the park, became a focal point when in 1978 the family paid $200,000 at auction for the most famous, and then most expensive, dollhouse in the world. They displayed it along with the dolls and other antique toys until 2006, when the collection was sold. This is not the only part of LEGOLAND Billund to have changed or disappeared over the years, and many new attractions have been added since. Despite this there's one attraction included in all the LEGOLAND parks that has endured and goes from strength to strength—Miniland.

Considered by most to be the heart of all LEGOLAND parks, the Miniland at Billund is where the true spirit of the LEGOLAND ethos lies. Boutroup's original intention was that the park would communicate the many possibilities the LEGO brick provides and the challenge it poses to our imaginations. And this challenge is no more obvious than in Miniland. GKC and Boutroup believed that visitors would enjoy seeing scaled models of real buildings and locations rather than fictitious creations from the designers' imaginations, and they were right. But for the designers charged with this task, there was an added level of accuracy and attention to detail required if they were to produce buildings that tourists from all over the world were to recognize.

Before the days of sophisticated computer design technology, in order to re-create a real Swedish village, designers spent time there taking thousands of photographs from every angle. They also recorded measurements to determine the true size and correlation of all the village's buildings. Back in the studio, hours were spent producing 1:25 scale models made from plaster and wood, before LEGO designs were drawn up on graph paper and allocated to individual builders. Dagny Holm's building team had far fewer brick styles to work with than designers today, but the models they produced were still impressive—the only real cheat employed by builders, which is still used today, was the use of glue to hold bricks together so that the models—that remained outdoors throughout the cold and wet Danish winter—could withstand the elements and the necessary handling and transportation.

Much like the real world, Miniland is always changing. As model designs have become more sophisticated and the LEGO parts collection has grown accordingly, more and more possibilities are open to designers. Models are checked frequently for wear-and-tear, sun and weather damage, and real-world accuracy on a regular basis. But whether it's changing one of the 11,000 light bulbs, fitting in a new building to keep up with the world's ever-changing skyline, or adding an entirely new Miniland installation, the LEGOLAND team endeavors to keep the park's central attraction fresh and exciting.

One such development took place at Billund in the 1980s, a one-year construction of Copenhagen's Nyhavn Harbour and the surrounding area. A locale of considerable public focus and recognition, there was no room for error, and eight designers

Bjørn Richter's Mount Rushmore at LEGOLAND Billund is still one of the park's most impressive LEGO sculptures. © Jeremy Tilston

were entrusted with the task of pulling it off. The resulting colorful installation made up of over three million bricks includes 123 buildings and forty-one ships floating in the water. A more recent attempt to top this feat was the 2004 completion of a mini Billund Airport, to tie in with the opening of the new terminal there. On completion it was the largest single structure in Miniland. LEGOLAND's designers' enthusiasm for the limitless number of new, clever ways to show off their skills means that the total number of individual bricks used in Miniland has shot from six million to twenty million in the last forty years.

One man who knows all too well what it means to use a lot of bricks is artist Bjørn Richter. Better known as the man who built Mount Rushmore (albeit out of LEGO bricks), he is a Danish LEGOLAND legend whose intricate designs have truly stood the test of time at the park. Commissioned in 1970 to produce three works on a scale never seen before, he was not limited by the 1:20 or 1:25 scale of Miniland, and was free to build as he saw fit. This was an instant attraction for the young artist who said, "I felt that it would be exciting to join a unique idea from the very start. There were almost no limits to travel for inspiration or research." Richter was inspired by the Native American culture he had seen on his travels, and began designing Mount Rushmore. He had never built from LEGO bricks before and while describing the material as similar to working with clay he had to use a more methodical approach than he was familiar with. "Because of the mathematical logic of the system it was possible,

Bjørn Richter spent two years working on his Chief Sitting Bull statue, which still stands in LEGOLAND today. Photo courtesy of Bjørn Richter

and necessary to design the layout on huge, printed sheets," he explained. "Then I drew outlines of the shell, which was built with DUPLO bricks to save time. After that, the shell was modeled in detail with ordinary-sized bricks."

Installed four years later, the rocky relief consisted of 1.4 million LEGO bricks and 40,000 DUPLO bricks. Bjørn Richter was a close friend of Dagny Holm's who worked on the buildings and stylized animals while he developed his large-scale structures. "Nobody had ever seen that kind of work, or thought it possible," he said. "I gather I broke some limits and rules." Not satisfied with his first record-breaking brick count, Richter topped it with the Great Bison Hunt relief, and the Chief Sitting Bull sculpture, which when finished stood thirty-six feet tall and required 1.75 million bricks. Describing the atmosphere working at LEGOLAND, Richter said, "Everything was new; nothing like LEGOLAND existed anywhere. There was a pioneering spirit at that time, which promoted the best of creativity." Not surprisingly, given their artistic credentials and impressive stature, Bjørn Richter's work still stands in LEGOLAND today, although they do get a fresh layer of lacquer every spring.

Slightly faded, after years braving the elements, Chief Sitting Bull observes the wonders of LEGOLAND Billund from his rocky perch. © Jeremy Tilston

Despite the summer tourist season being well under way by the time Billund was ready to open in 1968, the world's first LEGOLAND saw 625,000 visitors make the trip to the moors that year to witness the spectacle—a number that far surpassed GKC's expectations. This park made from LEGO bricks situated far from the nation's capital soon became the second most visited tourist destination in Denmark after Copenhagen and has remained so ever since. Today, LEGOLAND Billund's annual attendance is around 1.7 million with 44 million people having visited the park since it opened its doors over forty years ago.

With things not having gone quite to plan in Germany, it was understandable that GKC was reluctant to push forward with another park. His son, Kjeld, however, realized the potential to expand and promote the LEGO brand through the parks, and in 1989 set things in motion to develop a worldwide LEGOLAND building strategy. Most of today's major theme parks were built in the 1970s and it was throughout the 1980s that the theme park industry came into its own, adding new attractions and locations, drawing people to destinations all over the world in search of fun and thrills. While competing with the likes of Universal Studios, Disney parks, and Six Flags, LEGOLAND also stood out on its own, more specifically targeting a younger audience. Kjeld's plan was to seize this momentum and LEGOLAND's uniqueness and roll out the Billund model in a number of different locations. Rather than build the parks with outside help and outside funding, the LEGO Group decided to take matters into its own hands and run the show itself.

When, in 1992, Windsor Safari Park went into receivership, TLG leaped at the chance to buy up the land. The Safari Park, which had been at the site since 1969 (the year after Billund was opened), housed a large number of animals in outdoor enclosures, as well as Seaworld, an attraction featuring performing dolphins and a killer whale. Despite its prime location, visitor numbers to the park had trailed off and owner Themes International suffered crippling financial losses, in part due to expensive new developments at the park. New homes were found for all the animals and the LEGO Group moved in to renovate. Nothing of the original park was left behind except for a funicular railway.

LEGOLAND Windsor is now one of the U.K.'s top theme parks, and was joined in 1999 by LEGOLAND California in Carlsbad and in 2002 by LEGOLAND Deutschland in Günzburg. Each of these distinctive theme parks includes its own personalized Miniland attraction featuring iconic buildings from the country they are situated in. But Miniland is only part of the LEGOLAND experience, and all of these parks include a variety of rides and experiences for families to enjoy. LEGOLAND parks are aimed at three- to twelve-year-olds with roller coasters suitable for younger children, stunt shows and theatrical displays, driving schools, and activities that involve teamwork and interactivity so the whole family can participate.

In 2005, after a period of financial loss across its business, the LEGO Group decided to sell a 70 percent stake in the LEGOLAND parks to Merlin Entertainments

THE OTHER LEGOLAND

Many people wrongly believe that LEGOLAND Windsor was the second park to open, twenty-five years after Billund. In fact, it was only a few years after the LEGO Group was rightfully patting itself on the back for its success in Denmark that it decided to license out the LEGOLAND idea to a German company. With LEGOLAND Billund swiftly becoming one of the most popular tourist attractions in Denmark, there was no time for the Germans to waste, and they quickly set about building a park in Sierksdorf on the Baltic coast. Opening in June 1973, little is known about the park's initial reception. What is known, however, is that in 1976 the LEGOLAND license was pulled because of disagreements and, after just a few seasons in operation, the park was closed down. The Sierksdorf site was sold and transformed into Hansa Park—a family-oriented theme park. In the first few years of business, LEGO models could still be seen at Hansa Park. It was this negative experience with Sierksdorf that prompted GKC to refuse to expand the LEGOLAND parks arm of the company and the reason it wasn't until 1996 that a second park was opened by TLG in Windsor. This later expansion to the U.K. and California meant that finally, in 2002, LEGOLAND returned to Germany.

Group (MEG), a theme park and attractions operator owned by the Blackstone Group. While LEGO still has a share in the parks, MEG has developed the brand to include a new resort development in Florida, now the biggest LEGOLAND park in the world.

MEG is also responsible for launching a new LEGO experience. The first LEGOLAND Discovery Centre was opened in Berlin in 2007 and seven more have been rolled out since—one in Duisburg, Germany, four in the United States, one in Manchester, England, and one in Tokyo. These indoor attractions are suited to any climate and offer visitors more of an interactive experience based on the LEGO itself than rides and attractions. Still aimed primarily at young children, the centers include 4D cinemas, factory tours, model builder workshops and interactive classes, building zones, soft play areas, and LEGO shops to purchase all the latest toys. Of course the centers also include a Miniland (on a smaller scale than the outdoor parks), bringing the true LEGOLAND experience to many people who cannot make the longer journey to one of the LEGOLAND parks. Merlin Entertainments Group is looking at potential future sites in Europe, North America, and the Far East.

A view of Windsor's miniature LEGO world in the heart of the Berkshire countryside.
© Richard Ashworth

Some of London's most famous buildings and monuments are on display at LEGOLAND Windsor.
© Richard Ashworth

LEGO bricks are not the only thing on offer at LEGOLAND parks—rides and stunt shows like this entertain millions of visitors every year. © Richard Ashworth

What the LEGO System had managed to achieve, beyond being a less mechanical version of a Meccano set, was a play environment that lasted long after building, an inclusive building technique that encouraged girls and boys of any age to build from their imaginations. But there was something missing from the houses, cars, planes, and fantasy worlds these children spent hours playing with, and that something was people.

Known as "minifigs," "figs," and "LEGO people," those little yellow mini figures that populate LEGO creations the world over have as vibrant a history as the bricks they sit on. Despite now being one of the most recognizable elements in the LEGO universe, it wasn't until 1978—twenty years after the first stud-and-tube bricks came onto toy shop shelves—that the minifigures we know today were launched. Since then, they've evolved to become one of the most variable and collectible toys available, not to mention the world's largest population: Estimated at four billion, there are currently twelve times more LEGO minifigures than there are Americans.

But like all great civilizations, LEGO people did not start out as we now know them. Four years prior to the birth of the smiling minifigure, in 1974 the LEGO Group launched the Family set, which included parts to build five figures: grandmother, mother, father, and two children. Each figure had a set of opposable arms, hands that could be connected to other LEGO pieces, and small ears that formed connecting points for hair pieces. But unlike their descendants, their legs and torsos could not be moved. This LEGO family were also included in "home" sets, such as the 1974 Complete Kitchen sets (263), which included two figures. Adding a new dimension to the system of play GKC had developed, the figures were responsible for winning the LEGO Group its first British Association of Toy Retailers Toy of the Year Award in 1974 and were soon the biggest selling product, and a hit with girls and boys. Realizing they had struck gold, the company set about developing the LEGO figure, releezing variations on it that would go on to inspire the minifigure.

Jens Nygaard Knudsen had been working as a designer for LEGO Futura since 1968, creating LEGO cars, fire stations, and his first model that was brought to market: a police heliport (354). "After a while I started working on a small figure," he explained. "I thought the box sets needed more life in them. The figure consisted of three elements and had six different hats. It gave a spark of life to the box sets and a lot of new opportunities." Known as "the extra," or "stiffs," this simple angular figure had no facial expressions, no defined arms or legs, and served very little play purpose apart from being moved and attached. It could not hold onto other LEGO elements, and visually was a step backward from the more human form of the LEGO Family. Despite the original larger figures still being available, the extra appeared in a number of LEGO sets including Police Headquarters (370) and Texas Rangers (372). The scale of the figure was significantly smaller than the alternative figure design, meaning a set could more easily include enough pieces to make a house or plane that could accommodate these figures. But Knudsen hadn't given up on the little block people

"I am convinced that the minifigure will live as long as children play with LEGO," said designer Jens Nygaard Knudsen, pictured here during his time at the LEGO Group.
© Jens Nygaard Knudsen

The award-winning Family Set (200), released in 1974, injected characters and life into the LEGO System toys. © Pieter Stok

Set 277 was one of many "homemaker" sets that were released during the 1970s—with a more distinct dollhouse feel, they proved popular with girls as well as boys. © Pieter Stok

Released in 1975, these smaller police figures (659) with no faces, arms, or legs were the inspiration for the more detailed minifigures we know today. © David Martin

The smaller "stiffs" made sets like this 1976 Rescue set more playable, and opened the System up to new play theme ideas. © Jordan Schwartz

and as new ideas for exciting themes branching away from the town/home models were being developed, Knudsen was inspired to push his design further.

"I started designing a new figure with far more abilities than the old one that was on the market. I designed new moveable legs and arms with hands that could hold 3.2 millimeter accessories. I used the head from the old figure, as well as the hats." he said, In fact, around fifty prototypes (made from LEGO bricks and tin) were developed in the process of making the final figure.

Recalling the final stage of development of the first minifigure, Knudsen said, "Godtfred, who was known to us all simply as GKC, became more and more visible in our department. He was thrilled by the new ideas and the new figure. So after various alterations and adjustments the new minifigure was approved and we ordered the test tools for the production of it. Things really speeded up and GKC wanted us to push forward and get the elements produced quickly." This was also a top-secret matter at LEGO HQ and all designers who were given test elements for the minifigure had to sign a confidentiality agreement. The minifigure made its debut in the Town theme in 1978 and immediately became extremely successful. The first minifigure available in set 600 was a smiling figure with a yellow head, hat, black policeman's clothing, and moving arms and legs. Over thirty years later, that same policeman figure, updated, but very much the same, has morphed through over forty different versions, and appeared in more than 100 different LEGO sets, making it the most prolific minifigure of all time.

The first batch of minifigures included seven different figures across the Town, Space, and Castle themes. The famous policeman was followed by a fireman, a petrol station attendant, astronauts, and medieval knights. Despite original plans to avoid assigning gender to the toys—in the hope that children would use their imaginations—shortly after the first figures were introduced, a decidedly female-looking hospital nurse was launched. Since then a variety of hair pieces and clothes choices have given LEGO lovers the opportunity to develop a wide range of figures, both male and female, although there has always been a higher ratio of male to female minifigures.

From 1978 most Town sets were being marketed as LEGOLAND Town System, and TLG put out a large number of small sets introducing the new minifigure in its many guises. These sets' emphasis was less on big-scale building and more on playability, injecting color and characters into what was previously a vehicle-led world. Rather than continuing to produce large card boards to build models on, base plate sizes were increased and roadways made on them for LEGO vehicles. These were available individually and also as part of sets such as Bus Station (379) and 1980's Town Square Castle Scene (1592), which cleverly incorporated the medieval-style building being developed for the medieval knight-themed sets (covered in more detail later) with the modern Town style.

Released with the 1986 Police Command Base (6386), this policeman minifigure is one of many reincarnations of the first policeman from 1978. © StreetFly JZ

For a time, the LEGO Group released sets including both the old "family" size figures and the new minifigures (which featured as dolls or babies), such as this nursery set (297) from 1978. © Pieter Stok

One of the first few female minifigures released during the 1980s, this lady came with a convertible sports car (6501). © David Martin

Larger base plates such as this one from a 1981 fire station set (6382) included studs and railways and marked a departure from the traditional boards of the '50s and '60s. © David Martin

The minifigure celebrated its thirtieth birthday in 2008 and is one of the LEGO System's most collected elements. © Andrew Martin

MINIFIGURES BY NUMBERS

- Nine is the number of parts a minifigure is traditionally made up from. These are: head, torso, hip joint, two arms, two hands, and two legs. Some minifigures come with hair pieces or other accessories.
- Three is the number of parts a minifigure is typically packaged as. These are: head; torso, arms, and hands; hips and legs. Any headgear, including helmets, hats, and hair pieces, will not be attached in the packaging.
- Four is the number of standard LEGO bricks high a minifigure is, including its head.
- One is the number of holes that now exist in a minifigure head to reduce the risk of choking if the small part is swallowed.
- Seven is the number of points of articulation found on a typical mini figure: legs move back and forth, arms move back and forth, wrists swivel, and head swivels.
- Ninety is the number of degrees a minifigure can move its legs forward (they can only move them back about 45 degrees).
- And 3.9 is the number of minifigures sold every second in the world.

Police Command Base (6386), released in 1986. © StreetFly JZ

Throughout the 1980s, LEGO continued to update its various Town sets, adding in new building techniques and minifigure accessories. These can be seen in the archway garden wall and patio furniture of Holiday Home (6374), the signage and transparent pieces used for Motorcycle Shop (6373) and Cargo Center (6391), and the sheer scale and building versatility of larger sets such as Victory Lap Roadway (6395), Police Command Base (6386, pictured), and Big Rig Truck Stop (6393). The fast-paced, nonstop development of ideas and parts that Godtfred encouraged ensured these sets were a world away from the earliest stud-and-tube town sets of the late 1950s and incorporated emergency services, construction work, leisure activities, boats, and planes.

LEGO Train had emerged as a distinctive motorized theme of its own, and the introduction of minifigures to the vehicles set them apart from the model trains produced by the likes of Hornby and Lionel. Firstly, the minifigure scale was unique to LEGO Train—model trains are most popularly built in 1:87 scale—and secondly the primary colors and child-friendly appearance were markedly different from the more severe-looking models largely popular with adult hobbyists. The year 1980

Tug Boat (4005), released in 1982. © David Martin

Hamburger Stand (6683), released in 1983. © Andrew Martin

Emergency Treatment Centre (6380), released in 1987. © StreetFly JZ

Fire Patrol Copter (6657), released in 1985. © David Martin

marked the start of a new phase for LEGO Train, as it embarked on what is referred to as the "gray era." While still compatible with both the 4.5 and 12 volt lines, the tracks' familiar blue was replaced with a more natural gray color, and the trains themselves followed suit, adopting more realistic designs based on existing trains. The year 1980 also saw the launch of thirty-five sets related to the Train theme and while many of these were track parts, wagons, and accessories, there were a few engines to choose from, including a passenger steam train (7710), a diesel freight train (7720) and an electric goods train (7730).

It was during this period (1980–1991) that the LEGO Train theme moved beyond simply the trains and tracks themselves, perhaps to accommodate the more involved level of play the minifigures had introduced—the first railway station (7822) and level crossing (7834) hit stores in 1980, and were soon joined by a service wagon (7821), a goods station (7838), and a container crane (7823) by the end of the decade. The technology had also changed with a transformer that served an impressive array of remotely controlled functions including signals, points, and crossings as well as the introduction of lighting features on the trains and lampposts. The older blue-era trains were compatible with the new tracks, so Train enthusiasts could simply add to their collection.

This push-along passenger steam train (7710) was one of the first gray-era engines. It was compatible with 4.5 volt and 12 volt tracks. © David Martin

Released in 1985, this train (7715) included five minifigure passengers and a small platform. © StreetFly JZ

The 1985 passenger train (7715) included a platform with destination times. © StreetFly JZ

Sets such as this 1985 road crossing enabled fans to more easily merge Town and Train sets. © David Martin

While the introduction of trains to the LEGO world had been a departure from the original Town Plan building system, the contemporary designs and recognizable vehicles were a part of the larger LEGO Town a child would imagine. If you wanted a passenger train to drive past your police station or holiday cottage, now you could build one. But LEGO was about to go where no minifigure had gone before with the launch of a brand-new LEGO theme in 1978.

In 1962 United States President John F. Kennedy set a deadline. In a speech at Rice University in Houston, Texas, he declared that America would land a man on the moon by the end of the decade. Despite Kennedy's assassination a year later, the space program forged ahead and, as Kennedy had predicted, in 1969 Neil Armstrong spoke those infamous words as he stepped foot on the moon. It's not hard to see why in the late 1960s and 1970s, space travel held a fascination for the world. With the proliferation of international media and television news, the globe was united in this obsession of what was "out there." The toy industry, waking up to the influential power of the television, was quick to produce products that would appeal to the children of this new Space Age. The '60s saw the release of Mattel's Major Matt Mason astronaut action figures, the Ideal Toy Company's Zeroid robot aliens,

Set 358 was one of the first space-related sets to be sold in Europe. The nose cone of this model does not include the original parts, and an aerial is missing from the ground vehicle. © Pieter Stok

The iconic Classic Space uniform with planet logo. This logo has been repeated in various guises throughout the theme's history. © Owen J. Weber

and Colorform's Outer Space Men. The emergence of space toys helped breathe fresh air into the LEGO System, with a contemporary, new play theme as expansive as Town Plan. For LEGO fans who grew up on *Star Trek* and *Star Wars*, these were the sets which enabled them to play out their space adventure fantasies as the creators of their own ships, bases, and alien wars.

Perhaps because of the United States' heavy involvement with space travel, it was American licensee Samsonite who put out the first LEGO space toy in 1964. The set (801) was a small 98 cent packet that could make a simple rocket, but wasn't followed up with any bases or accompanying sets. The time from development to release of a new LEGO product could take up to three years, so it wasn't until 1973 that a rocket base (358) was launched in Europe. TLG seemed to be testing the ground, unsure if the space craze would hold long enough for them to develop sets and get them onto shelves. But they persevered and, despite the final Apollo moon landing taking place in 1972, released a set depicting a moon landing in 1975 (367) complete with a U.S. flag.

Jens Nygaard Knudsen was one of the designers who worked tirelessly to bring the new LEGO Space toys to life. "LEGO Space and was given top priority so we worked hard to finish the theme," he recalled. "We had to make many samples by hand, build models and make test tools, new decorations, a space logo, a new vacuum plate system (32 × 32 studs) and much more. After several months of hard work—I actually put in fourteen months of work hours in a year—the space theme was finished."

Commonly referred to as "Classic Space," the early space-themed sets of the 1970s and '80s were a design revolution for LEGO. Although later they would introduce a number of new parts in exotic colors to create dramatic spaceship shapes and set the tone for the science-fiction world of the new theme, these early sets were relatively simple but carefully designed to create a recognizable impression of space that children who knew all about Neil Armstrong could identify with. Gray was en vogue in Space and featured heavily in spaceships, bases, and new base plates

This moon-landing set (565 in the United States, 367 in Europe) featured some inventive astronaut figures and a U.S. flag. © Jordan Schwartz

(some of which included craters). The theme was called LEGOLAND Space System, and featured the same packaging style as the LEGOLAND Town System sets.

The original 1978 "Classic Space" sets such as Rocket Launcher (462) and Space Command Centre (493) were manned by some of the very first minifigures. Available in red and white uniforms emblazoned with a unique space logo, accompanied by the meticulously designed helmets and airtanks, the sets were brought to life as children could play real space games with real astronauts. The minifigure brought with it the opportunity for LEGO to sell smaller sets that could build a small buggy or spacecraft with as few as 19 pieces (885 Space Scooter); these cheaper sets made LEGO more accessible to lower-income families. Producing smaller, more economical sets forced LEGO to get creative with how they used the system's parts, as can be seen in 1980's Shovel Buggy (6821) and 1983's Seismologic Vehicle (6844). But LEGO did its best to keep larger set collectors happy, too, with some ingenious spaceship designs, including 1979's Galaxy Explorer (928) and its big brother, Galaxy Commander (6980), released four years later with a white and blue color scheme and mobile laboratory that fits onto the back of the ship for transport. Using the Electronic Light & Sound technology developed for LEGO train sets, a few sets were released with these battery-run capabilities. Sonar Transmitting Cruiser (6783) and XT-Starship (6780) were both available in 1986, and Sonic Robot (6750) in 1987. The

This space supply station (6930) released in 1983 is an example of the simple but effective sci-fi building Classic Space incorporated. © Owen J. Weber

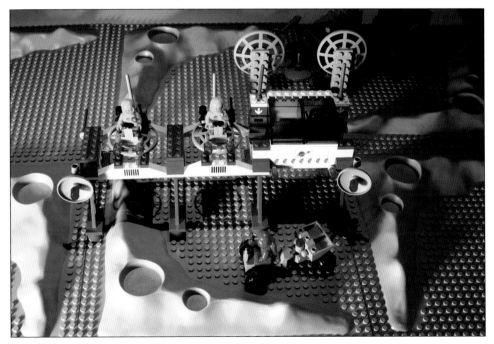

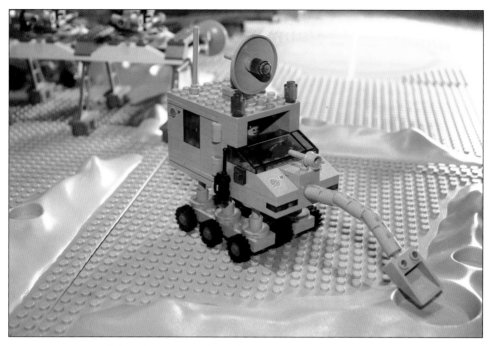

Mobile Lab (6901), released in 1980. © Owen J. Weber

The 1986 XT-Starship was one of a few Classic Space sets that incorporated the Light & Sound technology. © David Martin

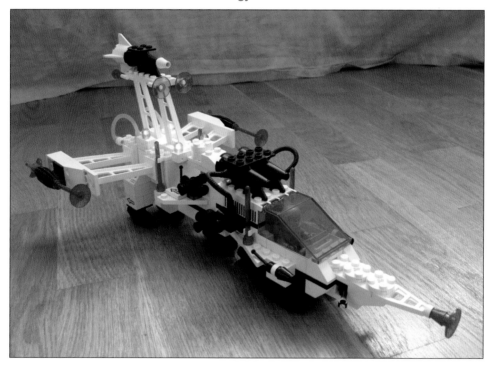

technology was ideally suited to the Space theme which pioneered the use of color-ed transparent parts and innovative design, and added yet another dimension to these sci-fi creations.

While the majority of Classic sets were imaginative and stretched the scientific truth of space technology at the time (and even since), some sets stand out for their imaginative spirit more than others. There was the Solar Power Transporter (6952), Walking Astro Grappler (6882) with its controllable trunk, and the Robot Command Centre (6951) that launched a rocket from behind while a spaceship docked in the robot's mid-section. LEGO's gamble in space paid off, and sets continued to fly off the shelves. "It became a huge hit straight away and generated hundreds of new jobs in Billund," Knudsen said. LEGO Space toys were a phenomenal success for LEGO and were subsequently named 1979's Toy of the Year by the British Associa-tion of Toy Retailers.

The unforgettable Space sets from this period still delight adult fans who fondly remember their childhood introduction to LEGO through this distinctive theme. LEGO sold smiling astronaut minifigures who busied themselves on space missions for eleven years before the next stage in the theme's evolution appeared at the end of the 1980s. Space was about to get all shook up with the emergence of good guys, bad guys, and very cold planets.

*   *   *

Uranium Search Vehicle (6928), released in 1984. © Owen J. Weber

For a company that set out in 1958 to produce simple plastic bricks to entertain and encourage development in children, TLG was unrecognizable twenty years later. By 1979 they had established themselves firmly as a producer of popular toys for children of all ages: From DUPLO's infant and preschool range celebrating its tenth year in production, to new jewelry sets for girls (see chapter 4) and the evolution of the Expert Builder sets from 1977 for advanced builders (covered later in this chapter), not to mention the Town and Space System sets that were growing in popularity. To an outsider it appeared there wasn't a toy-buying demographic the LEGO Group wasn't trying to cater to. But somehow they found a gap in the market. While the company encouraged parents to help their children make the transition from the large DUPLO bricks to smaller LEGO parts customer research showed that some children struggled to build the system sets—often palming off the building process to adults or older siblings—and would find it difficult to play, especially maneuvering the small minifigures without repeatedly breaking the models. While the Basic building sets, which had been a firm fixture since the late 1960s, offered children as young as three the opportunity to build simple models and use their imagination, there was no unified idea to make them marketable and attractive to young children.

FABULAND, first released in 1979, was the first LEGO theme to address this transitional group of LEGO fans. The sets, while including regular-size LEGO bricks, were assembled with the help of larger plastic parts, such as an entire house front with windows and door. LEGO bricks would contribute to the playability of the set, such as building the roofs, chimneys, or parts of small vehicles. The theme was also the first produced by LEGO to include specific characters. The peaceful community of FABULAND was made up of a group of anthropomorphized animals including dogs, cats, mice, sheep, pigs, monkeys, and even a lion. In some territories, the animals had names. Therefore, set 341 was known as Cathy Cat's & Monty Mouse's Cottage. These new minifigures were slightly larger than regular LEGO figures, and had looser joints and oversize heads, making it easier for small hands to grip and rotate them.

Despite their construction and color simplicity (with the exception of FABULAND figures, pieces were produced mainly in red, green, blue, and yellow), the sets were fairly detailed to keep small minds occupied. The earlier sets were largely based around building locations, and most included more than one character for imaginative play as well as sticker sheets to decorate the buildings. There was a FABULAND airport (in 1984, a year before the first LEGO Town airport appeared), petrol station, restaurant, bakery, and police/fire station. In 1983 small figurine sets were introduced, allowing children to add to their own FABULAND without their parents having to purchase large, more expensive sets. These were followed by vehicle-based sets in 1985 such as Police Car (3643) and Aeroplane (3625). Imaginative sets of the late 1980s such as Steamboat (3673) and two amusement park sets with Ferris wheels (3681 and 3683) turned FABULAND into a LEGO wonderland, focusing more on the fun side of life than the practicalities of policemen, hospitals, and airports more com-

FABULAND's Wally Walrus (released in 1984) came with a tricycle, flask, and umbrella in set 3791. © Fatima Pires Santos

monly associated with LEGO Town. FABULAND sets were also accompanied by little booklets which, as a 1985 catalog explained, introduced the inhabitants and the buildings of the FABULAND village. Parents were encouraged to use the booklet to inspire their children to tell their own stories.

FABULAND sold well throughout the 1980s, but perhaps due to strong competition from the likes of Fisher Price's Little People, Hasbro's new Transformers toys, and the popular Japanese craze Sylvanian Families, a toy which took the BATR Toy of the Year Award three consecutive years in a row (1987–1989), it was not to last. In 1990 no new FABULAND sets were released, marking the end of the range. Despite not being one of LEGO's longest-selling lines, FABULAND was a relative success and the first time LEGO stepped outside of minifigure territory to try and appeal to a marginal market. It would not be the last.

With FABULAND helping to bridge the gap between DUPLO and regular LEGO toys, DUPLO was being developed to bring children into the world of studs and tubes from the earliest age possible. The year 1983 was big for DUPLO and saw the range of toys expand to proudly take up six pages in what was named the "LEGO and DUPLO Catalogue." By this time, DUPLO had developed into a preschool range, providing a variety of toys suitable for up to five-year-olds. Despite targeting children as young as one in previous years, market research had found that the average age for children to receive their first DUPLO toy was two years old. Seeing a large portion of the infant toy market going untapped, the LEGO Group's research and development team, Futura, set about designing a range of products suitable for newborns and up. Research began in 1979, four years before the range would make it into the catalog. Its secret code name was "Project Baby." In his book, *The World of LEGO Toys*, Henry Wiencek describes how a trip to the British Museum inspired the research team. Having seen some of the world's oldest baby rattles on display, DUPLO designers knew that they wouldn't be able to invent a new product better suited to the mind and dexterity of a baby than the rattle, so rather than try and beat it, they decided to work with it to make the best DUPLO rattles they could. After various prototypes were made to appeal to babies at different stages of development, focus groups were held with mothers who ultimately informed some of the basic principles of the finished rattles. They were the ones to suggest handles, recommend reducing the size and weight of the rattles, and to make sure they could not be pulled apart, something the initial prototypes were capable of doing. While designers realized after the focus groups that the DUPLO rattles couldn't have the

This 1988 DUPLO Circus Caravan set (in the foreground) included the new articulated DUPLO figures, a dog (not pictured), and an elephant. © Pieter Stok

same construction play value of other DUPLO toys, they were built with studs at the top and holes at the bottom so that they could be integrated into the DUPLO building system when the child was older. The most well-known and well-received rattle from this range was the Duck Rattle-Teether. With its moving eyes, rotating central ball, and two handles, it proved a great success, and was sold virtually unchanged from 1983 to 1996.

The introduction of DUPLO figures with moving arms and legs, and push-trains with track pieces, as well as the introduction of dollhouse-themed play sets, enhanced DUPLO toys' appeal to the older end of the infant market. Sets such as Crane Set (2646), Play Farm (2655), and Play House (2770) show how, as much attention to detail was being paid to these products as to their System big brothers. Their constructional ability was carefully matched to the age range of children playing with them—all plastic furniture and accessories could be connected to something or have something connected to them, as well as being a non-intimidating, stand-alone toy. The range continued to develop and expand throughout the 1980s, adding new, innovative products for babies, toddlers, and young children.

It would be fair to say that the LEGO Group was covering all its bases: there should not have been a child out there, whatever age, who wasn't playing with some type of LEGO. A 1980 survey conducted revealed that 70 percent of all Western European families with kids under the age of fourteen owned LEGO Bricks, so the company was clearly doing something right. But it was those older children—the nine and up age group—the ones enticed by video games, 1980s action movie heroes, and *Star Wars* figures who LEGO wanted to keep interested into their early teens.

The Technic story begins in 1962 with the birth of the LEGO wheel. When the initial Small Wheels (400) and Large Wheels (401) were available to buy, children, for the first time, were able to build LEGO cars, trucks, and buses with real working wheels. LEGO bricks were finally in motion. Once the wheels were rolling, the LEGO Group moved on to design cog-style wheels and basic motors. These were initially sold by U.S. LEGO licensee Samsonite (a later version was sold in Europe) and were large by today's Technic standards. The round plates, with studs and tubes, would turn when connected to a wheel or a turntable. The gears were available in different sizes and colors and were designed to develop a child's interest in basic engineering principles. These first-generation gears were never sold in Europe, where LEGO started selling a new, updated version of the gear wheels. To provide more flexibility, gears were no longer attached using the stud-and-tube method, but rather a cross-shaped axle that the gear would fit over, as well as bearings and connectors to fit the axle into brick tubes.

This idea of "engineering" toys to produce a plaything that has working parts was the birth of the Technic range, which first emerged as a separate entity to the LEGO System in 1977 with the "Technical" sets. Early advertising declared they were "as technical as the real thing," and while this may not be entirely true—the models included helicopters, tractors, and fork-lift trucks—the design and appeal of the sets were much more mature than the LEGO System sets, at the time depicting Western scenes and moon landings. New bricks, beams, and connecting parts, produced predominantly in red, yellow, gray, and black, were inspired by and compatible with regular LEGO bricks but had the ability to connect in different ways. They made up the original lineup of four model sets, the largest of which was a 601-piece Auto-Chassis (853), and two supplementary sets, which included spare motors, pulleys, axles, bricks, and gears—many of which were new parts, such as the connector pegs, piston rods, and new Technic beam.

A year later the United States began selling the same products under the name "Expert Builder Sets"—"for experienced LEGO builders," and while these early sets still relied heavily on traditional LEGO parts, with each year designers developed new Technic components to increase building ability and minimize the space required for gears and motors. In 1980 the first Expert Builder Idea Book showed how much could be done with the parts already produced, and included instructions for mechanical dogs, a clock face, and a steam shovel. A year later a second generation of models were released. A second helicopter, tractor, and auto-chassis meant there wasn't much variety from the original 1977 models—these vehicles became synonymous with Technic, updated examples of which can still be found in the 2010 range.

In 1982, when Technic was officially named "Technic" in Europe (U.S. sets would not change from "Expert Builder" until 1986), the name first appeared on three sets

LEGO FOR ADULTS

Of course, Technic wasn't technically the first time the LEGO Group had produced a line geared toward the older market. In the 1960s, when Godtfred wanted to produce a scale model of a house he was designing, he realized LEGO bricks were not the right size to match other architectural model materials, so he simply had a new brick designed. These new bricks were 5/8 the size of regular LEGO bricks and formed the basis for a new building system Godtfred marketed under his new company Modulex. While the system was never a great success with architects, industrial planners found it useful and, in 1966, the product was available as the Modulex Planning System. Modulex would go on to produce interior signage systems and merge with an existing international signage company. Concurrently, the LEGO Group was developing three "architectural" sets targeting adults. The three sets included bricks and plates, but no special elements, meaning scale-model hobbyists were restricted in the style of buildings they could create. The range was not a success and was discontinued in 1965.

This U.S. Technic Universal Box (8020) released in 1984, still had the "Expert Builder" name—this wouldn't change in the United States until 1986. © Jordan Schwartz

called Universal Boxes (8030, 8050, and 8090). While the 1980s saw LEGO System sets becoming heavily themed, these Universal Boxes pushed builders to produce one of a number of sets, rather than trying to streamline their creativity. This was also the year a key Technic element was introduced—the friction connector—allowing two beams to be joined together in a secure connection, resulting in many of the frame-structures associated with Technic ever since. As the 1980s progressed, sets included more beams and less LEGO bricks—this move was especially evident in the 1984 Pneumatic series where sets such as the Fork Truck (8843) and Excavator (8851) included a pneumatic pump and cylinder and rubber tubing circuit system. By connecting the circuit and working the pump, builders could cause the vehicles to perform specific actions. In a market becoming increasingly saturated with licensed toys and electronics, the LEGO Group spent some of the decade trying to establish what kind of toy Technic was, and who it should appeal to. This can be seen with toys like 1987's Robot (8852)—a truck that transformed into a yellow and gray droid—quite obviously influenced by Hasbro's hugely successful Transformers line.

The release of eight new sets in 1986 was the largest release in the Technic line at that point, and that was in part due to the arrival of the first Technic "theme."

The Arctic Action series (8620, 8640, 8660, and 8680), while not straying far from the vehicle designs of the non-themed sets—they included a scooter, a helicopter, and a rescue unit comprising of a six-wheeled off-road car and a small snow plough—marked a significant move on Technic's part to make toys (rather than models) that children would want to play with. By creating a world and scenario as well as articulated figures to inhabit it, the system had moved from simply being about "expert builders" creating clever models toward the playability factor more commonly associated with LEGO toys. The set that stood out most from the group was Arctic Rescue Base (8680)—despite having wheels, and instructions to turn it into a helicopter transporter, this was the first building structure set to be produced using Technic parts.

While the movable Technic figures first included in the Arctic Action sets may not bear much resemblance to the LEGO minifigures fans had been introduced to eight years previously, the iconic yellow used for heads and the C-shaped hands made them unmistakable as TLG merchandise. Unlike their stockier predecessors, the Technic figures had more points of articulation (head, shoulders, elbows, wrists, hips, knees, and ankles) and with sculpted noses, ears, and even eyebrows, these folk were clearly the inhabitants of a far more technical world. For those keen to bring their older models to life, there were two sets released, each just including three

This 1988 Prop Plane (8855) originally included one Technic figure pilot dressed in red and blue with a white safety helmet. © Paul Tichonczuk

Technic figures. Set 8712 included a racing driver and mechanic with helmets—a third figure with red trousers had the common black bowl-cut hairpiece. The boys got a revamp in 1993 with set 8714 with three racing driver outfits, matching helmets, a pair of shades, and two mustaches!

Despite attempting to appeal to younger builders with the inclusion of these figures, the Technic models that followed continued to get more realistic and intricate. Even the 1988 box revamp, which saw the models posed in front of technical CAD drawings, played up the more mature construction values of the product over playability. While the LEGO Group would continue to include the figures in some sets throughout most of the 1990s, unlike LEGO minifigures they were not featured prominently on packaging or in promotional material. Instead the design and technical capabilities of the models were what drove their popularity and fueled sales. For ten years, Technic would continue relatively unchanged in appearance and intent—the LEGO building system for experts had finally found its place and it wasn't going anywhere. Popular sets from this period included 1989's Backhoe Grader (8862),—the back of which could be operated by three separate pneumatic cylinders; the Air Tech Claw Rig (8868) with 9 volt motorized pneumatic crane, and the mighty, 1425-piece Super Car (8880) that required a fifty-page instruction booklet to put together. The end of the 1980s saw the introduction of a 4.5 volt motorized set (8054), which was swiftly replaced the following year by the 9 volt Electric system (8720). This change in LEGO toys' electronics was the first since the 12 volt Trains were introduced in 1969, and soon filtered out from Technic sets across all of LEGO's electrical output. There were new flexible cables, the first Technic ship (8839), as well as various modifications to cables, hinges, gears, pneumatic parts, a new electronic control center (8485), and many new electronic elements. While future Technic sets would continue to push children to develop more advanced models, the 1990s would see the LEGO Group take the range down a more "playable" path to make the toys more appealing to a younger audience and some new technological advancements that would introduce Technic to a whole new generation of builders.

*   *   *

The same year the Technic name first appeared on toy shop shelves, the LEGO Group reached another milestone. Fifty years had passed since Ole Kirk Christiansen first started producing toys in his Billund workshop. A toy company that had started out of necessity for a struggling carpentry business was now celebrating its golden anniversary. And although so much had changed in that time, the true spirit of Ole Kirk's original toys lived on in the 1980s' bright, plastic designs the company was now producing. Where Ole Kirk had taken risks, embracing new plastic technology when the European market was so against it, the LEGO Group was now following suit with the introduction of new designs, new building systems, and new technology with the introduction of Light & Sound toys. Light & Sound was an electric system through

89

One of the more popular Technic sets from this period—the Backhoe Grader (8862), released in 1989. © David Martin

which LED lights and sound bricks were introduced to regular System models. The light bricks were capable of carrying different colored globes and could be set to flashing or continuous mode depending on their usage. There were two types of sound bricks that produced siren sounds—one more suited to Town sets and another to Space. Light & Sound technology was used through the 1980s and early 1990s.

With the unprecedented success of the new minifigures and Space System, the LEGO Group was ready to reward loyal fans with a brand-new theme. Jens Nygaard Knudsen was promoted to head of design in 1978 and put in charge of developing themes that were both futuristic and historical. After giving children the sci-fi play environment of Space, his department decided to concentrate its efforts on the past and a truly regal theme. Before the launch of the first Classic Space toys in 1978 and 1979, the LEGO Group had touched on the theme in earlier sets to gauge its popularity and success, as well as to develop building methods and styles for this new scientific frontier. The medieval world of LEGO Castle—one of the longest-running and consistently popular LEGO themes—was introduced in a similar way in 1978, with the release of a set simply named "Castle." Known to Castle collectors by its product number "375"—which indicates its categorization as a larger Town set, as opposed to a new theme—this three-turreted, bright yellow design featured a great variety of bricks to create the various slopes and walls, a drawbridge, a sticker sheet to decorate flags, shields and torsos with the Heraldic designs, as well as a record fourteen minifigures. This delightful set was one of the first to take LEGO building to another time period, and the addition of these knights and guards, with their helmets, horses, and weaponry, transported the castle model from historical relic to a living, breathing battlement.

Although 375 was the first castle set children were able to buy, it wasn't the first time the LEGO Group had encouraged them to build castles. Eighteen years previously, the first major LEGO Idea Book was released, emphasizing to children that they could build more than what was on the front of a set's box. Some of the larger illustrated models shown were actually produced by the professional model shops in Billund, Wrexham (U.K.), and Detroit (U.S.), to be bought and displayed by retailers. Of course, many children didn't own enough bricks to build the large designs, but it was something to aspire to; the idea being that if they kept collecting LEGO bricks they might be able to build what they saw—such as the blue and red five-story castle in the 1960–1963 Idea Book. Although the set itself wasn't sold, and the book featured ideas as opposed to detailed instructions, the spare parts packs sold through retailers meant they could potentially purchase all the bricks required to re-create a similar castle of their own. Other glued-together castle models were also sold

One of the most highly prized LEGO Castle sets is this yellow stronghold (375), released in 1978. © Owen J. Weber

through retailer magazines for display purposes, and some were built exclusively for advertisements and catalog photographs.

In 1979 two more castle-related sets were released, signaling a move toward the new theme. They were Knight's Tournament (383)—a small jousting set that included some rare parts (a large tree, two red decorated flags, and a female minifigure)—and Knight's Procession (677), a set of six knight minifigures and a small cart. The bright colors and harmless activities depicted in these three sets created a romantic, positive image commonly associated with the chivalry of the era. In the same way early Moon-landing Space sets were eventually replaced by space-cruising bad guys and police units, later Castle sets would feature more realistic colors and create factions, pitting knights (and other creatures) against each other in battle, making these early sets particularly unique.

As part of the theme's development, one of Knudsen's colleagues was charged with designing a horse figure for the theme (previously the horses had been built from an assortment of bricks). "After several handmade samples, we approved the horse with the design it still has today," Knudsen said. The theme's historical period required new levels of creativity, pushing designers to come up with all the elements required to create the medieval aesthetic, Knudsen explained: "We developed new accessories for the minifigure, such as helmets, visors, shields, swords, and flags, as well as developing new decorations and a (Tudor-style) wall element. We introduced grey bricks for this theme. Later we would go on to design a sorcerer, ghosts, skeletons, and an impressive dragon."

Maintaining fan interest in a theme that has run as long as Castle relies heavily on reinvention and the introduction of new factions. While the earliest LEGO guards from the first Castle set wore a blue and purple uniform with the crown on their torsos, other knights from the same set wearing different colors were also represented. It was not specified as to who the knights were, or whether they were on the same side. The release of a group of Castle sets under the LEGOLAND banner in 1984

WEETABIX CASTLE

Before 375, in 1970, British cereal eaters had the opportunity to own the first-ever LEGO castle set. In exchange for Weetabix box coupons, LEGO fans could send off for a 471-piece castle. Although smaller than minifigure scale and not as uniformed as its yellow ancestor—it included gray base plates, white turrets, a yellow corner tower, red walls, and blue finishes—it introduced the idea of using sloped bricks at the base of towers and 1 × 2 bricks to create the battlements. Due to its limited availability and its place in LEGO Castle history, this set is highly sought after by collectors.

A massed army of Black Falcons show off their blue uniforms with black and silver design. Collectors regularly trade minifigures from this era as they are no longer in production. © Ruben Salanda

saw the emergence of two distinct groups of knights. With more specific names attributed to sets and castles, and with identifiable uniforms and flags, it became commonplace for fans and LEGO literature to refer to these groups by name. Here, we explore the sub-themes of "Castle" released during the 1980s, their identifiable crests and clothing, and some of the sets in which they feature prominently. The date in brackets indicates the time period that each sub-theme was available.

Black Falcons (1984–1992)

Of the earliest sets released, the predominant shield design was that of a bird on a black and white crest. Although never officially named in LEGO literature, their 1986 castle, Black Falcon's Fortress, and this crest are the reasons fans have given them the moniker. This castle, encouraged by fan support, was re-released in 2002 as part of the LEGO Legends series. The majority of sets were sold until the early 1990s, and the last new set to feature a Black Falcon crest was a 1992 Black Knights set, the box of which happened to feature two Black Falcon minifigures with their swords raised—indicating that the two factions were enemies.

Crest: A black and silver bird (presumably a falcon) spread-eagled on a contrasting black and silver background.

Dress code: Their crest appeared on a blue torso, while their arms and legs were usually black. Some knights wore (painted/stickered) silver breast plates, and had black or gray helmets with slotted visors and colored plumes.

Find them: At home in Knight's Castle (6073), fighting off the Crusaders in Battering Ram (6062), and manning the catapult in 6030.

Crusaders (1984–1992)

The same year the Black Falcons saddled up and rode out, the King's Castle appeared, adorned with the image of a lion, protected by red and blue knights and guards. Some of the sets from this era including King's Castle (6080) feature guards with a crest of two crossing axes, as well as those wearing the lion crest, working together, and these are often referred to as Lion Knights sets. In 1992 LEGO referred to the lion-wearing "Crusaders" by name, but officially only a few LEGO sets from 1990–1992, including King's Mountain Fortress (6081), are considered "Crusaders." Given the similar appearance of the earlier sets, it's common for people to consider all the lion-crested sets as Crusaders.

Crest: Either a blue lion on a yellow background with a red border, or a yellow lion on a blue background with a red border.

Dress code: Red and blue are predominant with the ax-crested minifigures wearing red torsos with blue arms and legs, and their lion-crested friends wearing red torsos and legs (sometimes gray) with blue arms. Painted/stickered silver breastplates were worn by some, while others were decorated with chain mail. Later Crusaders usually had black legs. The Crusaders in King's Mountain Fortress were the

The impressive King's Castle (6080) in gray bricks could be opened out, as shown, to create a formidable defensive line against their enemies. © Owen J. Weber

An armor-clad Crusader brandishes his LEGO sword and shield—just some of the many accessories the LEGO Group designed to bring this medieval theme to life.
© Jordan Schwartz

This simple civilian setting (Guarded Inn) is one of the most popular LEGO Castle sets of all time, and was re-released in 2001 as part of the LEGO Legends series.
© David Martin

first to try out the new knight's full face helmets more commonly worn during the Crusades.

Find them: Haunted by one of the first glow-in-the-dark ghosts in King's Mountain Fortress, protecting a maiden in Guarded Inn (6067/10000) and rowing a boat in Viking Voyager (6049).

Forestmen (1987–1990)

While previously focusing on the pomp and privileged of the knight class, the LEGO Group turned to the outlaws of medieval times with the introduction of Camouflaged Outpost (6066) in 1987. This set was the first to feature the Forestmen—a group of merry bandits who lived in tree-covered caves and castle ruins. In some countries, the Forestmen were directly associated with the legend of Robin Hood—with 6054 (otherwise known as Forestmen's Hideout) referred to in some territories as Robin Hood's Tree Hideaway. They fought mainly with brown bows and arrows and the odd sword or wooden spear and while not technically a "Castle" subtheme, they could be seen launching an attack on the Black Knights and the Black Falcons in the 1989 catalog.

Crest: Not all the Forestmen were lucky enough to be carrying shields—but some of their bases proudly displayed the crest of a noble stag on a green background with a brown border.

The Forestmen brought vegetation to LEGO System in a big way, especially with this hideout set, Camouflaged Outpost. © David Martin

Dress code: The most common Forestmen minifigure, was the "Robin Hood" of the pack. His green torso and legs with red tunic and brown/green hat with a red feather make him unmistakable as the legendary folklore figure. Variations on the same outfit with blue, gray and black tunics made up the rest of the bandits, including a female minifigure with green bodice and necklace (only available in set 6071).

Find them: Hiding stolen treasure in Camouflaged Outpost, battling a lone Crusader in Forestmen's River Fortress (6077), or keeping lookout from the rope bridge in Forestmen's Crossing (6071).

Black Knights (1988–1994)

Although not strictly referred to as a "Black Knights" set, Black Monarch's Castle (known in the U.K. as Black Fortress—not to be confused with the Falcons' 6074) was the first set to feature knights holding the Black Knights' shield. The castle was essentially a black revamp of King's Castle with octagonal turrets, but was capable of being hinged open to attach smaller sets and build up a larger structure. The move from building gray castles to introducing the distinctive black structures is something designer Jens Nygaard Knudsen remembers well. "We kind of liked it, but it didn't please GKC (Godtfred)," he recalled. "Maybe it brought back memories he had from the War, I don't know. It did take us a long time to convince him, though, and prove that the black castle brought a dramatic aspect to the theme—not an evil aspect."

In 1992 that drama was embodied by Black Knight's Castle, perching atop a rocky hill with drawbridge and Tudor-style wall piece. The sub-theme was official, and the knights had even more to contend with, fighting off the Forestmen. The Black Knights were included in new sets until 1993, and were replaced by the Royal Knights in 1995.

Crest: Sets released prior to 1992/1993 usually featured smaller shields, the same shape as previous sub-themes', with a yellow and blue dragon on a red background with a blue border. Marking the official launch of the Black Knights in 1992, a new oval-shaped shield was introduced and the dragon design was changed, including the color arrangement—it was now a blue and red dragon with a yellow background and blue border. The Sea Serpent (6057) flies a sail with a red dragon design on it, too.

Dress code: An official Black Knight, as seen in 6009, wore all black with a red belt and gray detachable breastplate. His helmet was a new design for LEGO with an intimidating black visor, capable of attaching new dragon-style plumes to the top, and plumes to the side as well. This knight donned a wispy red mustache and beard. The Black Knights were the first Castle sub-themes to have minifigures with facial hair.

Find them: Rowing a boat under the watchful eye (and crossbow) of a Black Falcon in Battle Dragon (6018), preparing for catapult fire in Knight's Stronghold (6059), and getting spooked by Black Monarch's Ghost (6034).

By the late 1980s, business was booming. The LEGO Group had been inventive and selective enough with its new product lines to increase sales, despite the changing toy climate. They had developed a wide fan base who excitedly picked up each new LEGO catalog to discover what new products were going to be reaching a toy shop near them soon. For the true LEGO fan, there was the option to be a member of a LEGO Club—such as LEGO U.K.'s LEGO Builder's Club, which started releasing a eight-page magazine *Bricks 'n Pieces* in 1981 (the magazine had been going in a smaller newsletter format since 1974). In 1988 a LEGO U.K. catalog advertised that in exchange for a £2.95 check postal order, lucky British LEGO fans could receive a LEGO Club badge, a membership card, a sew-on patch, LEGO Club stickers, and three copies of the magazine. By joining you also had the opportunity to enter LEGO Club competitions and receive special offers.

This was not a new concept—A. C. Gilbert had encouraged Erector fans to sell subscriptions and submit ideas to *Erector Tips* magazine to earn the title of "Master Engineer," while Frank Hornby's *Meccano Magazine* was originally distributed free to fans. Before the age of the Internet, fan clubs were the way children communicated with a company or product, interacted with other fans of LEGO toys, and felt like they were part of something special. For a toy manufacturer releasing new products twice a year, the LEGO magazines served as both a platform to encourage creativity and community and as an advertisement for new sets. The LEGO Club today still offers a free magazine to kids (as well as a junior version for builders under seven) and also includes online material such as videos, building tips, and competitions. Despite *Bricks 'n Pieces* running LEGO building competitions in its pages throughout the 1980s, the wider LEGO community had its first opportunity to come together in 1988 at the first LEGO World Cup competition held in Billund, where fourteen countries were represented by nearly fourty children.

The 1980s saw LEGO tackle fantasy worlds and technical building and introduce niche ranges like FABULAND with great success. The development of Space and Castle themes proved LEGO's versatility as a toy capable of portraying vastly different environments. The idea that if you could imagine it in LEGO bricks, you could build it from LEGO bricks was starting to take hold, and as the company and its minifigures turned the corner into the next decade, it seemed that with LEGO toys anything was possible.

Making LEGO

Although LEGO will always be a Danish toy from a Danish family, its appeal is nothing short of universal. Early on in the company's history, local sales offices were established all over the world and with LEGO products being shipped to more and more countries, it wasn't long before the production of LEGO toys went global, too. Surprising to some, the main LEGO headquarters and one of its factories are still in

Billund, Denmark, where the whole story began, although the production facilities and processes have changed significantly since the first LEGO bricks were made.

Rapid expansion, universal customers, and dramatic changes in the world's economy have had an immediate impact on the production locations of not only LEGO, but the entire toy industry. In 2007, 60 percent of the world's toys were made in China, which means LEGO remains one of the few large toy manufacturers still producing toys outside of Asia. But Billund is not the only place proud to manufacture LEGO parts. Over the last fifty years, plants have existed in South Korea, Brazil, Switzerland, Germany, and the United States. In 2000, after thirty-five years of production and distribution, it was announced that the Enfield plant in Connecticut would be closed and the warehouse and packing responsibilities moved to Mexico. A large proportion of domestic production in Billund was also moved to the Czech Republic where costs are lower, while the manufacturing of LEGO Technic and BIONICLE products was retained in Denmark. In 2006 production was contracted out to Flextronics, a Singapore-based company with facilities in Eastern Europe and Mexico. The plan was to retain the production of specialized and highly technical products (such as Technic and BIONICLE) in Billund, while the production of more wage-intensive, voluminous System products would be outsourced to lower wage-paying areas. This restructuring aimed to secure LEGO's financial position in the toy market after reporting its first deficit in 1998, and then facing tough competition from cheaper rivals, such as the Canadian-based Mega Bloks. But after three years of working with Flextronics, LEGO ended the contract, regaining control of production. Stating that after a successful run with Flextronics, they felt LEGO was better off handling global manufacturing itself, rather than outsourcing, they relocated the Mexican plant from Juarez to Monterrey (also in Mexico) and negotiated with Flextronics to take over its Hungarian plant. Today, the LEGO group also retains sites in Kladno, Czech Republic, and works with other manufacturers in Hungary, Poland, and China.

Before LEGO is made, however, it needs to be designed, and this itself is a multistage process. After a theme has been selected for development, designers work together to draw inspiration from the world around them (for themes such as LEGO City, Technic, etc.), popular culture and technology (for more unusual fantasy themes like Space Police and Atlantis), or existing characters and locations (for licensed LEGO themes such as *Toy Story* or *Harry Potter*) to get a range of possible ideas for how to develop the theme. A mood board is often created to help consolidate all of these ideas and focus on the best ones, which are then developed into potential LEGO sets to serve a variety of price points.

To develop an individual set, designers must consider any functions or specific mechanics of it that will need to be incorporated, and how best to incorporate them. With about 6500 different elements to choose from, the "sketch model" stage gives the designer an opportunity to flex his muscles and come up with a range of ways to build a sellable LEGO set. All designers work differently—some draw out their

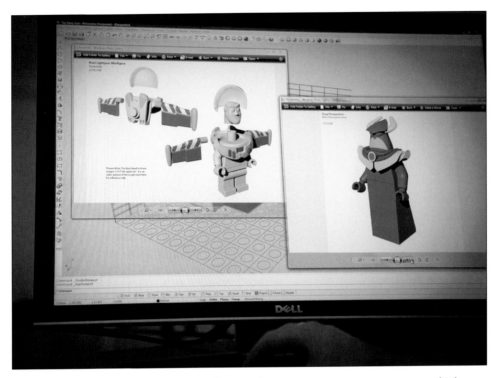

Designs for LEGO Toy Story minifigures shown on a computer program, which illustrates how the various elements would fit together and their size. © Alex Howe

ideas or build a virtual model on their computer, while others "sketch" immediately in LEGO bricks. Unfortunately, their options are not unlimited. In the designing of a model, certain factors must be taken into consideration, the most important of which is cost. Unusual or new elements can be expensive to produce, especially if they are not required for any other set/theme. If a piece does not exist that a designer feels is necessary for the success of the theme, he can design one, but must consider safety standards, compatibility with other LEGO elements, and the cost of manufacturing, packing, and supplying the part (some parts can take longer to mold than others).

With more recent themes and licensed themes, the characters and story behind them have been an integral part of the launch of the theme, and these are developed in conjunction with the sets to create a complete play experience. If a license is involved, models must be approved by the licensor, who may make suggestions to make sure the model is staying true to the brand. Once a viable sketch model and its characters have been designed, the LEGO Group often presents models to focus groups of children to see what they like and dislike about the products. Sometimes children's suggestions can influence the final design, or the focus group can highlight potential problems with a set when it is being built and played with by a child.

The designers will also test the model and rebuild it multiple times to make sure every part included is essential, and every part required is present.

All of the LEGO designers' precision and perfection means nothing if a toy is unsafe for the child who plays with it. TLG's international sales mean its toys must comply with safety standards all over the world, so a whole array of tests are carried out on each piece and product in a stage called "Model Review." Not only are the building instructions designed to make sure that children of the target age group will be able to reconstruct the model, but tests are carried out by machines that imitate a child's bite, attempt to twist objects, and drop them with a measured force, all of which are required to make sure the product is safe. The materials are also tested for heat durability and toxicity. Despite no LEGO products ever leaking any chemicals, a scare in the 1970s surrounding cadmium metal used in many toys including LEGO yellow and red plastic bricks caused a health and safety and environmental concern. TLG proved that there was no danger from its bricks, but made the costly decision to change the specifications of its plastic to make sure it was cadmium-free. After designing, testing, and rebuilding, and when everyone is happy with the model, it goes into production.

One of the LEGO Group's most astounding factors is the meticulous attention to detail given to each individual part produced. How often have you had to return a LEGO toy because some of the parts are missing? Do you remember the last time you couldn't fit two LEGO bricks together? LEGO bricks have to stand the test of time, perhaps twenty years or more. In addition, bricks made twenty years ago have to be able to fit perfectly with a brick made today. The "clutch power" of a LEGO brick is the pulling force required to pull two bricks apart, and it is the molding techniques and materials used by the LEGO Group that mean the bricks maintain clutch power over their long lives. The quality control in a LEGO factory ensures this, and it is not taken lightly—arguably, it's the cornerstone for the LEGO Group's success.

Many people have described their visit to the LEGO Kornmarken factory in Billund as something straight out of a sci-fi movie and there's a good reason why. In 1959 LEGO production was considered advanced when only one operator was able to manage two machines at once, while today vast areas of factories are run by a computerized system which requires robots to do most of the work, while a couple of human workers oversee entire warehouses.

In one of Billund's giant warehouses, there are fourteen silos each three stories high, constantly being refilled with raw plastic granules that arrive from Germany, Italy, and the Netherlands. Deposited into the silos from frequently arriving truckloads, the granules come in fifty-five different colors (which can be mixed to produce more colors) and are the size of grains of rice. They are soon vacuumed up again by large nozzles and transported via tubes to the molding machines in one of twelve adjoining molding halls. Every twenty-four hours fifty tons of raw plastic are processed in an ongoing cycle of LEGO production. Despite the vastness of the factory itself

One of the fourteen silos at Billund's Kornmarken factory is refilled with ABS granules.
© Alex Howe

and the volume of production, the molds are very modest and can produce a small number of parts at once providing a high degree of accuracy. LEGO bricks have a diameter variation of two hundredths of a millimeter, to ensure bricks made years apart for completely different sets will all fit together perfectly.

In total there are 775 molding machines—their job is to melt down the granules to a temperature of 455°F and inject the liquid plastic into the specific mold they are programmed to. These molds are capable of applying anywhere between 28 and 165 tons of pressure (depending on the element being produced) and maintaining that exact pressure for the time required, due to a hydraulic system. LEGO engineers also designed a cooling system to keep the molds within one degree of the necessary temperature, and the molding rooms themselves are climate-controlled. The parts harden and cool within fifteen seconds and are dropped onto a conveyor belt and into a bin at the end of the machine.

The Kornmarken factory makes parts twenty-four hours a day, all year round, but normally during the "low season" when there is less demand for sets, 40 percent of the molding machines are turned off, with the remaining machines producing basic bricks and plates to feed the ongoing demand. Specialist parts are not made all year round but respond to seasonal demand, which is less predictable. It is only after a brick has been produced that the true efficiency and resourcefulness of this LEGO factory comes into play. When the container of molded parts reaches a pre-

Each molding hall includes approximately sixty-five molding machines, but only one human worker. © Alex Howe

cise weight, the central computer alerts a robot via a radio signal to come and put a lid on it, give it a barcode, and replace it with an empty container so the process can begin again. Because of the level of accuracy required, and the dangerous conditions, there are rarely any people present in the molding rooms, unless they are checking machines for quality control or performing maintenance work. One person, supported by a group of maintenance workers, will oversee the work of seventy-two molding machines. The robots themselves find their way around by following grooves on the factory floor.

OLD MOLD

After many years of hard service, all LEGO molds are put into retirement. Made from hard steel and polished with diamond dust, the friction of the plastic and the extreme heat and pressure these molds have to endure mean eventually they have to be replaced at a cost of tens of thousands of pounds. They work hard, though, with some molds producing over 120 million bricks before they can take it easy.

A retired 2 × 4 brick mold on display at the LEGO Museum in Billund. © Ian Greig

The LEGO Group's ingenuity can also been seen through its recycling methods. All the leftover plastic from the mold that helps form the unique stud system inside a LEGO brick, and any elements that accidentally find their way onto the factory floor, are not thrown away but are reground and reused to make more parts. The same happens with faulty bricks and clear melted plastic that is used to "clean" the inner tubes of The machines before a different color plastic is used. Together the machines at Billund produce approximately 2.4 million individual bricks every hour, and for every one million bricks produced, only eighteen fail to meet the high-quality standards, so nothing is wasted—not time or resources. In addition, boxes that are damaged or sets with missing pieces are used for donation boxes given to underprivileged children organizations around the world.

The molding machines have built-in sensors to detect if there's a change in pressure or temperature that might cause faulty bricks to be produced, setting off an alarm to alert technicians. If the molding machine detects flaws, the faulty pieces are pushed aside, but some flaws are too subtle for even these robots so there's always a pair of human eyes working the floor. The technician's job is to take a sample of the molded output to the inspection station and inspect them for faults and variations often so small they're unnoticeable to the untrained eye. Faults that occur are abnormal studs, a tiny hole in the brick where the light shines through, variation in color or

Nothing gets wasted at the LEGO factory—unused plastic and faulty bricks are melted down to make new parts. © Alex Howe

plastic thickness at any point on the brick, or even an excess of plastic (known as a "high gate") caused when too much plastic was injected into the mold.

After the robots have deposited the filled containers onto the conveyor belt, they are sent through to a sorting room where a robotic forklift takes them to a check-in station and then, depending on the computer's orders, they are either sent to the storage facility or straight to the assembly line in the packing hall. LEGO is known for turning giant buildings into mini-models, but when it comes to storage it's chosen to supersize.

The Billund factory has four storage chambers: Two stand at twenty meters (65.6 feet) high, and the other two at thirteen meters (42.65 feet) high. With no humans in sight, the storage facility is operated by eight logical motion machines and fifteen automatic cranes that are directed by the mainframe computer as to what to shelve, where, and what to retrieve. Powered by compressed air, these robots float up and down the aisles at a speed of 2.5 meters (about 8.2 feet) per second, in a nonstop aerial performance. LEGO makes the most of this 170 square kilometers (65.6 square miles) of shelf space, stocking 420,000 boxes of parts at any given time, which is only 80 percent of the towers' overall capacity.

But for those LEGO bricks that are needed immediately (or for those picked from the shelves by the machines), the next stop is either decoration or straight to packaging. Not all parts require decorating, luckily, as it is the most expensive part of the LEGO production process. Tiny minifigure heads are held individually by machinery while facial details are printed on. Any special coloring/markings you see on a piece are created by going through this intricate process. Pre-assembled parts are also put together here—such as clicking minifigure arms and hands into place.

As mentioned earlier, it's very rare that a LEGO customer will open his or her purchase and find faulty or missing pieces. That is due to the meticulous checks in place to ensure no LEGO set goes out the shipping door incomplete. Unlike other packaging rooms, where workers count pieces into boxes, almost the entire packing process is automated to ensure an almost flawless level of efficiency. Every single LEGO part that finds its way into the packing room is weighed individually. Twenty billion of them each year are poured into a vibrating funnel which, using optical sensors, shakes each piece out of the top one by one so they can be weighed on the scales. This measurement checks that the piece is the precise weight it should be, assuming there are no faults. If it passes the test, it makes its way along the conveyor belt to be packaged in a polyethylene bag, or if not, it is dropped into a bin to be ground down to begin the whole process again.

For the lucky pieces, the wait is almost over. The correct amount of each piece required for the set are dropped into a small box that moves along the conveyor belt collecting the rest of the pieces required. As the box makes its journey it is weighed to ensure the correct number of pieces are present at any given stage. If there is an inconsistency, an alarm will alert a packaging worker to come and check the box

Each box in the vast storage "cathedral" has a unique barcode to tell the computer what parts are inside. © Alex Howe

Tiny minifigure heads are given their unique facial features in the decorating room. © Alex Howe

With so many parts coming through the decorating room at once, technicians have to keep track of the variety of minifigure faces being made each day. © Alex Howe

A LEGO employee checks the correct packets of parts as they make their way into the boxes with their instruction booklets. © Alex Howe

and make any corrections. Then, once all the pieces have been grouped together, they are wrapped in a polyethylene bag. Two types of bags are used by LEGO, as you may have noticed. Some bags are perforated, and although these are more expensive they tear less easily, so are used for groups of pieces that are more likely to tear the packaging. Perforated bags can be compressed more easily, so take up less room in a smaller box. Smaller pieces are usually inserted into solid bags. After filling, the bags are weighed again to check for any inconsistencies.

The cardboard packing boxes that contain LEGO sets are assembled and a book of relevant instructions is dropped into it. The boxes are weighed at this stage to check the instruction booklet is not missing any pages. The appropriate polyethylene bags are then dropped into the set, or placed in by assembly line workers, before it is weighed for a final time. If it makes the grade, it gets boxed up with other sets just like it and sent to the shipping department.

BONUS BRICKS

It is better to have too many (you might have gone wrong in your assembly) than to have too few. There are two reasons for this. Firstly, some pieces (e.g., 1 × 1 tiles) are so small the scales do not always pick up when more than the required amount have dropped in, and secondly LEGO knows how easy it is to lose these pieces under the sofa, so they try and throw in a few extra where possible.

onto a moonlit sea where a pirate ship approaches. For many children, this was their first peek at the next play theme the LEGO Group would try and conquer—the swash-buckling world of pirates. Stories such as Robert Louis Stevenson's *Treasure Island* and the adventures of Peter Pan have long inspired children and informed their playtime. In the 1980s and '90s, films such as *The Goonies* (1985), Roman Polanski's *Pirates* (1986), a 1992 re-release of Walt Disney's *Peter Pan*, and Steven Spielberg's Oscar-nominated *Hook* (1991) contributed to the popular culture pirate tapestry, so it seemed the next logical step for the LEGO Group to embark on these uncharted waters. Unlike many themes that followed it, Pirates has stood the test of time, only disappearing from toy-shop shelves in the mid-2000s, before returning in time for their twentieth anniversary in 2009.

"After all the work on Space and Castle we were about to launch a new theme," explained then Head of Design Jens Nygaard Knudsen. "We decided on LEGO Pirates and it became the biggest of all the themes." The earliest 1989 sets were an immediate success, and introduced fans to new parts and new approaches to the building system. As with the creation of all LEGO themes there were various decisions that needed to be made. "We decided on designing a hull for a pirate ship," Knudsen said, "but we had to decide whether it should be able to float or not. GKC and I quickly agreed that the ship was to be designed for floor play. We also designed rope ladders and masts, rowing boats and cannons. After some discussion about whether the cannon should be able to shoot or not, we made one that could shoot." And even though pistols and guns were things that LEGO had refused to produce for previous themes, minifigure Flintlock-style pistols

Captain Redbeard ruled the LEGO seas from 1978 until he was replaced by Captain Brickbeard (who also had a red beard) in 2009. © Jordan Schwartz

and muskets were included in sets featuring the Imperial Soldiers. The pirates themselves were infamously the first minifigures available without the original plain smiley heads. As Knudsen explained, "For the minifigure we designed a wooden leg, a claw instead of a hand, a patch over the eye as well as new hats and decorations for role play." Their eye patches, facial hair, peg legs, hooks, and headgear made them unmistakably pirates and they were the first minifigures to have multiple facial expressions, hair, and features. There was even a female minifigure in this range—something some of the Space and Castle ranges were missing. "We also invented the palm building system for Pirates," said Knudsen of the first LEGO palm trees sold with sets such as Shipwreck Island (6260) and Eldorado Fortress (6276). They would become a mainstay for Pirates and also apper in other themes such as the Paradisa line.

Decorative base plates had been seen as part of Space and Town sets (such as the crater-covered plate in set 6970 Beta-1 Command Base) but TLG developed new vacuum base plates with ramps and crevices decorated with painted rock designs for children to build sets on. These Pirate "islands" are seen by some as the first signs of LEGO dumbing down its sets to appeal to the Game Boy generation. Whereas previous generations may have created their own impressive LEGO structures on which to build castles and space stations, soon LEGO was rolling out vacuum base plates across its product line and they became fairly common, in some form or another, in Town, Space, and Castle sets. These base plates weren't the only new parts designers got to work on for Pirates. "Along the way we added natives, crocodiles, new masks, new headgear, and new great decorations for the pirates theme," Knudsen recalled. "We also added a suspension bridge and a canoe. A new snake, however, didn't get the official approval!" The introduction of all these simple yet effective parts as well as LEGO monkeys, parrots, sharks, and material sails added color and interactivity to this appealing new play world.

PIRATE SHIPS

- The first ship the pirates helmed was the Black Seas Barracuda (6285, also known as Dark Shark). This large vessel with its five-sail formation was made up from an impressive 909 pieces, and is still considered one of the best Pirate ships to date. With its skull-and-crossbones flag, red and white sails, and human figurehead brandishing a chalice (presumably filled with rum), this was a ship for Captain Redbeard to be proud of. The ship was so popular it was re-released in 2002 as part of the LEGO Legends series with a few minor changes, the most noticeable of which was the use of nonfiring cannons.

- LEGO fans (and Redbeard) had to wait until 1993 before they could get their hands on another ship for the pirates—and this time they had a choice of two: the smaller Renegade Runner/Seastar (6268) or the six-sail Skull's Eye Schooner (6286), also know as the Black Skull—a set that eclipsed the Barracuda in size. This time there was no mistaking the pirates—both ships carried black and white sails emblazoned with the skull-and-crossbones design. Armed to the teeth with muskets and a cannon, the Runner may have been small, but was packed with details including a moving rudder, real compass, and four pirates. The Schooner, meanwhile, had a nine-strong crew, manning four cannons (with the capacity for four more), as well as a working winch and rudder.

- In 1996 Captain Redbeard was seen toppling off the back of the Red Beard Runner (6289), the first pirate ship in three years, also known as the Marauder. While the Skull's Eye Schooner and Black Seas Barracuda had been fairly similar in shape and style, this ship caused some controversy among avid Pirates fans with its more playful design (e.g., fishing net, tattered sails) and mechanical gimmicks. The front mast, featuring the Imperial swords emblem, had a trapdoor underneath it which, when released, lowered the mast to the side revealing the skull-and-crossbones sail and the pirates' true identity. The ship's quarterdeck with skull design could also be triggered to fall away if the ship was "attacked"—the cause of Redbeard's toppling on the box photograph. The ship lacked the realistic detail of its predecessor: There was no anchor and only limited armament. It was re-released in 2001 alongside the Armada Flagship (6280) from the same year.

- In 1997 only four Pirates sets were released—these would be the last new pirate-themed sets for twelve years, with the exception of DUPLO and 4+ sets. Unfortunately, LEGO didn't put out a large ship set this year, so fans of Pirates vessels had to settle for the more modest Cross Bone Clipper (6250)—a small craft similar to 1993's Renegade Runner.

- A new ship was long overdue by 2009 when LEGO unleashed its new Pirates line. With Redbeard hanging up his hook for retirement, the ship Brickbeard's Bounty (6243) was named after a new red-bearded pirate who looked remarkably similar to Old Red. The ship itself carefully incorporated some of the best elements from previous designs into an exciting new home for the pirates: the red and white sails from Black Seas Barracuda (without the traditional thread rigging); the winch and net from Red Beard Runner; and the return of firing cannons from the early sets. New details included a mermaid figurehead, vinyl pirate flag, a new shark large enough to eat a minifigure, and a large Captain's cabin with impressive quarterdeck.

The 1989 set Forbidden Island (6270) incorporated many of the new elements introduced for Pirates—a shark, parrot, monkey, firing cannon, and the palm tree building system. © StreetFly JZ

The rope bridge element first used in Forbidden Island would later be used in Forestmen, Adventurers, and other Pirate sets. © StreetFly JZ

Of course, pirates wouldn't be pirates if they didn't have some soldiers locking them up for stealing treasure, so TLG also released sets that included "good guys" to defend forts and islands from the pesky buccaneers—although it was common for children to be rooting for the pirates. In the 1989–1991 sets Captain Redbeard (or "Captain Roger," as he was also known) and his cohorts took on the boys in blue— the Imperial Governors, who came armed and ready in sets such as Sabre Island (6265) and the grander El Dorado Fortress (6276). Their ship was the modest Caribbean Clipper (6274), also known as the Seahawk, but occasionally they would sail ashore on a smaller vessel to arrest the pirates (as in Rock Island Refuge (6273).

In 1992 the blue "soldiers" were replaced by the Imperial Guards, who dressed almost identically, but in red. They answered to the Admiral (recognised by his smart red and white uniform, white gloves, and black bicorne with white plume)—and while their red and white striped flag was colored differently from the Governors', they fought under the same crossed cannons and crown insignia. The U.K. name for the trading post set 6277 was Port Royal—a real seventeenth-century Jamaican port town captured by the British in 1655. The set itself provided a port hub for the guards who were very busy seizing treasure from the pirates on Skull Island (6279), protecting the Imperial Outpost (6263), and manning their weapons at Cannon's Cove (6266).

New helmets, weapons, and epaulets were designed for these boys in blue. © Jordan Schwartz

IMPERIAL GOVERNORS

- Referred to as "Governors" in the 1990 catalog, this group is often called Imperial Soldiers.
- The soldiers' colors were blue and white, and their flag had a blue background and a white cross with two cannons crossing underneath a crown (symbolizing the head of the empire the soldiers fight for).
- The lower ranks wore red epaulets and shako hats while their senior officers' shoulders were dressed in yellow and wore bicorne and tricorne hats with plumes.
- The Caribbean Clipper had a yellow parrot as its figurehead.
- Governor Broadside himself was only available with the ship and the El Dorado Fortress—he could be recognized by the large white plume on his hat, mustache, and different tailoring on his torso.

On the cover of a 1994 LEGO catalog, a minifigure with a painted face and grass skirt catches a ride on a seaplane with a knight, while narrowly escaping attack by a LEGO Space Spyrius robot. In an effort to expand the playability of the Pirates theme, LEGO introduced the "Islanders" sets. These locals provided another enemy (or ally) for the pirates, and added some native flavor to the naval military backdrop. The six Islanders sets did not feature any Imperial Guards but did include adventurous pirates who had ventured from their ships in search of treasures. The Islanders sets were bright and inviting; draped in foliage, vines, and palm trees, they were a series of small alcoves such as King Kahuka's Throne (6262) and Forbidden Cove (6264). Great attention was paid to small details such as native shields, fire torches, and weapons—the Islanders carried bows and arrows and spears, and locked trespassing pirates up in wooden cages. The largest set was 1994's Enchanted Island (6278), the base for the Islanders; it included two boats (one of which belonged to the pirates) and a drawbridge that could be swung to topple the person crossing it.

The Islanders' dress code had a Polynesian feel with necklaces made from bones and plants, grass skirts, and animal horns protruding menacingly from their black, top-knotted hair. The male Islanders had their faces painted, and there was also a female Islander available only with Enchanted Island—one of the few female minifigures available with a Pirates set. King Kahuka (the Islanders' leader) stood out with his large red mask and white plume. Underneath, his face was painted white, red, and blue.

But the LEGO Group was not done with Pirates for the '90s and in 1996 a line of new sets welcomed some more regimental colors to the high seas. Flying blue and white striped sails with a red and yellow insignia on their "Armada Flagship" (6280),

El Dorado Fortress was home to the Imperial Governor and his guards and came with a treasure chest, cannon, and prison cell. © StreetFly JZ

it's commonly thought these seafarers belonged to the Spanish fleet—their flag was a crown resting atop an anchor. The Armada was not as grand as previous ships, but had a collapsible mast, and a cannon capable of rotating and moving along a track. This ship was also re-released in 2001 alongside the Red Beard Runner. They didn't have an outpost or fort to protect, unless you include the seventy-four piece Armada Sentry (6244), but one brave sailor can be seen attempting an attack on the crocodile-infested pirate hideout Shipwreck Island (6296), while another two risked their lives at the Pirates Perilous Pitfall (6281, North America only) with its booby-trapped falling boulder. The Armada sailors themselves dressed in red with blue lines on their torsos. There was a green minifigure with a detailed ruffle and gold medallion, and a captain with a silver neck chain and detachable metallic breastplate. Typically, the Armada men's faces featured pointed mustaches and inquisitive eyebrows.

Unfortunately, despite the initial success of Pirates, the Armada sets seemed to mark the end of the theme's life as LEGO designers pressed on with the development of more unusual themes. With the exception of re-released sets in the early 2000s, it wasn't until 2009 that LEGO Pirates would raise the anchor and take to the seas again.

Action-driven sets, such as this 1991 Coastal Cutter, were introduced to the Town theme in the 1990s. © StreetFly JZ

From 1991, most LEGO sets were marketed as "LEGO System" regardless of their theme, including the new Pirates sets. Back on dry land, certain ranges, such as Space's Spyrius or Western, were clearly identified by extra branding on the box, but most LEGO Town sub-themes, with the exception of a couple (e.g., Paradisa) were not. Throughout the '80s and '90s, the LEGO Group produced an almost continuous stream of basic Town sets, constantly updating its emergency services, construction, and transportation ranges. These resulted in action-driven sets such as 1989's Coastal Rescue Base (6387) and 1991's Fire Rescue (4031) to everyday infrastructure such as service stations, pizza places, and airports. Initially, LEGO catalogs integrated the various arms of Town with photographs incorporating different sets and ranges, but as these ranges grew larger and more distinct, they were often given their own pages to attract fans of that particular sub-theme, such as airport-related sets and those revolving around a harbor. There were sets that focused specifically on getting away from town life, such as Rocky River Retreat (6552) and Amazon Crossing (6490) as well as a small range of Australian Outback sets in 1997.

The Breezeway Café (6376), released in 1990, is a fan favorite from this period. It showed LEGO toys weren't just about spacemen and warring knights, and that building a cheerful café could be equally entertaining. © Andrew Martin

The LEGO Group also launched the Paradisa line to appeal to girls, and action-driven sets such as 1993's Aerial Acrobats (6345) and 1997's Roadblock Runners (6549) to make Town less about refuse collection and milk trucks (although 6693 and 1581 are great examples of those) and exciting to a generation of children more accustomed to action movies and computer games. Between 1986 and 1995, Town sets received the Light & Sound electric treatment on eight different sets—one tactic LEGO employed to make the toys more interactive and appealing to tech-savvy kids. By 1991 Light & Sound had been renamed Electric System and two sets, including a police patrol vehicle and an airport fire truck, were fitted with the battery packs. These were followed by a coastal patrol boat in 1994 and the F1 Hauler (6484) in 1995—both these vehicles also included small motors, rotating the radar on the boat and moving the crane on the hauler. These were the last Town sets to include the Electric System, although LEGO Trains would continue to keep minifigure towns moving into the new millennium. Here are some of the more significant sub-themes that were produced under the Town name during the 1990s.

While there were many traditional Town sets full of policemen, firemen, and construction workers, this era introduced a number of new occupations to LEGO Town, including this TV crew (6661). © Andrew Martin

Paradisa (1992–1997)

Inspired by the sunny building style of the popular 1990 Breezeway Café (6376) and earlier horse-riding sets including Riding Stable (6379) and Derby Trotter (6355), the LEGO Group released a holiday-themed range of pale pink, green, and white sets featuring lots of horses, palm trees, and female minifigures in an attempt to draw more girls to the brand. With not a policeman or road sweeper in sight, and the first use of pink pieces such as seats, fences, gates, and even cups, this was a big leap for TLG, and the inventiveness of some of the designs is a testament to how much they wanted it to succeed. Popular sets include Poolside Paradise (6416) with its swimming pool and curving stairway and the horsey Rolling Acres Ranch (6419). After five years of sipping cocktails and relaxing in the sun, the range ended, and no LEGO Town set has returned to such "girly" territory since. For more on the Paradisa line and other LEGO products targeting girls, go to page 164.

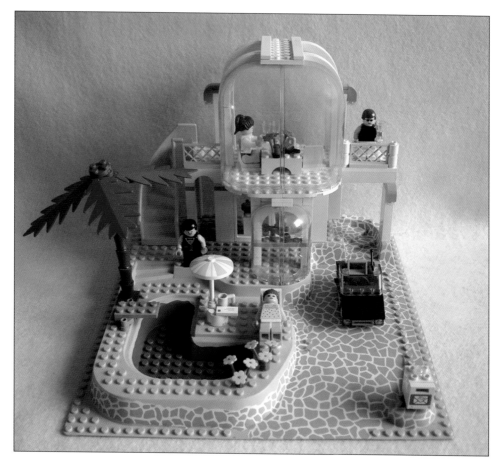

Poolside Paradise (6416) was one of the first Paradisa sets released in 1992.
© StreetFly JZ

With a hint of pink, Paradisa brought pure leisure to LEGO Town, and some wonderful new female minifigures. © StreetFly JZ

Race (1992–2000)

Before car theme LEGO Racers appeared in 2001, the good folk of LEGO Town supported their favorite racing drivers down at the track. With the invention of the LEGO wheel, it was inevitable that designers would build a race car. LEGO racing car designs went back as far as the mid-1970s with a Formula 1 car (392) and various racing car sets throughout the 1980s, some with "Shell" sponsorship. By the 1990s LEGO racing drivers had switched their sponsorship to Octan as can be seen in 1992's Checkered Flag 500 (6551), one of the first Race sets of this period. The previous year LEGO had released some smaller Race car/minifigure sets including Red Devil Racer (6509), Screaming Patriot (6646) with a stars and stripes design on the back of the car, and Mag Racer (pictured below). More of these small sets were released in 1992 and 1993, which saw the addition of a new F1 racing car (1990) and a set of two dragsters (1992), as well as the Victory Cup Racers set (6539) complete with winners' podium and racing cart transporter. Other memorable 1990s Race sets included the Hot Rod Club (6561)—the ideal location for these colorful drag racers to get fixed up—and 1995's F1 Hauler, the only 9 volt Electric System Race set. The

Road Racer (6605) was one of a number of small racing car sets released in the 1980s.
© David Martin

Before LEGO Racers, the simple race car designs of the 1990s, like Mag Racer (6648), were available as small, affordable sets for car fans. © David Martin

LEGO Group took a break from Town Race sets in the late '90s, although racing cars continued to feature prominently in the Technic range, and then launched a small collection of sets in 2000, boxed with a new checkered flag "Race" logo. These included a motorized Rocket Dragster (6616) and Grip 'n' Go Challenge (6713)—a competitive set that saw two cars with pincers tackling each other to score goals with a plastic boulder. These were the last Race sets; as of 2001 Racers was launched—a new theme independent from Town.

Launch Command (1995)

With only five sets to its name Launch Command is a "blink-and-you'll-miss-it" range. The centerpiece of the space travel action was front and center of page five of the 1995 catalog—an impressive 562-piece Shuttle Launch Pad (6339) complete with working crane system, detachable fuel tank, and rocket boosters, as well as a scientist minifigure with security clearance tag. The realistic colors and designs were repeated in 1999 with Space Port, but Launch Command did it first and was the only range to have a shuttle transport plane (6544) and an evacuation unit

This Launch Evac 1 vehicle (6614), with a revolving yellow hose, bears the Launch Command rocket logo. © StreetFly JZ

complete with flame-busting hose (6614). Launch Command's logo—a white circle with red and blue outline and space shuttle image—appeared on astronauts' space suits, the shuttle, and other vehicles, and was the basis for the Space Port logo a few years later.

Divers (1997–1998)

With Aquanauts, Aquasharks, and Aquaraiders all diving onto the scene as brand-new themes in the mid-1990s, Town soon picked up its own flippers and oxygen tanks and took to the deep seas. A heavy dose of sea life in the form of sharks, stingrays, and octopi, combined with the realistic Town colors of white, blue, and yellow for the mini-subs, stations, and boats, made this an original new sub-theme for Town fans. Memorable sets include Diving Expedition Explorer (6560), with its subterranean ruin, diving cage, and large boat; Deep Sea Refuge (6441), which included an underwater station complete with portholes; and Discover Station (1782) for its helicopter and crane that could lower an observation pod down into the water.

RES-Q (1998–1999)

The year 1998 saw the release of two action-packed Town sub-themes. RES-Q was a high-octane emergency response team comprising of water, air, and land vehicles designed to evacuate people from disaster zones—similar to System Coastguard sets released between 1989 and 1995. In the 1998 American catalog a LEGO display to introduce the theme featured a collapsed bridge in a lightning storm. The photograph displays the different elements of the RES-Q team sent in to remove debris from the road, save drowning survivors, and air lift the injured to safety. The RES-Q color scheme was yellow and black with transparent blue and their black and red logo is visible on all their vehicles and on the back of their white and orange uniforms. The whole team came together at the Emergency Response Center (6479), a set similar to previous waterside police bases such as 1996's metro PD Station (6598).

Extreme Team (1998–1999)

This group of adrenalin junkies made up the other turn-of-the-century Town release. The Extreme Team members are easy to spot with their recognizable black jumpsuits with colored sleeves, visor shades, and bright red "X"s on their backs. Their outfits were reflective of the vibrant colors used for their vehicles and equipment, setting the stunt team apart from other less adventurous Town ranges. Whether they're trying to break the land speed record in Land Jet 7 (6580), performing gravity-defying stunts in Daredevil Flight Squad (6582), or risking life and limb in Extreme Team Challenge (6584) with its abseiling zip line and rocky rope bridge, they always look like they're having a good time.

Space Port (1999–2000)

While LEGO Space was stretching the imagination of planetary travel with the likes of UFO and Insectoids—themes that featured colorful alien creatures—LEGO Town took on the more realistic Space Port. With a renewed public interest in space travel due to Mars missions, these sets were fresh and exciting, and the first real-world space designs to come out since 1995's Launch Command—Space Port's logo was an updated version with a shuttle veering across a blue and yellow circle. The astronauts' white jumpsuits, similar to those available with the first Classic Space sets, were modernized with a full-face gold visor. The space shuttle itself in Mission Control (6456) and the satellite-bearing rocket in Countdown Corner (6454) both featured electric bricks with light and sound capabilities.

The new Space Port logo can be seen to the left of this minifigure scientist, as he prepares his instruments for liftoff in Mini Rocket Launcher (6452). © Kent Quon

City (1999–2002)

Having developed distinct Town sub-themes such as Divers and RES-Q, the LEGO Group decided to rebrand the more traditional town sets as "City." The new logo featuring a Manhattan-esque cityscape was the image that encompassed sets relating to emergency services including police and fire service (Super Rescue Complex 6464) and coast guard (6435), as well as construction sets such as Roadside Repair (6434) and other iconic Town staples such as 2001's Octan Gas Station (6472). In 2000 a number of smaller, easy-to-build sets aimed at five-to eight-year-olds were released, which included a fire station (6478) and a highway construction set (6600) made up of large ramp pieces and 2 × 4 × 3 bricks. The sub-theme logo was altered to show a city surrounded by greenery.

*   *   *

While Town was diversifying, Space was giving children of the 1990s exactly what they wanted—really awesome spaceships. In a decade of Power Rangers, Buzz Lightyear, and toy-store queues for Thunderbirds' Tracy Island, this period was dominated by sci-fi, monster-fighting heroes, and action-packed cartoons. The LEGO Group's own TV commercial campaigns were reflective of this, with increasingly cinematic and dramatic realizations of the products, such as a Futuron and Blacktron commercial which included a desert canyon chase sequence reminiscent of many popular sci-fi/action movies. Some of the most memorable advertisements from 1988 to the mid-1990s centered on a boy called "Zack the LEGO Maniac" (sometimes he was referred to as Jack or Mac). The commercials showed Zack—dressed in shades and a LEGO jacket, playing with the latest LEGO sets—accompanied by a catchy theme tune, demonstrating the technical capabilities of sets in an effort to make the building toy appear contemporary and exciting, an easy task for Space sets, which often featured in Zack commercials.

The 1990s were a busy decade for Space and a tough time for Space fans who had the unenviable task of having to choose between a large number of new sets (unless their pocket money could stretch to all of them, of course). Not only were fans able to buy some of the most realistic and scientifically accurate space travel sets with Town's Launch Command and Space Port, designers were throwing caution to the wind with a continuous outpouring of fantastical and unusual Space ranges. The charm and creativity of Classic Space has never diminished, and these sets remain some of the most collectible and well-loved by adult fans. But since Classic sets were phased out in 1987, the theme has expanded to include good guys, bad guys, alien guys, and everything in between. With some sub-themes only lasting for a year or two, the late eighties and nineties space sets stand out for their use of color, design, and varied minifigures. With some timeline crossovers and color palette similarities, it's forgivable to confuse the different factions of LEGO Space's intergalactic world. Below is a guide to the space sets of the period ranging from 1987's Futuron civilians to 1998's Insectoid cyborgs and their bug-shaped spaceships.

Futuron (1987–1990)

The phasing out of Classic Space is hard to spot if you take the minifigures out of the equation. Considered to be a "civilian" space race of worker astronauts, the name Futuron was never referred to on the boxes of the sets, causing some confusion with the last Classic sets due to the continuation of the blue and white color scheme. Futuron designs were markedly more sci-fi than the Classic sets—they even included brick-built robot droids—and would inspire and shape much of LEGO Space in years to come, although the simplicity associated with it would slowly be replaced by more heavily themed ranges.

Minifigures: Although Futuron astronauts' torsos had the same gold planet logo as their Classic predecessors, their uniforms could be recognized by the diagonal zip that ran across their torso, separating a colored top half (yellow, red, blue, black) from a white bottom half. Their trousers, arms, and helmets matched their main body color, except all of their visors, which were transparent blue.

This 1988 Hovercraft (6875) exemplifies the white and blue futuristic design of the Futuron sets. © David Martin

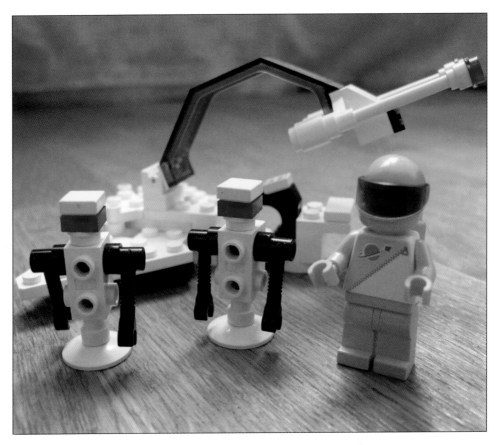

Futuron's uniforms were only subtly different from Classic Space—notice the diagonal zipper and half-white torso. © David Martin

Significant sets: Futuron made a big impact with the 1987 release of its monorail system (6990), bringing more movement and interactivity to the theme than Classic Space had. Although the monorail was updated under the Unitron sub-theme in 1994, this remains a popular early set. The building style of Futuron's base, Cosmic Laser Launcher (6953), and the control center for the monorail displays the LEGO Group's first use of large dome-shaped transparent pieces to create arches, and spherical structures, something that would be a recurring feature in LEGO space.

Blacktron (1987–1988)

Released the same year as the new Futuron designs, the original Blacktron sets were one of the LEGO Group's earliest attempts to market a truly unified sub-theme. Although the 1987 and 1988 sets or catalogs never openly refer to the Blacktron members as "bad guys," they did little to avoid the reputation with their sleek black and yellow ships, and it became quite clear they were up to no good in 1989 when

The design of this Blacktron Alienator illustrates the stark contrast of the Blacktron sets from any other previous Space sets—even the Blacktron visors were black.
© David Martin

they started appearing as Space Police prisoners. Although Blacktron sets were few, designers would return to the sub-theme in 1991.

Minifigures: Blacktron members are true to their name when it comes to picking out their wardrobe. And designers made sure the attention to detail paid to the Blacktron ships was reflected in their dress code. These spacemen wore black all over with a silver space suit design printed on their torsos.

Significant sets: Blacktron is one of the darkest space themes, with only a hint of transparent yellow adorning their black ships, vehicles, and base. Released a year after Futuron's laser launcher, Blacktron's Message Intercept Base (6987) was the largest space base yet, and is considered one of the best of its kind. From its large open dome and futuristic corridor to its two accompanying vehicles and spacecraft hanger, this is a complete base with a multitude of functions. Other well-loved sets from the first Blacktron era include Alienator (6876)—a land vehicle with a leg-walking mechanism, and the racing-car rover Battrax (6941).

Space Police (1989)

The LEGO Group made it clear Blacktron were not behaving in space when they created a police team to keep them in line. The original police sets were not dramatically different from Futuron—white as the main color had been replaced by black and blue with transparent red—but chunky "POLICE" tiles made it clear who was in charge. By introducing "good guys" and "bad guys" into the theme, designers opened the door for other similar sub-themes and what every sci-fi LEGO fan enjoys—space battles.

Minifigures: Unfortunately, TLG did not design a distinctly different uniform at this stage for the police—perhaps to help show their allegiance with the Futuron civilians—and they were kitted out in black and white Futuron torsos, (with black sleeves and white hands), black hips (giving the impression of a belt), and white trousers. They are most easily identified by their white helmets with red visors.

Significant sets: Of the original six Space Police sets on offer in 1989, there are a couple worth a special mention. The Space Lock-up Isolation Base (6955), where the police took their Blacktron criminals, was an original base design, which included a launch mechanism for the small police cruiser and housed the portable prison cell pods that were available with other smaller sets such as the Galactic Peace Keeper (6886). The police patroller SP-Striker (6781) was the only Space Police set to include a battery brick system—a light-up computer and lights across one set of the ship's wings, which could be set to flash or remain on.

M:Tron (1990–1991)

The new decade brought with it a shiny new range of LEGO workers. With no weapons to fight or defend, the M:Tron race were considered to be civilian workers replacing Futuron. Their functional black and red vehicles with gray trim and neon-green transparent parts stood out from the space teams that came before them. They were also the first space range to utilize magnets for increased interactivity. To facilitate the use of magnets, designers devised various manual work for M:Tron around the idea of searching and recovering precious raw materials from the sandy planet they were based on. This was the first space theme not to feature any kind of base set and is made up entirely of vehicles. This was also the last space theme to be marketed under the "LEGOLAND" banner, replaced by LEGO System from 1991 onward.

Minifigures: It's difficult to confuse an M:Tron minifigure with any other space men because of their distinctive red torsos with black and red "M" logo. They had white arms and legs, and black helmets with their signature neon-green visors.

Significant sets: The sub-theme's space ships were Particle Ionizer (6923, pictured) and the slightly larger Stellar Recon Voyager (6956), but one of the best-remembered M:Tron sets is the Mega Core Magnetizer (6989), also known as the Mobile Recovery Center, which served as a sort of base unit for the M:Tron team. With its quarter-dome, neon-green cockpit with stadium-style seating for three, magnetized crane, chunky durable wheels, and abundance of mining accessories, this is M:Tron at its best.

An M:Tron worker mans the controls of 1990's Vector Detector (6877). © StreetFly JZ

The Particle Ionizer (6923) was just one of the M:Tron sets to incorporate the use of magnets—seen on the crane on the back of the ship. © StreetFly JZ

Blacktron II: Future Generation (1991–1992)

The M:Tron minifigures were working hard ionizing particles and detecting vectors, but 1991 saw the Blacktron bad guys crawl out from whichever space rock they were hiding under. With a flashy new logo and chunky black and white spacecrafts (with the same neon-green transparencies as M:Tron), it was clear Blacktron were looking for trouble. These new sets were essentially an upgrade of the 1987/'88 sets, which saw the angular, delicate designs replaced by military-inspired vehicles and ships with cockpit pods that could be switched between sets.

Minifigures: Unlike their Vader-esque ancestors, 1991 Blacktron militants sported white torsos with the new black and green "B" logo. They had white legs, black arms and hands and the same black and green helmets as their enemies.

Significant sets: With obvious comparisons to the original Blacktron designs, Blacktron II managed to carve a distinct identity for itself with the introduction of more spherical cockpit pods, which were the centerpiece of the more popular sets. Alpha Centauri Outpost (6988), with its use of lights and landing pad, is generally not as celebrated as other base sets, but the Aerial Intruder (6981) fared better,

The Grid Trekkor (6812) was one of a number of smaller sets that made up the Blacktron II fleet. © StreetFly JZ

Blacktron II's Alpha Centauri Outpost, released in 1991. © StreetFly JZ

thanks to the cockpit, which opens to lower a ramp for two roving buggies. There were also a number of smaller sets, including the Tri-Wheeled Tyrax (6851) and Super Nova II (6832).

Space Police II (1992–1993)

Sensing trouble, TLG unleashed a new Space Police sub-theme, to begin what the coppers had started a few years earlier. In the 1992 catalog, the Space Police can be seen flying in to stop trouble as M:Tron workers wave their wrenches in the air to scare the Blacktron bad guys. This time, there was no mistaking the Space Police for ordinary civilians. With their black and gray ships with red trim and dark green transparent pieces, these guys meant business. Despite only releasing six sets over two years to most territories (a further two sets were available in the United States), these Space Police did not have a base or station to take Blacktron back to, although they maintained a form of detachable jail cells like the earlier police sets.

Minifigures: Setting them apart from other space characters, these were the first space-themed minifigures to have non-standard faces. The smiley staple was replaced with a brown-fringed face with raised eyebrows and a headset microphone. They had green torsos (with the Space Police logo and what appear to be tech devices), green arms and legs, black hands, and a black helmet with a dark green visor.

Significant sets: Despite not having a black and red police station to house all the Blacktron II criminals, Space Police II made up for this with its fleet of vehicles. There was Rebel Hunter (6897), with its releasable prison pod hinged in the mid-section, and Solar Snooper (6957)—a ground vehicle with a reconnaissance aircraft that could land on the back. The largest Space Police II set was the Galactic Mediator (6984), which despite not having the armament associated with a crime-fighting unit, is known for its size, playable space, and sleek wing design.

Ice Planet 2002 (1993–1994)

By 1993, Blacktron's techno-stealing tendencies had driven them far from the dusty M:Tron plains to a frozen wilderness dubbed "Ice Planet 2002" inhabited by a team of rocket-wielding, ice-tunneling scientists. The blue and white color scheme harked back to the days of Classic Space and Futuron's monorail, but was cleverly revitalized with the injection of transparent neon orange. Ice Planet 2002 was a futuristic sub-theme for a whole new generation of 1990s space fans, and the sets were detailed and eye-catching.

Minifigures: In the 1993 catalog a Blacktron thief is caught frozen in a block of ice—their clothes and equipment inferior to the local inhabitants'.

The Ice Planet 2002 minifigures with their bright orange skis and helmets and warm-weather clothing brought new life to LEGO Space. © Jordan Schwartz

Ice Planetiers' black torsos decorated with a blue, white, and silver design featured the Ice Planet 2002 logo, and a zip revealing a warmer second layer beneath. Larger sets included a second torso design with gold trimmings intended for the "chief" minifigure with his scowl and white mustache. Taking the torch from Space Police, other minifigure heads included a floppy-fringed Ice Planetier and a red-headed girl with bright red lips and hoop earrings—just what space was missing. To handle the extreme climate, the inhabitants wore neon-orange goggle visors with attached antennas on their white helmets, neon-orange skis, and carried matching chainsaws to break through the ice.

Significant sets: The Ice Station known as both "Krysto" and "Odyssey" (6983) was an impressive half-dome structure atop an icy formation base plate. Serving as more of an outpost than a complete base, its primary function was the transporting and launching of rockets with satellites attached to them. With the use of magnets and movable parts, there was lots of interactivity with this set, and two vehicles—a sled and a rocket transporter. The Deep Freeze Defender (6973), also known as Ice Cruiser Zycon IV, was Ice Planet's largest spacecraft but was capable of dividing into multiple combinations. The dual cockpits were fitted out with large white skis and there was even a rocket sled for the chief to drive and park inside the ship.

Spyrius (1994–1996)

With Blacktron out of the picture, Space was ready for a new set of villains and the Spyrius people and their evil robot droids were more than happy to fill the spot. The Spyrius home planet is desolate and covered in dark gray jagged rocks, while Spyrians themselves are war-raging, technology-hungry destroyers who used giant robot machines and small droids to demolish and steal as they like. Their unluckiest victims appear to be Unitron (see below), as can be seen in the 1994 and 1995 catalogs. While the Spyrius color scheme is almost identical to M:Tron's (with the addition of transparent blue in some sets), its design is certainly not. The sets launched in 1994 featured robot vehicles looming over mischievous minifigures, and flying saucers replacing more traditional fighter jets.

Minifigures: Space fans were not disappointed by the new minifigures on offer with the Spyrius sets. There was a mean-looking male figure with red hair flopping over his techno headband, an even meaner-looking chief with a mustache and stubble (both dressed in blue and black military garb), and then there was the robot. Long before the *Star Wars* team got the LEGO treatment, the Spyrius droid, with his black head, silver smiley face, and transparent helmet, was the first minifigure robot.

Significant sets: LEGO had made big robot space machines before, with Classic Space, but 1994's Recon Robot (6889) and Robo-Guardian (6949) were truly original designs, built to move on wheels (rather than the legs of Classic Space and 1997's more clumsy Roboforce). In a TV commercial, the swift Saucer Centurion (6939), which split down the middle, could be seen deploying a space buggy from the air, and the Lunar Launch Site (6959), the Spyrius base set, kept a secret missile weapon hidden inside a rock—a technique designers would use again with Unitron's base.

Unitron (1994–1995)

In 1994 a monorail set appeared in catalogs not part of the current Ice Planet 2002, Space Police, or Spyrius lines. It would be the first of four Unitron sets (the other three of which would only be available in the United States). In the 1994 catalog, while the Space Police were busy protecting Ice Planet 2002, Spyrius attacked the Unitron monorail and its workers. Despite their military apparel and weapon-launching outpost, they appeared to be a more covert operation than an official crime-fighting force. Sets had a black, gray, transparent blue and transparent green color scheme and no "Unitron" logo on the sets. Although their home planet is unnamed, all the Unitron boxes featured an image of a planetary body similar to Earth in the background. Unitron remains the most underdeveloped Space set, but despite the impressive monorail, and introducing dark gray to the theme (in their Zenon space station, 1793), failed to create the design impact of other '90s space ranges.

Minifigures: Dressed in gray (a first for space minifigures), with dark gray, yellow, and black details, they had blue hands and yellow helmets with blue visors. There were two head variations available—a red-headed male with raised eyebrows and a headset and a "chief" figure with wraparound silver eyewear and a modified helmet.

Significant sets: The 9 volt Monorail Transport Base (6991) is how Unitron is most fondly remembered. The gray tracks and blue transparencies are reminiscent of Futuron's 1987 monorail, although the touches of neon green bring a more sci-fi feel to the set, and its design in general is more advanced, with a two-story track and cockpits that double up as spaceships, which can be launched from the top landing pad or transported away from the bottom.

Exploriens (1996)

In 1996 Space minifigures were no longer mining for raw materials or taking chainsaws to ice rocks—they were looking for fossils. The science-savvy adventurers known as Exploriens brought color and light back into the dark world Space had become, with their bright white and blue spacecrafts and base. Tracking the planets from the Earth and skies for new finds, the Exploriens theme had a fresh, new look to it. Incorporating the magnet technology used in other space themes, as well as some Technic parts to further functionality, Exploriens also introduced the use of holographic stickers on the ships, and fossil magnet pieces that when viewed under blue red transparent "scanners" revealed different fossil designs. Exploriens sets are remembered fondly for their inventive use of parts and giant starship.

Minifigures: Designers developed the use of droid workers with Exploriens by creating a new robot considered the second female in Space after being referred to as Ann Droid in *LEGO Mania Magazine* in 1996. Only available in three Exploriens sets, this white and silver female fossil hunter is a rare find. Exploriens dressed for work in gray with a hint of yellow. Their rocket-shaped logo features on both worker and chief torsos, and all heads feature some kind of communications gadget. Some Exploriens come with special breathing apparatus helmets.

Significant sets: It would be wrong to mention Exploriens without commenting on the 678 piece Starship. For this large and detailed ship, designers reverted to a one-man cockpit, and with its moving head, wings, radar, and rockets, not to mention the four different Exploriens minifigures that accompanied it, this ship was an impressive addition to any space fleet. The Exploriens Android Base (6958), although only large enough to hold its telescope-carrying vehicle, featured a moving radar dish, which also controlled the base's doors, and a holographic communications screen. The Scorpion Detector (6983) and smaller Hovertron (6815), which was the centerpiece for the 1996 catalog cover, are both noted for their interesting use of parts and playability.

Roboforce (1997)

The year 1997 saw a departure from the traditional space-man base/starship ranges Space fans were used to with the introduction of Roboforce and UFO. Roboforce was another four-set theme for the LEGO Group and consisted of four black robot vehicles; two with orange transparencies and two with neon yellow. The orange robots appeared utilitarian with their practical arms and legs, and chainsaws, while the yellow robots were more aggressive with weapons and shaped in non-human forms. Roboforce is one of the less popular space sub-themes—perhaps due to its lack of definition and purpose, unlike the incorporation of robots in Spyrius, which was more successful.

Minifigures: Two minifigures were available with Roboforce. The two orange sets featured black and gray uniformed robot operators, with a detailed yellow and red "Robo" design that extended from the torso onto the legs. They wore orange helmets and breathing apparatus with black visors and had black hair and stubble. The two yellow sets included a similarly dressed figure. The yellow set heads were the same as Unitron "chief" heads, and they had neon-yellow breathing apparatus, black air tanks, and black helmet visors.

Significant sets: Robo Master (2154) and Robo Stalker (2153) both used wheels to get around, while the other two robots had more static legs. All the sets apart from the dinosaur-shaped Robo Raptor (2152) included a detachable spacecraft of some kind—the largest of which belonged to Robo Master, with its long utility arm and scorpion-esque tail. Robo Master also had a cockpit pod similar to those used by Blacktron II.

UFO (1997–1998)

It wasn't until 1997 that LEGO decided to go where no LEGO Space theme had gone before and introduced aliens. The UFO sets were inhabited by cybernetic beings and droids whose new, technological way of life posed a threat to the human race; consequently, their ships were strikingly different from their predecessors. They appeared to inhabit a vast, rocky, green planet, although without a base or many land vehicles it's more logical to assume they were a nomadic race, living in their spaceships. To create the sleek curves of these flying saucers, designers used large prefabricated parts to build up the structure of the ships, knowing this would be the easiest way to achieve the desired look. These large plates, with their UFO-themed decorations, are fairly controversial in collecting circles, as they don't require building and are harder to build other creations with. For colors, designers stuck to an old Space favorite—red, gray, and black with neon yellow transparencies. Despite fan opinion being widely split over the range, more UFO sets were created between 1997 and 1998 than had been for any other space theme since Blacktron II in 1991.

Minifigures: Accompanying ten UFO sets were five different minifigures. Three of the race's alien beings were available in blue, gray or red. All three had different torsos and legs heavily decorated with silver and gold detailing, while their heads varied according to color: blue aliens had blue or trans-yellow heads while gray and red aliens had different trans-red heads. They all came with a large black or gray shoulder armor piece and a contrasting black or gray helmet that completely covered and disguised their faces.

Significant sets: Unlike other space sets which had divided their attention between bases, land vehicles, and spaceships, UFO was made up almost entirely of airborne spacecraft. One of the most popular UFO sets was Warp Wing Fighter (6915). It's not the largest spaceship in the range, but one that is admired for its sturdy construction and rare printed parts—UFO sets also featured holographic and heat-sensitive stickers. Alien Avenger (6975) had the look of a typical flying saucer, the top of which was connected by magnets, and could be removed leaving a command center on land and a smaller saucer to fly away. Set 6999 not only included the smaller Cyber Saucer (6900) but came with a UFO mask so you could look like the aliens, too.

Insectoids (1998–1999)

The LEGO Group pushed ahead with the release of another non-human space sub-theme in 1998. These aliens, however, presented less of a threat to humanity, as they busied themselves on the planet Armeron searching for Voltstone rock—rock which has been struck by lightning used as fuel by the Insectoids. As seemed to be the fashion in space at this time, the humanoid cyborgs had robot drones helping them with their work. Their equipment and spacecraft was designed around an insect theme with ships resembling large bugs with cybernetic wings, legs, and bug eyes where cockpits normally appear. The color scheme was gray, blue, and transparent yellow.

Minifigures: According to a U.K. 1998 catalog, some key Insectoid team members were: Captain Sec who commands the Space Swarm (U.S. name: Celestial Stinger), Inspector Leon, Commander Webb, and the third "female" in space, Inspector 2 (also known as Gypsy Moth). These figures had human features—hair, eyes, smiles—but their technology was integral to their look. Gray and black dominates, with blue, green, and silver details. The Insectoids droid was gray and silver, similar to Ann Droid, but wore the same transparent helmet as Spyrius's robotic friend.

Significant sets: The largest Insectoids set was the crew's fueling station, the Arachnoid Star Base (6977). Shaped like a spider, it could be split to form two vehicles, one of which had light and sound functions. This was also included in other sets in the series, such as the Celestial Stinger (6969)—shaped like a large hornet, it had a pointed orange front that lit up and delicate blue wings with multi-directional maneuverability.

* * *

Unlike Space, LEGO Castle sets had started to develop clear factions as early as 1984. The introduction of the Black Falcons, Crusaders, Black Knights, and the Robin Hood–ish Forestmen meant moving into the 1990s. LEGO had already given fans plenty of play options around this theme. Rather than risk repeating themselves and losing fans, the LEGO Group took Castle in a more extreme direction, as would later be repeated with the Insectoids and UFO Space sets. As with Space, the armored minifigures and their trusty steeds were not immune to the fantastical influences of popular culture, which resulted in some unusual sub-themes during this period.

Wolfpack Renegades (1992–1993)

Despite featuring heavily in 1992 catalogs, waving their swords and being attacked by the Black Knights, Wolfpack Renegades was one of the smallest Castle sub-themes ever released. With just three sets to their name and a total of five Wolfpack members across all three sets, they were not as threatening a force as the Forestmen. Preferring to reside in a tower, rather than tree-covered castle ruins, the Wolfpack were a group of thieves trying to avoid capture by the Black Knights. The Wolfpack sets were some of the first to feature a glow-in-the-dark ghost minifigure (available in 1992), signaling a move toward more supernatural Castle sub-themes.

Crest: They may have been a motley crew, but they had a uniform and a smart crest all the same. Stamped with the white face of a dangerous wolf, their shields were black with a red border.

Dress code: With no obvious armor, the Wolfpack wore simple brown, black, and gray tunics with the wolf-face logo, and black or brown hoods. One member had a sleek, black mustache while his friend wore an eye patch (covering the mark of an unfortunate run-in with a Black Knight, perhaps).

Find them: Hiding out with a gray parrot and a ghost in Wolfpack Tower (6075) and Ghostly Hideout (1596) or smuggling treasure and a barrel in their cart in Wolfpack Renegades (6038).

Dragon Masters (1993–1995)

By 1993, the Wolfpack and the Black Knights had a new enemy to worry about: a giant fire-breathing dragon called Ogwen and his magic master. The Dragon Masters (or Dragon Knights, as they are also known) were ruled by a white-bearded, wand-waving magician who went by the name Majisto and sometimes Merlin—a reference to Arthurian legend, although there were no accompanying characters from the story. This was the first Castle sub-theme to venture into the realms of fantasy, and although it was short-lived, it was the predecessor for fantasy sub-theme Fright Knights.

The dragons themselves (of which three were available across all the sets) were a new addition, as well as glow-in-the-dark wands, and dragon headpieces for the horses. The largest set was Fire Breathing Fortress (6082), a small castle with a large battlement roof for Majisto to control the flying dragons from.

Crest: A fire-breathing dragon in green and red is the crest displayed on the Dragon Masters' yellow oval-shaped shields and flags—a more dramatic and threatening version of the Black Knights' crest.

Dress code: While Majisto opted for bright blue robes, black belt (with pouch), black cape, and blue pointed wizard hat, his knights were extravagantly dressed. They featured corresponding blue and black arms and legs, red and black torsos with a dragon face logo, yellow and red capes with the crest's green dragon, and large black helmets with dragon plumes. Other guards wore more simple red, blue, and gray clothes with the dragon face logo and black helmets.

Find them: Taming a fire-breather at the Dragon's Den (6076), taking one for a ride in Dragon Wagon (6056), or cooking up a potion at Majisto's Magical Workshop (6048).

Royal Knights (1995–1996)

Majisto and his dragons were given a king and a new group of knights to breathe fire at in 1995, when the Black Knights were replaced by the Royal Knights. Referred to in some territories as "King Richard" or "King Richard the Lionheart" the new LEGO king with his army's lion crest was a reference to the twelfth-century king of England, Richard I, who was also known by this nickname. The king had a large castle similarly colored to the Black Knights' that included a pop-up skeleton (the Royal

Knights were the first Castle sets to include these new figures), a ghost, a trapdoor, a catapult, and a drawbridge. It was the first castle to feature long, thin turrets on the battlements with flags. The castle could be added to with the Royal Drawbridge (6078), which included a Dragon Knight on horseback holding (oddly enough) a Black Knight's shield.

Crest: The Royal Knights proudly displayed their crest all over their castle. The yellow and black face of a lion wearing a crown sat on a red and white background with a blue border.

Dress code: The king himself was a rare find (only available in two sets), and had a red and white torso with the lion face on the front and a gold necklace and gold studded belt. He had a metallic golden helmet with a white plume and silver sword—the king available with the castle set also included a lion-logo cape. The King's men wore a combination of red, white, blue, and gray clothes with their torsos displaying the lion logo or covered in chain mail.

Find them: Bowing down to their mighty leader in King's Carriage (6044), being scared by a rather skinny fellow in Skeleton Surprise (6036), and ruling over all they survey in Royal Knight's Castle (6090).

Dark Forest (1996)

The Forestmen of the late 1980s must have been tugging on the heartstrings of LEGO designers by the time 1996 came around. Dark Forest was a continuation of the earlier Forestmen sub-theme but, true to their name, had a slightly darker edge to it, tying in with the direction Castle had gone in over the previous few years. The sets featured more weapons and traps, and similar to the three Wolfpack sets, focused less on the tree-top hideouts of charitable outlaws and more on fighting and thieving. The use of the Forestmen's crest allowed collectors to tie these new sets in with their previous outlaw collection. Unfortunately, Dark Forest only released three sets and, with the introduction of Fright Knights in 1997, was never fully integrated into the Castle theme.

Crest: No change was made to the deer crest first seen in Forestmen's Hideout in 1988.

Dress code: The Dark Forest minifigures' wardrobe was a fusion of Wolfpack and Forestmen. While previously most of the Forestmen outlaws had worn hats, the majority of Dark Forest wore the Wolfpack hoods. Green was still a popular color for torsos, but brown was also prevalent, including a rather distinctive brown armor worn by one of the minifigures. There were no female minifigures in Dark Forest.

Find them: Toppling a booby-trapped tree on a passing Dragon Knight in Dark Forest Fortress (6079), loading a catapult in Bandit Ambush (6024), and taking on the King's Royal Knights in their Hemlock Stronghold (6046).

Fright Knights (1997–1998)

The same year LEGO Space turned into a home for walking robots with Roboforce, LEGO Castle decided to return to the fantasy realm of Dragon Knights in a big way. Rather than revive the theme, they took the basic elements: dragons, a magician, and knights, and stretched their imaginations. Fright Knights were led by Basil the Bat Lord, and had a witch instead of a magician wielding her power over them with the help of a crystal ball. It was not entirely clear if Willa (the witch) was on the same side as Basil or against him, especially in sets such as Fright Force (6031) where Basil and his knights appeared to be cornering Willa. Other "enemies" are scarce in this sub-theme—although the odd Dark Forest or Royal Knight minifigure did appear in some of the sets. There were black dragons with bright orange wings in this range (as well as the original green dragons), and bat wings decorated the Fright Knights' castles and carts. The theme was short-lived, however, and the LEGO Group would not revisit the idea of a fantasy Castle sub-theme until 2007.

Crest: The Fright Knights carried white shields with black and red bats on them. Basil, the Bat Lord, also wore the same crest on his cape.

Dress code: The most striking thing about the Bat Lord's apparel was his helmet— black and full-faced, it was finished off menacingly with a bat wing on each side. His clothes were red, black, and gray and in some sets were available with his cape. His knights and guards dressed in a combination of these colors, and designers introduced some new gray-patterned armor designs. Willa the Witch was one of the first female minifigures to wear a skirt one-piece brick instead of legs. Her black and red dress with yellow buttons and spider brooch was complemented by her red cape with black spider logo and black witch's hat.

Find them: Avoiding the traps at Witch's Magic Manor (6087), ready to lock someone up in Traitor Transport (6047) and take them back to Night Lord's Castle (6097), while Willa's green dragon gives her a lift in Witch's Windship (6037).

Ninja Knights (1998–2000)

After Fright Knights, LEGO Castle returned to the more realistic realm of ninja warriors, set in a mountainous Japanese region, with a new style of medieval architecture. They produced a large number of small one-minifigure Ninja Knights sets for promotional purposes, making Ninja one of the largest Castle sub-themes. The sets revolved around three different groups—the ninja themselves (led by a shogun), the samurai, and the robbers—providing children with multiple minifigures and battle options. The sets were numerable and varied from boats and cannons to fortresses and bridges, with six sizable building structures released over two years. Despite the fact that "ninja" are not technically knights, and although the theme didn't conform to the European medieval traditions, Ninja Knights was officially part of the Castle theme.

Crest: The ninja opted for the symbol of a black wingless Japanese dragon on a yellow crest—a symbol of a water deity—as can be seen on the Ninja Fire Fortress (3052). The Samurai's blue flags and banners bore the image of a golden fan, while the robbers retreat (6088) was adorned with the red, black, and silver image of a bull's head.

Dress code: The Ninja minifigures were as diverse as their crests. For the ninja, designers created a hooded scarf to keep them disguised, and they wore jackets with overlapping lapels tucked into their trousers with belts (a knife discreetly tucked away). The ninja were available in black, gray, red, green, and white—the color favored by the ninja shogun with gold detailing. The samurai were mainly dressed in blue and black with silver armor and gray helmets. Both ninja and samurai shoguns came with gray shoulder plates. The Robbers were recognized by their angry faces and red and green shredded clothes. One older Robber wore an eye patch and was protected by some tatty old armor—a sign that maybe he was once a samurai, too.

Find them: Taking a boat ride with a shogun in Shanghai Surprise (3050), whizzing down a zip line at the Emperor's Stronghold (3053), and getting away from it all at Robber's Retreat (6088).

*   *   *

Between the mid-1990s and the first few years of the new millennium, the LEGO Group began to experiment more with ranges unconnected to its "evergreen" themes. While Town, Space, Castle, and Pirate sets continued to be popular, new and unusual themes began to appear; some moved away from the core building values of the company's past and struggled to find their place in the fiercely competitive toy industry, while others embraced them, quickly built large customer bases, and joined the LEGO hall of fame. Here we explore some of the more recent additions to the LEGO catalog.

Aquazone (1995–1998)

Before LEGO Town decided to send minifigures under water to wear flippers and explore ancient ruins, Aquazone were already below sea level doing just that. The release of two distinct Aquazone sub-themes simultaneously in 1995 was a first for the company, and helped to establish the popular theme that lasted for three years.

Aquanauts (1995–1996)

As the heroes of Aquazone's undersea adventures, the Aquanauts were exploring the seas looking for crystals and studying their properties using state-of-the-art underwater technology. They had a yellow submarine logo to match their bright yellow and transparent blue base and submarines and wore blue, white, and yellow uniforms. Their base, the Neptune Discovery Lab (6195), utilized vacuum base plates similar to most 1990s Space bases, but was distinct in design and included a number of unusual features—swinging doors, a crane, and a conveyor belt to carry the crystals. The Aquanauts also had a few individual vessels for carrying out their work such as the Crystal Explorer Sub (6175) and the Crystal Crawler (6145) with their insect-like pincers and Sea Sprint 9 (6125)—a mini sub with its own flippers.

Aquasharks (1995–1998)

Of course the Aquanauts did not have an easy time of it in the big blue with the Aquasharks around—a group of scuba-diving bandits looking to steal the crystals for their own personal gain. True to their name, the Aquasharks' underwater vessels such as Spy Shark (6135) and Deep Sea Predator (6155) were black, blue, and transparent orange and designed like sharks—the fronts were decorated with the jagged-teeth faces of the angry predators, as well as their blue shark logo. The Aquasharks wore black and yellow, with orange helmets to match their submarines. Unlike the Aquanauts, the bad guys didn't have an elaborate deep sea base, but a cave where they hid their stolen crystals (6190), which came with their largest vessel.

Aquaraiders (1997)

This year saw the release of a third force in the ocean. Only three Aquaraiders sets were made, making them one of the smallest LEGO sub-themes, and by design, one of the most distinctive. The Aquaraiders' vessels were a bright yellowy-green force to be reckoned with. Preferring power over prowess, these guys bulldozed their way around the ocean floor detecting crystals with their Scavenger (2160), scooping them up with their Aqua Dozer (2161)—a vessel that would look more at home on a farm—and generally making a mess with their Hydro Reef Wrecker (2162). Their ships and equipment were predominantly green and black, with transparent yellow features, and were decorated with eyes and jagged teeth—similar to the Aqua-sharks. The eye was also their logo. The Aquaraiders wore gray, black, and yellow, with silver and blue detailing and transparent yellow helmets; one Aquaraider also had a yellow hook.

Hydronauts (1998)

The final year of Aquazone saw the Aquanauts and Aquasharks replaced by the Hydronauts and Stingrays. This new conflict brought with it a sci-fi style of deep-sea building—with larger bases and vessels, as well as new octagonal cockpits. The Hydronauts with their brighter, friendlier color scheme and impressive Hydro Crystalization Station (6199), are widely considered the "good guys" in this second era of Aquazone. The minifigures' faces had painted-on breathing apparatus and were dressed in blue with hi-tech silver detailing and transparent yellow helmets. Their largest ship was the Hydro Search Sub (6180), which came with a detachable vessel with two suction tubes, and they also had a substantial ground vehicle (6159) for hunting down those crystals.

Stingrays (1998)

The Hydronauts may have had a base with a prison, but their enemies' impressive Stormer (6198)—a large underwater ship shaped like a stingray—measuring at approximately 45 by 55 studs, pretty much eclipsed the Hydronauts' station. The Stormer's dramatic double-fronted cockpit and sliding magnetic rear doors made it one of Aquazone's sleekest and most unusual designs. Gone were the cartoon shark facial expressions of Aquasharks and Aquaraiders, and in their place menacing Stingray eye slits. The ships' color scheme of gray, black, red, and transparent yellow was reminiscent of Space's Blacktron sets, and the minifigures' demonic red eyes, bizarre black mouths, and gray and brown uniforms marked them out as a new breed of underwater baddie. Other significant sets included the Sea Scorpion (6160) and the mini Sea Creeper (6140).

Western/Wild West (1996–1997)

The 1960s and 1970s saw the classic Cowboy and Indian stories reinvented with the production of spaghetti Westerns in Europe. Directors such as Sergio Leone and stars including Clint Eastwood and Henry Fonda did their bit to put the genre back on the map, re-popularizing the Wild West for a whole new generation. Keen to offer children contemporary and exciting toys, this theme was one of the first to be experimented with by the LEGO Group. Its efforts to capture its play value can be seen in 1975's Wild West Scene (365) and 1976's Cowboys (210 and 617), Stagecoach (697), and Western Train (726). But unlike themes such as Castle and Space where Classic sets soon evolved into distinctive minifigure themes, it wasn't until 1996 that a minifigure Western theme emerged.

The first wave of sets focused on the conflict between the local cowboys and bandits and the U.S. cavalry living in LEGOREDO Town (the same name given to the Wild West–themed area at LEGOLAND Billund). There was also a Sheriff who did his best to keep the criminals at bay in sets Sheriff's Lock-up (6755) and Sheriff's Showdown (6712). Larger sets in the series included Bandits' Secret Hideout (6761) and the mighty Fort LEGOREDO (6769), where the cavalry, dressed in bright blue and gold with smart white gloves, fired upon a bunch of rowdy bandits. Incidentally, those bandits were some of the first minifigures to be granted non-smiley facial expressions. While facial hair, hair pieces, and lips (for the ladies) had been featuring on minifigures since the Pirates appeared in 1989, the bandits were the first to show grimaces, as in Gold City Junction (6765) where one can be seen looking rather angry that he might not make a clean getaway from robbing LEGOREDO bank.

Despite not being a long-running theme, Western (later referred to in catalogs as Wild West, but returning to Western in 2001) was significantly the first to include rifles and revolvers as weapons. While Castle, Space, and Pirates had all featured their fair share of weaponry—from crossbows and lasers to swords, muskets, and even pistols—the LEGO Group had not provided handguns for contemporary themes such as Town. The period setting of the Wild West could be the reason behind the LEGO Group's diversion from its previous "no war toys" policy. Western was also the first theme to include plastic snakes. While designers had tried to have snakes approved for the first Pirates sets, it wasn't until Western that the public got to play with them.

The 1997 sets centerd on the First Nations people living near the frontier town in Rapid River Village (6766)—a large camp set with two tepee, a river, totem pole, canoe, and decorated horses. Unlike the Polynesian locals from 1994's Islanders sets, these minifigures had more expressive faces an attempt to depict an ethnicity for the first time in LEGO elements. Their traditionally painted faces were the first to have larger eyes with eyebrows, detailed mouths, and even noses. Their torsos and legs were particularly colorful with ornamental necklaces, fringed clothing, and realistic colors. The chief had a large feathered headdress, and most of the other characters had long black hair worn in two plaits. Their tepee, shields, and horses were also carefully decorated to create a very detailed landscape. Other sets released this year included Chief's Tipi (6746) and Boulder Cliff Canyon (6748) with its falling rock and healthy dose of vegetation and snakes. Notably, there were no First Nations sets released with cavalry/cowboy minifigures and vice versa. The 1998 Canadian catalog shows both ranges side by side, with no interaction between the two.

Despite many of the Western sets being sought after today, TLG has yet to release any new sets since 1997 but in 2002 it re-released three of the most popular sets—Fort LEGOREDO, Rapid River Village, and Sheriff's Lock-up.

Time Travel (Cruisers/Twisters) (1996–1997)

This was another theme that seemed to appear as quickly as it vanished. Based around the idea of time travel, it sees the Cruisers (a scientist and his apprentice) travel through time to clean up the mess wrought by the meddling Twisters (Tony Twister and Professor Millennium). Due to their time-traveling antics, the laboratory where the Cruisers carry out much of their work is a mix of LEGO building styles, with nods to Space, Pirates, and Castle themes. Time travel occured with the aid of specially decorated umbrella pieces, known as Hypno-disks, and a hat from the era the wearer wanted to travel to. Hats appearing on the various time-traveling devices belonged to pirates, bandits, forest-dwellers, knights, and spacemen. Dr. Cyber and his Cruiser sidekick, Tim, not only had unusual minifigure faces with large eyes and noses, but a rather impressive choice of gray and yellow transportation: There was the swift Rocket Racer (6491), which bore some resemblance to *Back to the Future*'s DeLorean; it's pumped-up older brother the Hypno Cruiser (6492); or the ultimate airborne ship the Flying Time Vessel (6493).

The Twisters, who traveled with the aid of a cylinder filled with artifacts from various time periods, appeared in three different sets in 1997. The two characters were

151

dressed in black military garb with epaulets and although Professor Millennium had a grimacing face, both minifigures had the traditional facial features, sans noses. Unlike the Cruisers, these two have no base, but instead the blue and black Twisted Time Train (6479), which had its very own resident ghost and skeleton, the Time Tunnelator (6496), and the Whirling Time Warper (6496) with its numerous moving parts.

Adventurers

Desert (1998–1999)

Before Indiana Jones made his mark on the LEGO world in 2008, there was another adventurer who roamed its most dangerous territories looking for treasures. His name was Johnny Thunder (in some countries, Thunder was referred to as Joe Freemann or Sam Grant). Seen escaping from a sphinx tomb with a red ruby stone on the cover of the 1998 U.S. LEGO catalog, Johnny (an Australian explorer/archeologist) wore a wide-brimmed brown hat with khaki shirt and red neck scarf. The theme was based around the adventurer who unintentionally got himself in trouble while looking for ancient wonders in various tombs, desert oases, and ruins. Adventurers Desert sets were the first to use such a wide array of sand-colored parts, as can be seen most dramatically in the large ruined temple set 5988. Johnny wasn't alone in the desert, and, just like Indy, had a girl along for the ride known as Miss Pippin Reed (Miss Gail Storm/Linda Lovely, in some countries), an elderly intellectual called Dr. Kilroy (Dr. Charles Lightning/Professor Articus), and daredevil pilot Harry Cane. The foursome was pursued by the evil Lord Sam Sinister in a black top hat and his friend, Baron Von Barron. Other sets included Oasis Ambush (5938) and Sphinx Secret Surprise (5978).

Jungle (1999)

A year later Johnny and friends, bored of the Egyptian wilderness, headed west to the Amazonian jungle to explore its ruins and rivers. The bad guys on their tail were the money-grabbing Señor Palomar, his pirate assistant Gabarros, and treasure-thief Rudo Villano. The jungle sets included the first-ever LEGO blimp (5956) branded with the Adventurers' logo and piloted by Harry Cane; a river boat and tribal shrine (5976); and some ancient Amazonian ruins where Johnny and his allies take on the bad guys (5986). There were also a fair few spiders, snakes and bats, and foliage to create that jungle atmosphere. This was not the end for the Adventurers team, who still had a good few years of travel ahead of them.

LEGO for Girls

When GKC drew up his list of ten basic qualities that a good LEGO product should possess, there was no doubt in his mind that it should be suitable for girls and boys. From a business point of view, this seems obvious—it wouldn't have made sense to exclude half of the toy consumers—but to Godtfred, the decision to push forward with LEGO bricks as the company's primary product was almost entirely due to the limitless possibilities of play and unisex nature of imaginative construction toys. In a 2008 *Telegraph* article reporting on the announcement that LEGO bricks were voted Britain's favorite childhood toy (Argos survery, 2008), the journalist comments on how the toy's unisex appeal probably helped it take the title. Before the days of Barbie and G.I. Joe, LEGO sets were packaged with images of girls and boys playing together. The 1958 boxes show both sexes happily building Town Plan sets. It was only in 1971 that TLG marketed some sets with just girls playing on the box—these sets, which included a dollhouse-style living room (260) and kitchen (261) happened to be more domestically themed than some of the company's other output from this time. These dollhouse-type sets were further improved with the release of the LEGO Family (200) in 1974 and minifigures in 1978.

In 1979 the "Scala" name appeared for the first time on a LEGO product and marked the first time the LEGO Group intentionally marketed a product line specifically toward girls. These Scala jewelry sets consisted of 2 × 2 plates with hinges, which could be linked together to make a bracelet or necklace, and 2 × 2 colored tiles with numbers, patterns, and pictures on to decorate the jewelry. In 1980 these were followed by Scala rings and a mirror. But the products were not a big success and were discontinued in 1981.

A female minifigure tends to her horse at Rolling Acres Ranch (6419), released in 1992.
© StreetFly JZ

When the Scala jewelry line failed to take off, TLG took its time to return to gender-specific toys for girls. In 1992 they made a conscious attempt to interest more girls in the LEGO System with the release of LEGO Town sub-theme Paradisa. The theme centered around a cosmopolitan beach-side community where minifigures sipped smoothies at the Sand Dollar Café, went windsurfing or horse riding, and cooled off at the pool. Five sets tested the tropical waters and they included the Seaside Cabana (6401), which came complete with the first LEGO windsurfer; Poolside Paradise (6416), with its unusual swimming pool baseplate and pink spiral staircase; Sunset Stables (6405); and the more impressive Rolling Acres Ranch (6419)—the largest Paradisa set ever produced with 366 pieces. These 1992 sets were fairly successful for the LEGO Group, and were kept in production for four years, the same sales period allocated to Space Police, Pirate, and Technic sets released that year. TV commercials for the new line didn't involve much building and focused on the play appeal of the sets as girls maneuvered the horses and minifigures around this delightful holiday village to the sound of a sing-songy jingle. Although no LEGO set is "just for girls" or "just for boys," one thing's for sure—you never saw Zack the LEGO Maniac playing with Paradisa.

The Sand Dollar Café (6411), released in 1992. © StreetFly JZ

Paradisa was the first System theme to feature light and dark pink plates, and other pink pieces and a new light green. With male minifigures outnumbering females by quite a lot, Paradisa attempted to redress the balance for the girls. Each set included a female figure for every male, and introduced new hair ponytail pieces, new female faces, and even a strapless top. Two Paradisa sets from 1996 are sought after because they include a small brown pony exclusive to this line. Between 1992 and 1997, TLG produced eighteen Paradisa sets, and despite never having revisited the line, elements of the Paradisa world and its influence can be seen in later Town sets.

A new brand targeting girls joined the LEGO System ranks alongside Paradisa in 1994. Belville sets were made up of regular LEGO bricks, as well as some decorative parts made specifically for the Belville range. For example, the Pretty Wishes Playhouse (5890) included a parrot and palm tree, more commonly associated with the Pirate theme, as well as a DUPLO crib, and Belville pink wall lattice pieces. The Belville figures were larger than minifigures and articulated at the head (both vertically and horizontally), shoulders, elbows, wrists, waist, knees, and ankles.

The largest Paradisa set—Rolling Acres Ranch (6419)—came with three LEGO horses.
© StreetFly JZ

In 1986 Godtfred Kirk Christiansen resigned as chairman of LEGO System A/S and LEGO Overseas, and his son Kjeld Kirk Kristiansen, whose smiling face had appeared on many a Town Plan set as a child, took over. By 1990 the LEGO Group was one of the world's ten largest toy manufacturers with 7,500 employees, five factories, 10,000 molding machines, and a popular theme park to its name. Despite the success of the previous decade, TLG was not resting on its LEGO bricks—far from it—as the company saw this position and success as an opportunity to push its toyline even further, expanding the LEGO System but also introducing new lines targeting girls, developing programmable bricks, and providing stimulating toys for all age groups.

The same year Kjeld took the LEGO reins, fans saw the introduction of some of TLG's most accurate models yet. While Technic sets strived for engineering accuracy, the new Model Team sets were all about aesthetic precision. The first three sets, released in 1986, included a yellow 4 × 4 off-road vehicle (5510), a red Formula 1 racing car (5540), and a lorry (5580). Even the smallest set was made up of 288 pieces and the constructed toys were the most realistic vehicles TLG had produced. After this initial launch, one or two Model Team sets were released almost every year throughout the 1990s. They became known for their attention to detail as well as their impressive part counts—at one point Model Team set 5571, also known as Giant Truck, was the largest LEGO set ever with 1,757 pieces. Targeted toward keen builders, rather than children who wanted to play, the sets were fairly expensive but represented good value for money because of the pennies-to-parts ratio. They were also versatile, with instructions included to build more than one model—for example, 1995's 5541 could be built as a Hot Rod or a Roadster. This set was re-released in 2004 as part of the LEGO Legends series.

The 1990s also gave the LEGO Group the chance to reassess the playability of the Technic line where it made some radical changes to keep toys relevant and exciting to the target market of young teenagers. The first half of the decade saw the introduction to Technic of the new 9 volt electric system—the first new electric development since the 12 volt Train system in 1969—the Flex-system that allowed force to be transmitted where bulkier gears and cross axles could not, and 1994's Super Car (8880)—one of the most complex Technic sets every produced. But things were about to get a bit less technical. The year 1995 saw the release of a new gear box to simplify gear assembly for younger builders, and complex sets such as the 1995 Pneumatic Crane Truck (8460) and 1996 Space Shuttle (8480), while considered high points of Technic design especially by the older Technic community, were gradually phased out to make way for toys children could build more easily. This was achieved at first through the introduction of models such as 1996 set Convertibles (8244) that relied heavily on the Modul System. This set instructed children to build nine models, the base of each made up primarily of 2 × 4 LEGO bricks that had connectors at each end to help them snap together with Technic parts including the new rounded,

In addition to these more traditional Technic toys and the Competition range, LEGO also introduced Technic Slizer—a series of elemental robots made from some Technic pieces, but other parts such as their head pieces and a specially designed throwing arm were not really compatible with other Technic sets. These were followed with a similar product called RoboRiders in 2000. Both Slizer and RoboRiders are covered in more detail in Chapter 5.

MINDSTORMS: RCX

The year 1998 was a significant one for the LEGO Group. Not only did it mark forty years since the birth of the LEGO System, but it was a year of new product lines such as Aquazone's Hydronauts and Stingrays, Adventurers, a rebranded Scala line, and even new building systems such as Znap—a flexible plastic connecting toy similar to the American brand K'Nex. Unfortunately, this was the year TLG reported its first deficit of $24.5 million, and as a result many of these new lines did not survive long. There was one new product, however, that, despite making its debut on the eve of some of the LEGO Group's toughest financial years, created a following and carved out an educational niche unrivaled by any other LEGO product. LEGO MINDSTORMS was named after Seymour Papert's 1980 book *MINDSTORMS: Children, Computers, and Powerful Ideas* in which the author proposes the benefits of a computer-based learning environment for children. Not only has MINDSTORMS weathered the financial tempest of the early part of this century, but it has filtered into school and extracurricular learning environments around the world.

The life of MINDSTORMS' original programmable brick started some years earlier in 1984, when TLG began providing funding for research at the Media Lab at the Massachusetts Institute of Technology (MIT). Part of this partnered research included the development of a programmable interface to control LEGO robots. The technology developed at MIT was then used by the LEGO Group to produce a commercially viable product, known as RCX. While TLG had dabbled in electronic products with LEGO Trains and Light & Sound toys, this was by far the most technologically complex product they had ever produced: A plastic casing (covered in LEGO studs) with LCD panel, function buttons, and six electrical connections (three output motors and three input sensors) housed a battery space, microprocessor, and the brick's 32K of memory. A program to control the robot's behaviour was created by the user on a computer using a programming language (although TLG provided software with its MINDSTORMS products, many third-party languages were developed and used to similar effect) and uploaded using infrared technology.

The first MINDSTORMS product was 1998's Robotics Invention System or RIS (9719), now known as version 1.0. This kit contained all the components required to build and program a robot including the RCX, the infrared transmitter, two touch sensors, a light sensor, two motors, various cables, a manual, and software for your own computer (the essential component not included in the set!). On Jim Hughes's thorough Technic history website, Technica, he says that while other themes were becoming more character-focused and sets more elaborate, the RIS manual provided suggestions and parts of models, leaving the builder free to create and construct his own individual robot—similar to the earlier LEGO sets of the fifties, sixties, and seventies.

Although the robots were constructed largely from Technic parts only "LEGO MINDSTORMS" appeared on the box. Usefully, however, that meant other Technic parts were compatible with the kits. LEGO also produced its own Mindstorms SDK (software development kit) to embrace the creativity of programmers rather than compete against them. LEGO followed up the 1998 RIS with two upgrade versions (1.5 in 1999 and 2.0 in 2001) as well as a number of expansion kits that included more sensors, motors, and programming capabilities before introducing the next generation of robots—MINDSTORMS NXT in 2006.

Initially the models were fairly realistic, too, with the launch of the Crocodile Locomotive (4551) and the Metro Liner (4558) alongside the accompanying bright yellow Metro Station (4554) with its delightful platform lampposts, station clock, and vendor windows. But by the mid-1990s, the designs had taken on a life of their own, result-

The Load 'N Haul Railroad (4563) was one of the first 9 volt engines, released in 1991.
© StreetFly JZ

Sets such as this 1991 Metro Station (4554) helped to further integrate Train with the Town theme. © StreetFly JZ

ing in futuristic-looking creations such as 1996's Cargo Railway (4559) sold in some territories as "Shuttle Express 2011." Although the 9 volt trains were now compatible with the other 9 volt LEGO System sets, and the tracks were cheaper, signaling capabilities were nonexistent and many of the favored remote-control components from the 12 volt sets were not incorporated, reducing the complexity of track layouts and the level of interaction.

Elsewhere, technical developments were being made of a different kind. The year 1992 saw the introduction of DUPLO Toolo—a screw-driver construction set for three-to six-year-olds, and in 1994 a group of pink-packaged sets appeared with a "family at home" theme. Throughout the 1990s, efforts were made to remarket DUPLO, perhaps to highlight the different age ranges available under the theme's umbrella name. In 1995 DUPLO PRIMO (later LEGO PRIMO) appeared covering products suitable for children aged six to twenty-four months. Although the majority of PRIMO products were non-construction toys, the line had its own brick with a spherical knob in place of the usual studs available in 1 × 1 and 1 × 2 sizes. PRIMO also had its own elephant logo, similar to DUPLO's rabbit. The age range varied for some products between zero years and thirty-six months and in 2000 the name changed to LEGO Baby.

Despite the addition of DUPLO PRIMO and licensed infant products, TLG continued to sell more traditional DUPLO toys, such as this 1994 Ambulance set (2682).
© Otto-vintagetoys

Toward the end of the 1990s, LEGO produced a huge range of products for the infant market, many of which didn't conform to its own original guidelines. The extremes of the range at this time included larger plastic dolls wearing cloth clothes (2001), which came with their own miniature DUPLO version and accessories, and licensed products for Little Forest Friends (1999), Winnie the Pooh (1999), and Disney's Baby Mickey and Minnie, creating a rather chaotic picture of the company's attempt to produce everything and anything, rather than sticking to what they knew best.

It seemed no area of the LEGO catalog was safe from the pitfalls of expansion, even the pages for themes that no longer existed. FABULAND may have provided three-to seven-year-olds with a viable alternative to DUPLO and LEGO sets, but despite its success, 1989 was the last year new FABULAND toys were released. Over the next decade, nothing effectively filled the gap. The Basic sets were given a facelift in 1990, color-categorized into different age brackets (3+, 5+ and 7+), and then again in 1996 with the release of the Freestyle sets. These focused more on individual creativity rather than the construction of traditional ideas presented on the box. Models built for the packaging included a plane shaped like a duck, a house with a man growing out of it, and a tortoise creature carrying a pink house on his

A LEGO minifigure gets a piggy back from Jack Stone himself. As well as their different sizes, Jack Stone figures also had sculpted noses and ears. © Miwaza

back. FABULAND ideas were also incorporated into the Belville sets for girls, which combined regular LEGO bricks with larger pieces. In 2001 the LEGO Group found a new way to add that extra page back into its catalog and incorporate its bricks into play-oriented sets for children not as capable or interested in building. This new range was called Jack Stone.

Although not released in the 1990s, Jack Stone is worth mentioning here, given that it was clearly a theme dreamed up in this era. In the LEGO fan community, Jack Stone is somewhat of a running joke, because of its unpopularity. With the 1990s focusing on the development of the LEGO System sets, it was with heavy hearts that adult fans saw the arrival of the new "juniorized" theme in 2001. On LEGO forum Eurobricks.com, one user described Jack Stone, named after its daredevil life-saving lead character, as FABULAND crossed with James Bond. Certainly there are some similarities with the '80s animal kingdom—Jack Stone, targeted at children aged four and upward, mixed LEGO bricks with specially made parts and larger minifigures; incidentally the same figures were used in Creator sets also released in 2001—but this new theme was more action-oriented and less infantile in its appearance.

The majority of sets released between 2001 and 2002 (when the theme was discontinued) were based around vehicles and emergency rescue operations. While FABULAND had appealed to many post-DUPLO children with its colorful characters and engaging designs, Jack Stone was more marginal and masculine in its approach. All but one of the minifigures included were male (the exception is a female helicopter pilot in set 4618) perhaps putting off young girls and their parents. With the blue and yellow box design, these were clearly designed as "boys' toys," leaning heavily toward transportation sets such as fire trucks (4605, 4609), aeroplanes (4614, 4615, 4617, 4619), or police vehicles (4604, 4611). Unlike FABULAND, which had centered on town- and community-based locations, buildings were scarce and the action centered around one character and his escapades. The failure of Jack Stone could be largely to do with its focus on a character children were not familiar with. With TV shows and films licensing out characters to toy companies more and more, children had become used to playing with toys they knew through some other medium. Jack Stone was not a Teletubby, Spider-Man, or Mickey Mouse, and with so many other toy ranges providing children with non-constructive action-figure play, the competition was too strong. Despite being discontinued, however, the legend of Jack Stone lives on, largely due to its unpopularity. Parts and minifigures are occasionally used by adult builders in their humorous creations and stop-motion films.

* * *

In 1999, *Fortune* magazine named the LEGO Brick one of its "Products of the Century." While there is no denying that humble brick's place in the 1900s history books, the company itself was about to face its darkest time. After suffering a personal loss in 1995 when Godtfred Kirk Christiansen passed away, more bad news came in 1998 with the report of the company's first deficit. To someone on the outside, the LEGO

Group was still a company at the top of its game—LEGO.com (launched in 1996) had just opened for business selling sets through its online shop, LEGOLAND parks in Billund, Windsor (opened in 1996), and California (1999) were some of the world's most popular family attractions, and LEGO was developing new technologies and releasing new sets like there was no tomorrow. But as the world waited for the Millennium Bug to hit, TLG was preparing for some huge corporate changes to ensure that there would be a tomorrow, changes that would help to pull the company out of debt, steer a global recession, and get back to the brilliant basics that the LEGO Group does best—building with that humble brick.

CHAPTER 5

2000–2011 Foundations for the Future

LEGO CEO Jørgen Vig Knudstorp once said in a televised interview that most businesses fail not from starvation, but from indigestion. When the thirty-six year-old Dane took over from Ole Kirk Christiansen's grandson in 2004, the LEGO Group had a bad case of indigestion, and he was just what the doctor ordered. The 1990s and the first few years of the new millennium saw the company take giant leaps and hard falls while the old adage of "quality not quantity" was one they seemed keen to ignore. Not to say all the products were failures, far from it—this period saw the launch of MINDSTORMS brilliant robot building system, and the Technic-inspired BIONICLE—but the System building sets loyalist LEGO fans had grown to love had become character-driven play sets filled with larger bricks and pieces that minimized building. The themes themselves were wackier (Time Cruisers, anyone?) and did not attract the dedicated following associated with LEGO themes of old. Some themes were on toyshop shelves for such a short time (or not at all, if retailers did not have the room to display the company's entire catalog) that children did not have time to collect sets, even if they'd wanted to.

Ultimately, the quality of a product means nothing if the business model behind it is not profitable, and the LEGO Group had reached a stage, after years of success, where the purse was empty. The company itself was not entirely to blame—the market had changed dramatically since the 1970s when minifigures and bricks were the coolest thing out there. Now Toys 'R' Us superstores were selling everything from musical instruments and sports equipment to karaoke machines and laptops. As personal electronics became more affordable, children's wish lists began to read like a technophobe's worst nightmare—gone were the Christmas Days of helping to construct a plastic spaceship, as parents found themselves installing computer software and downloading MP3s to make their children's holiday gifts run smoothly.

But, as Knudstorp believes, any CEO worth his salary can't blame bad business entirely on external factors, and LEGO couldn't either. Somewhere along the way, the LEGO Group had lost sight of what they were really good at. Management was spread thin across the company's various off-shoots (clothing, theme parks, computer games, brand stores), leaving the toys themselves as an afterthought. Non-core product lines like the Adventurers, a new secret agent theme, BIONICLE, and even a Steven Spielberg–endorsed movie theme were just some of the results of this busy period in TLG's history.

Adventurers

Dino Island (2000)

The 1990s LEGO Adventurer Johnny Thunder reappeared just a year after his Amazonian trek in his most unbelievable adventure yet—the *Jurassic Park*–esque Dino Island. Pilot Harry Cane was replaced by dino enthusiast Mike and the evil Baron Von Barron made his return, aided this time by the beer-bellied Mr. Cunningham and Alexis Sinister (sister of Sam from the Desert sets), who spent their time trying to capture the dinosaurs from the research facility (5987) with the use of nets as in All Terrain Trapper (5955) and the sea-faring T-Rex Transport (5975). A whole range of molded dinosaurs were produced for the sets including a large green Tyrannosaurus Rex and baby, a gray Triceratops, a brown Stegosaurus, and a red Pterodactyl— these dinosaurs are similar but not the same as those that featured in the Dinosaurs sets of 2001.

Orient Expedition (2003)

After a few years away from the adventuring life, Johnny Thunder returned in the Orient Expedition line, no longer referred to as Adventurers. Set on a journey across Asia, the team (Johnny, Dr. Kilroy, and Miss Pippin Reed) with the help of some new friends traveled to India, Tibet, and China in search of Marco Polo's treasure, the Golden Dragon. Never far from trouble, Lord Sam Sinister tracked them across the continent. The three largest sets were available with a board game that revolved around the Adventurers' story. Those sets were the Scorpion Palace (7418), the Temple of Mount Everest (7417), and the Dragon Fortress (7419). The range, targeting 7+ incorporated various building styles seen in other themes, such as the fortresses from 1998's Ninja Knights. Orient Expedition marked the end of Johnny Thunder, although it's not hard to see how these sets influenced the 2008–2009 Indiana Jones licensed range.

Dinosaurs (2001) Dino Attack/Dino 2010 (2005)

Perhaps because they had lots of Dinosaur ideas left over from working on the Adventurers' Dino Island sets, or perhaps because it was a popular children's play theme they had not covered yet, 2001 saw the release of a few individually packaged Dinosaur sets. Of the eight different designs, four were packaged in plastic canister-style boxes (popularized as a packaging form by some of the Technic toys) and were capable of building four different dinosaurs each. For example, the Brachiosaurus (6719) also had instructions to build a Diplodocus, Plateosaurus, or a Plesiosaurus. The four other sets were baby versions of these, intended to build just one dinosaur. All the sets included between twenty and forty pieces.

Not quite done with the ancient beasts, they reappeared in 2005 in a short-lived theme split into two sub-themes. Sold to different territories, Dino 2010 and Dino Attack had different takes on futuristic worlds where dinosaurs roamed freely. Dino 2010 sets such as Dino Buggy Chaser (7262) and Dino 4WD Trapper (7296) showed dino-hunting minifigures trying to trap the escaped dinosaurs and return them to safety, while Dino Attack took a more aggressive approach with each set seeing an attack team vehicle pitted against a dinosaur, surrounded by the fires of an apocalyptic earth. While the contents of corresponding sets were fairly similar (2010's Urban Avenger vs. Raptor set was almost identical to the Buggy Chaser, with the addition of a large mounted gun), the tone was significantly different.

Alpha Team (2001–2005)

It may not have been as popular as City or *Star Wars* but Alpha Team was one of the LEGO Group's longest-running themes from the 2000s. Sticking around long enough to make a name for itself and influence the later Agents theme, Alpha Team were a group of secret agents whose mission was to stop the evil Ogel ("LEGO" spelled backward) from turning regular people into skeleton drones using mind control orbs. The majority of the futuristic theme's stories were told through the LEGO Alpha Team PC game and various online games and comics. The original sets were based around an attack on Ogel's base (6776)—a floating island control center far out at sea. The Alpha Team made up of leader Dash Justice, lasers girl Radia, explosives expert Crunch, mining master Diamond Tooth, and a few others descended on the base in a fleet of vehicles including their helicopter (6773), the Alpha Team ATV (6774), and the Cruiser (6772). The Alpha Team bomb squad set included a little robot gadget made of minifigure legs, a TV for a torso, and gear sticks where his head should be. The sets, while fairly simple and less original than other new ranges, were strong on playability and construction, and included lots of black and transparent blue and yellow parts.

The Alpha Team's logo, a globe with a red ring around it (similar to the Classic Space logo), was printed on all their vehicles, while Ogel had a skull face on his ship and control center. A skull face was also used to mark the entrance to the center, similar to Pirates sets such as Skull Island (6279) and Volcano Island (6248). Unfortunately none of these sets came with both Ogel and Alpha Team members.

Ogel himself was recognized by his one red eye, gold visor, and dramatic black shoulder armor, contrasting nicely with his half-black/half-red-dressed skeleton drones with skull faces and smart black caps. The Alpha Team, distinguishable by their faces and hairstyles, all wore different coordinated uniforms (usually black with silver and an element of color and the team logo) and often had one colored arm.

Mission Deep Sea (2002)

Alpha Team action was relocated to beneath the ocean's surface in 2002 and centered around Ogel's new underwater base (4795), a set that, this time, came with an Alpha Team submarine as well. Ogel's mind-controlling powers now extended to sea creatures, as could be seen in sets Mutant Ray (4788), Mutant Squid (4796), and Mutant Killer Whale (4797), organic sea life vessels driven by Ogel and his skeleton drones. This time, the bad guy's left hand had been replaced with a red hook and his signature color scheme of black and red could be seen on the base, the mutant fish, and the Ogel Shark Sub (4793).

The Alpha Team sets were a collection of yellow and black sub-surface vehicles to hunt down and attack Ogel and his drones. They included a navigational vehicle with mini-sub (4792), a one-man robot diving device with articulated arms (4790), and the team's command center submarine (4794). In the Alpha Team mythology, the heroes managed to revert the sea animals back to normal, but Ogel escaped, enabling him to return in 2004 for the most recent revamp of the theme.

Mission Deep Freeze (2004–2005)

The new range released in 2004 featured a similar Alpha Team lineup (although two of the original team had been replaced), but a new logo and packaging style, to fit in with the Antarctic setting of the new mission. Alpha Team sets were technically upgraded with more computer parts and gadgets. These even included a droid minifigure only available in Mobile Command Center (4746)—a step up from the early TV android—and a number of hi-tech-looking control panels and ice scanner arm. Alpha Team had a rubber-ball-firing mechanism built into both their command center and the small car that came with Ogel's base. They were also equipped with the flying Blue Eagle (4745)—a scout plane ready to stop the skeleton drones from carrying out their work—and ground vehicles to cut through the ice, even when team members themselves got frozen in it. The team's job was to find Ogel who was planning on freezing the whole world and then time itself using ice orbs. His new hideaway was a mountain fortress (4748) shaped like a human skull with a dramatic icy baseplate and ice blocks marking the entranceway. To help fend off the Alpha Team, he had an insect-shaped helicopter, available only with the base set, and the snow crawler (4745) with its pincer arm for collecting ice orbs.

In 2005 both sides got an upgrade of one set each, which could transform into three different creations. Alpha Team got the Blizzard Blaster (4770), memorable for its distinct android qualities, similar to a Hasbro Transformers toy. The cockpit included space for special agent Zed (the AT member responsible for saving the team and battling Ogel), and a top-mounted cannon for firing at one of Ogel's minions in a small vehicle similar to the Snow Crawler. The bad guys' three-in-one design was the Scorpion Orb Launcher (4774)—a six-legged, two-armed ground vehicle with a large articulated tail. The set also came with Alpha Team's Flex flying a hand glider. Despite the online story and comic showing Ogel himself trying to escape in the Scorpion Orb Launcher, he was not included with this set.

*   *   *

While the Alpha Team theme lasted longer than other new themes of the period, the sub-themes themselves were distinctly different and introduced within a short space of time of each other, similar to the Adventurers sets. Unlike 1980s/1990s Space sub-themes, which had introduced new factions for children to develop their own storylines within the framework of spaceships and bases, Adventurers, Alpha Team, and other LEGO themes have since dictated specific characters and storylines through comics, video, and online media, perhaps to encourage children to buy more sets to complete the story. In a sense, this could discourage creative thinking, as children merely build the models from the instructions and re-enact stories they've read online. LEGO has continued to create worlds beyond the sets themselves, most successfully with BIONICLE.

By 1999 the Technic building system was a secure fixture beside LEGO sets on toy shop shelves. Regarded almost as a separate entity, Technic had built up a large following of older fans who were choosing LEGO's technical system over rival brands K'Nex, Meccano, and Fischertechnik. Unlike LEGO sets, where building themes were becoming more disparate, Technic sets had managed to avoid straying too far from the fundamental building philosophy that appealed to fans. Perhaps the only exception was 1998–1999's Znap (which never bore the Technic logo)—a flexible building system made of brightly colored parts that were snapped together to build structures, similar to K'Nex. Despite the simplification of some sets at the end of the 1990s, the majority of Technic toys such as race car Road Rebel (8247), motorbike Sonic Cycle (8251), and helicopter (8444) were not that dissimilar from the Technic toys of the 1980s, encouraging children to build fast cars and construction vehicles. There was one noticeable difference in the 1999 Technic catalog, however, and that was the introduction of Slizer (or Throwbots as they were known in the United States).

Each Slizer was a robot created and abandoned by an alien race. In the toy's mythology there were eight "continents" or "zones" each inhabited by a different robot, who were designed to suit the climate and conditions of their home, e.g., Ice Slizer (8501) moves on ski-like feet and Sub Slizer (8503) has breathing tubes to facilitate his underwater lifestyle. The robots would come together and battle each other using their disc-throwing mechanisms. Certain figures could also be combined to produce "Super Slizers." This "elemental" story technique would be employed later for Robo-Riders and also BIONICLE, allowing the LEGO Group to essentially repeat and improve on the same idea. Each toy consisted of one Slizer robot constructed using some Technic pieces, but predominantly new decorative parts. One of these new parts was an arm with a molded spring in the center to allow the robot to "throw" the included disc. This was one of the first examples of Technic designers developing a piece for such a specific function, making it only really suitable for the Slizer range, rather than the Technic system.

Slizer was superseded in 2000 with the introduction of the RoboRiders—small vehicle robots with similar elemental associations leading to names such as Swamp, Lava, Frost, and Dust. Unlike Slizer, these toys were packaged in plastic canisters—a successful product innovation that would translate to other themes, notably BIONI-CLE. Some of these canisters, when exposed to cold temperatures, would reveal codes to access an online game. It was these two significant departures from the Technic product line that led to the launch of BIONICLE in 2001.

BIONICLE

In 2003 the best-selling LEGO product was BIONICLE, a range spawned from the style of Technic building and the character-led story of Slizer. BIONICLE, however, was built not around bricks and toys, but around a story that became the centerpiece of the product line. In a 2004 *Guardian* article, a marketing manager for BIONICLE said that when the idea for the range was proposed in 2000, the appropriate term for some of the more traditional executives' reaction was "skepticism." What the team behind BIONICLE was proposing was a multichannel, multi-media toy format where the story and the characters led the brand, rather than the toys themselves. Not only was this a method of selling toys the LEGO Group had not encountered before, but they were also wary of the theme's inherent violence—the story is based around two warring factions of part-organic, part-machine beings in a subterranean world. The setting was initially on a mysterious island called Mata Nui where the bio-mechanical locals faced attacks from the evil Makuta (a being who controlled the island's wild creatures). The theme's heroes were the six Toa—elemental power-wielding warriors who washed up on the island's shore in canisters. The villagers believed they would help to awaken the good spirit of Mata Nui and save them from Makuta's wrath. Over BIONICLE's history, new characters and locales were introduced, creating a diverse and imaginative universe for the BIONICLE story.

The LEGO Group took a leap of faith, launching the storyline on the BIONICLE website before any toys were available to buy. In 2001, under Technic branding (this was dropped a year later, helping BIONICLE to establish its own identity), the first BIONICLE toys were released. Similar to Slizer, the majority of BIONICLE sets were buildable action figures of varying sizes mainly sold in canister containers (to tie in with how the Toa arrived on the island), but there were also larger sets sometimes containing more than one buildable figure; Battle Vehicles—canister-size figures packaged with a larger vehicle; and more traditional play-sets featuring minifigure-scale versions of the action-figure characters with structures such as the gateway in Battle of Metru Nui (8759) made from LEGO bricks and Technic parts. Each character had a name and unique identity as well as physical abilities often wielding the power

The popular canister packaging was still being used in 2010 for the BIONICLE Stars sets. © Christopher Doyle

This 2010 set of the villainous Skrall (7136) was one of the last BIONICLE figures available. © Christopher Doyle

of the elements. While many of the parts used to construct BIONICLE figures were theoretically "Technic," over time many original parts have been built and colors introduced that do not feature in classic Technic sets, seting BIONICLE apart as an independent building system.

While the story was initially established online along with character bios and an episodic game, the website became the hub that drew together multiple elements that built the BIONICLE mythology. These included storylines within the instruction booklets for each toy, CD-Roms featuring movie clips and games, comics, and books, as well as four DVD movies beginning with 2003's *BIONICLE: Mask of Light*, one of the top 10 DVD premiere titles that year. The storyline was developed by eight individuals from different continents working for TLG. They would convene to write the next part in the story, distributing the various developments between the different media. In 2004 a producer for TLG's Web division admitted that the BIONICLE story was planned out for 20 years, so it was a shock to some fans to learn that the release of six BIONICLE Stars sets in 2010 would be the last. In a press release addressed to the fans, that appeared on BIONICLE fan-site BZPower.com, LEGO announced that although there would be no more toys, the BIONICLE story would not be ending, with experienced BIONICLE writer Greg Farshtey continuing to contribute to the theme's mythology on BIONICLEstory.com. The statement explained that a fresh start was necessary and acknowledged the fact that it was only by embracing uncertainty and innovation that LEGO has had some of its greatest successes—BIONICLE included. TLG urged fans to continue to be a part of the universe they helped to create, emphasizing the integral part the stories and multimedia platforms that brought BIONICLE to life had played in its popularity, longevity, and success.

Not ready to give up on that success too quickly, the LEGO Group had a new lineup of Technic-type action figures ready to pick up the torch in 2010—Hero Factory. The new characters were similarly built and designed like BIONICLE, but with a more robotic and contemporary feel to blend in with their futuristic city surroundings. Known as the Alpha Team (no relation to the minifigure theme mentioned earlier), these robotic heroes worked for the Hero Factory—an organization that built and trained them using the most advanced technology—and took on the galaxy's most evil monsters and villains. As with BIONICLE, online material heavily supported the launch of the line, including a build-your-own-Hero game.

* * *

While BIONICLE heroes may not have wielded light-up weapons or robotic body parts, their creation was still a technological advancement in terms of LEGO design. Developing a Technic-compatible fantasy theme to create their own range of action figures was just one of the risks TLG had taken by investing its money in the production of these new parts and the continuous mythology they were part of. But in terms of pushing the techno envelope to bring children interactive toys that embraced their computer-savvy lifestyles, the LEGO Group looked to other areas of the business to ensure it didn't fall behind other manufacturers, such as Bandai and their Tamagotchi virtual pets and Tiger Electronics Toy of the Year winner Furby. Computer games, handheld electronic devices, and robotic creatures with sound, light, and movement sensors were becoming increasingly affordable. While TLG was developing computer games (see Chapter 6), and had released its MINDSTORMS RCX brick in 1998, its core product was still just simple plastic building bricks. Rather than try and compete directly, the company introduced new ways to bring its bricks up to date.

In 2000 TLG formed an alliance with acclaimed film director Steven Spielberg to launch a brand-new theme that would allow children to play with LEGO toys from an entirely different perspective. At a glance, Steven Spielberg's MovieMaker Set (1349), with its street scene, minifigures, and angry dinosaur, may have looked like a

177

slightly unusual Town scene, but when you noticed the minifigure holding the camera, the clapperboard, and the boom mic, it became clear that this was a movie set. The bricks and pieces were packaged with a PC camera with USB connection and editing software co-produced by the LEGO Group's media arm and editing software developer Pinnacle Systems.

But the filming of LEGO toys using stop-motion animation was not the LEGO Group's idea first. The creative phenomenon had become a fan hobby toward the end of the 1980s, and with the growing availability of cheaper cameras and editing software, as well as the introduction of video-sharing site YouTube.com in 2005, making "brickfilms" (as they are known) became an established form by 2000—with entire websites dedicated to the appreciation of the films (for more, see Chapter 6).

This original Steven Spielberg set, available between 2001 and 2002, was the only one to contain the camera and editing software, but whether a child chose to use the camera provided, their own existing equipment, or simply play with the sets as LEGO toys, the additional LEGO Studios sets introduced lots of new parts and scenarios to the LEGO landscape.

LEGO Studios

Film Production (2000–2001)

Perhaps the most interesting of the LEGO Studios toys were those that focused more on the behind-the-scenes aspects of the film industry. Alongside the Movie-Maker Set, there were a few other larger sets released that same year and in 2001, these included Explosion Studio (1352) with a collapsible bank for a bank heist chase scene, Car Stunt Studio (1353), and a studio scene with a moving backdrop powered by a motor, allowing the filmmaker to capture an in-car driving scene and helicopter chase (1351). A number of smaller sets featuring stuntmen (1356), cameramen (1357), and small on-set vehicles (including a director's helicopter and camera car) were also available, some of which were sold with comic books. A large number of minifigures and on-set props and equipment were available as promotions with corporations including Coca-Cola, Nestlé, and Kabaya Sweets.

Jurassic Park III (2001)

While the film-production-related sets may have alluded to popular movie scenes (Spielberg's *Indiana Jones and the Temple of Doom* is clearly being referenced in set 1355 Temple of Gloom), no films were actually cited. In 2001 two sets were released to tie in with the cinematic release of *Jurassic Park III*; a film executive produced by Steven Spielberg who had a well-known relationship with the franchise, having directed the first two movies. The two sets, Raptor Rumble and Spinosaurus Attack, focus more on the action taking place in the film but a cameraman is included in each set. The dinosaurs that feature in these sets, while not officially considered part of the LEGO Dinosaurs range also released in 2001, are constructed using similar parts.

While these were the only two widely released sets connected to the movie, it is also believed that the scene depicted in 2000's MovieMaker is a reference to Spielberg's *The Lost World: Jurassic Park*, in which the climax of the film sees a distressed T-Rex wandering around San Diego.

Spider-Man (2002)

Despite Steven Spielberg not being involved with the film, the LEGO Studios theme was used to introduce Spider-Man to the world of LEGO toys (perhaps testing the water for the 2003 official LEGO Spider-man theme). Again, only a few sets were made—Green Goblin (1374) and Action Studio (1376), as well as a third set Action Pack (10075) that included the first two. Green Goblin showed a scene between the movie's villain and Spider-Man's friend, Mary Jane—this set did not include any film production crew or even a camera. Action Studio depicted a chase scene in the movie and included a director, camera, and light rigs. The director was the same minifigure who had featured in earlier sets (often assumed to be Steven Spielberg because of the beard, glasses, and baseball cap), despite the fact that the movie was being directed by Sam Raimi. It was sold with a CD, including suitable sound FX for the scene.

Classics (2002)

In addition to the Spider-Man sets, the last four LEGO Studios toys were released in 2002. These "Classic" sets depicted stock scenes from classic horror films. They included: a couple being surprised in their car by a lycanthrope in Werewolf Ambush (1380), a Dracula lookalike being chased from the grave by a garlic-waving gentleman in Vampire Crypt (1381), a crazy scientist trying to control his monster creations in Scary Laboratory (1382), and an Egyptian tomb complete with mummy in Curse of the Pharaoh (1383). All of the sets included landscape backdrops but only two featured film crews. Despite the rising popularity of brickfilms, and the use of stop-motion film technology by TLG in its own advertisements, no new LEGO Studios sets have been released.

*   *   *

With the development of MINDSTORMS, the LEGO Group was careful not to put all its programmable bricks in one basket. Instead, designers experimented with the possible route robotics could take LEGO products in. The first "programmable brick," albeit not as advanced as the RCX, was Codepilot and appeared in a 1997 Technic set called Barcode Multi Set (8479). Sold in only this one product, the microprocessor read and stored bar codes, which when scanned caused the Technic vehicle to perform various functions. The same year MINDSTORMS was released, two boxes targeting younger robo-fans branded Technic Cybermaster were also sold. This system's brick used radio frequencies to communicate with the computer, but despite having a greater range, was more limited technically than its big brother, the

A MINDSTORMS generation NXT robot on display at the company headquarters in Billund. © Alex Howe

RCX. There were also four Spybotics sets released in 2002, which explored the use of a robot spy theme to generate interest in the Technic-based sets. Each remote-controlled robot came with CD-Rom software that contained ten preset missions to complete and the ability to create new missions. While innovative, none of these products provided the functionality and versatility of MINDSTORMS, or its educational value.

The new NXT Intelligent Brick released in 2006 had more memory, USB, and Bluetooth connectivity (allowing users to instruct their robot from a mobile phone), light, sound, and touch sensors, and a new icon-based programming language "NXT-G." This was upgraded in 2009 to NXT 2.0, which improved on the robots' ability to detect colors and light, as well as the programming software. The LEGO Group's aim was to make robotics so simple that someone could build and program their first working robot in one hour using LEGO MINDSTORMS NXT 2.0 (recommended age 10+).

German construction toy company Fischertechnik had long been the European leader in educational robotics, with programmable sets available as early as the 1970s. Before LEGO had even considered the RCX brick, Fischertechnik's kits were being used by engineers to simulate industrial robotics. The early MINDSTORMS sets faced tough competition, especially in Germany, but with Fischertechnik's higher prices and the LEGO Group's secure footing in the huge U.S. market, combined with the improved technology of the 2006 NXT system, MINDSTORMS established itself as an effective classroom resource to rival the German brand. Children around the world now compete in local, national, and international competitions to demonstrate their engineering skills such as the *FIRST* LEGO League, an annual school program where children design MINDSTORMS robots and compete against each other in teams to solve technical and scientific challenges. In eighteen years of competitions, the League has seen some 150,000 students participate from fifty countries around the world. The networking power of the Internet has enabled MINDSTORMS fans to be part of a global community of builders of all ages, competing, sharing ideas, posting online tutorials, and uploading videos of their latest inventions.

BIONICLE and LEGO MINDSTORMS were some of the most innovative and popular children's toys to emerge from the LEGO think tank in recent years, in spite of the company's stretched resources at the time of their inception. But the creation, development, production, and promotion of huge new product lines such as these did not come cheap and after a few years of reported losses, 2004 was the year the LEGO Group reported a record deficit of nearly DKK 1.4 billion ($230 million), with company debts amounting to more than DKK 5 billion ($827 million). The company was losing money fast, not helped by the cost of constructing theme parks and legal actions taking place around the world. Since the patent on the company's iconic brick expired in 1975, TLG had fought tooth and nail to prevent rival brands, essentially copying the design of the brick, from producing cheaper imitations to LEGO bricks. These lengthy legal battles, not all of which have been successful, have cost the LEGO Group and other brands enormous sums of money, and while they continued to be fought, a different kind of action was being taken at Billund HQ.

LEGO fans feared the worst—with the company so clearly on a knife's edge it would have come as no surprise if a toy giant like Mattel had made a convincing enough offer to let CEO Kjeld Kirk Kristiansen off the hook—the brand still had great customer loyalty and, according to an independent survey carried out by Young & Rubicam, it was the sixth best-known brand in the world for families with children age up to eleven. But, like his father and grandfather before him, Kjeld was not a quitter and, rather than give up on the problem, he resolved to fix it. He announced a new financial plan in 2004 and then brought in an outsider to save the company: Jørgen Vig Knudstorp—a senior employee with three years at the LEGO Group under his belt, who had graduated with a Ph.D. in business economics just six years previously, a young man with no CEO experience. An odd choice, perhaps, for a multi-national company on the brink of collapse, but Knudstorp knew he was an unlikely candidate, and took a humble approach to the organization and its customers, looking to them to show him what needed to be put right. He set to work immediately, as he explained to Diana Milne from *Business Management* magazine in 2009.

"In 2003 we pretty much lost 30 percent of our turnover in just one year. The decline continued in 2004 with another fall of 10 percent. So one year into the job, the company had lost 40 percent of its sales. And of course we were producing re-

Jørgen to the rescue! Senior LEGO employees, including CEO Jørgen Vig Knudstorp, now have minifigures in their own image to hand out as business cards. © Alex Howe

cord high losses and cash flows were negative. My job was to look at how to stop the bleeding, how to stabilise sales and how to cut costs dramatically to deal with the new reality of selling 40 percent less than you did two years earlier. . . . We had too much capacity, it was sitting in the wrong countries, our products weren't sharp enough and the retailers were very unhappy."

Part of the new boss's seven-year strategy involved selling off the LEGOLAND theme parks to Merlin Entertainment Group (LEGO retained a 30 percent share in the parks and Knudstorp is on the management committee), discontinuing less successful product lines, and cutting more than 1,000 jobs in Billund. The slogan he used to describe the strategy was "We changed everything but the brand." By revamping the business and the product portfolio, the company's profitability increased—figures for 2008 showed that sales were up nearly 20 percent and the net profit had risen to DKK 1.35 billion ($270 million).

Part of the company's 2004 financial plan referred to a new focus aimed at the classic product lines of DUPLO/Baby, classic play themes, LEGO Technic, and LEGO MINDSTORMS, and the importance of achieving a balance between these and story-based products such as BIONICLE, *Star Wars* and *Harry Potter*. Here we explore the development of these classic product lines and their narrative-driven alternatives through the last decade.

*   *   *

Of all the evergreen themes, Town had remained a constant best-seller for the LEGO Group, and as a result, conceptually it had changed the least. Even so, designers were still finding ways to introduce new real-world play environments to Town as can be seen in 2000's Arctic. Branching off from the familiar world of diggers and fire engines, Arctic channeled the adventurous spirit of 1998's Extreme Team with the design aesthetic of Space sub-theme Ice Planet 2002. The Arctic explorers' home was Polar Base (6575) and a mobile outpost (6520) and scouting sled were also available; all three came with a polar bear. One of the more unusual sets was the Ice Surfer (6579), a wind surfer designed to whiz along the icy terrain. The team wore a mixture of red, blue, and green outfits with the Arctic logo (a snowy mountain)—and

---

HOUSES AND HOMES

While the pre-minifigure Town range had included lots of "build-a-house" sets, there were less post-1978. Some examples of these include the original 1978 Town House with Garden (376), 1981's Summer Cottage (6365), 1982's Town House (6372), and 1985's Weekend Home (6370). Throughout the 1990s, there was a heavier focus on more action-based ranges, and only a couple of "house" sets were released. Since 2003, basic building Creator sets (also known as Designer Sets 2003–2005) have revisited house building on a larger, more detailed scale, sans minifigures. 2007's Model Town House (4954) included 1,185 pieces to build a three-story home with adjoining garage, and 2008's Beach House (4996), which, while smaller, was an inspired yellow-brick design with a balcony, skylights, and barbecue patio. Recent home-building additions to the Creator range include Family Home (6754) and Apple Tree House (5899)—a truly modern family home with lawn mower, basketball hoop, and satellite dish. The most recent City range included City House (8403)—a three-story white-brick structure with a garden. Other recent buildings to house minifigures are above the special-edition Green Grocer (10185), in the loft space of the City Corner pizzeria (7641), or the Winter Village Bakery (10216). Failing that, you could always build your own.

---

for those out in the cold, there was a warm fur hood attachment. From 2003 onward, there was a return to the slightly more traditional definition of Town, although this time minifigures had moved to a larger metropolis.

Before the LEGO Group settled on "City"—the current incarnation for what was LEGO Town—there was a brief fling with World City (2003–2004), a fictional international location with a futuristic design to appeal to LEGO fans all over the world. The skyline of World City was made up of skyscrapers, and crime and transport were the two main focuses of the sets released. Two World City trains were available— passenger and cargo—as well as additional train cars and a grand central train

While Apple Tree House (5891) is not available with minifigures, this photograph gives an idea of the scale of Creator's recent detailed house sets. © Richard Wyatt

station in the popular yellow-brick style (although slightly modernized and with a skateboarder). The majority of sets, however, revolved around Police HQ (7035), the bleakest-looking police station yet, with its three-story tower, black glass windows, security camera, and heavily armored vehicles. Other police sets included Surveillance Truck (7034), Armoured Car Action (7033), and a criminal hideout complete with shark-decorated hovercraft (7045). World City also had a fire brigade and a coast guard called Coast Watch.

This fire service helicopter (7238) was released in 2005. © David Martin

From 2005, Town was a town no longer; LEGO City was here to stay. This new umbrella name encompassed all the LEGO sets existing in a contemporary real-world setting, from fire engines and police cars to hospitals, airports, service stations, and contemporary trains. The unified theme has been running for over five years and at the time of this writing, toys are categorized in the following sub-themes:

Emergency Rescue

There have been many LEGO fire stations over the years, most notably 1994's Flame Fighters (6571), but 2007's offering to the men in black was an impressive addition to the existing collection. This 600-piece City set (7945) included two large garages with working doors for the fire truck and chief's car, as well as control and alarm rooms. The year 2010 saw the release of another station (7208) with living quarters, a fireman's pole, and a kitty stuck up a tree. The fire brigade's fleet has expanded to include a helicopter (7238), off-road vehicle (7942), fire boat (7906), and even a hovercraft vehicle (7944) that moves on wheels to create the appearance of hovering.

Police

One of the first 2005 City products was the Police Motorcycle (7235)—a sleek, realistic design that set the tone for the new style of LEGO policing. The new Police Station (7237) was a supersize version of the 2003 World Police headquarters, utilizing

185

The LEGO policeman got a revamp and stylish new bike in 2005 with this set (7235). © Owen J. Weber

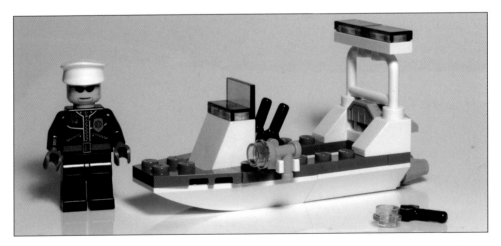

One of the most recent additions to the LEGO police fleet was this 2009 patrol boat. © Christopher Doyle

a similar three-story tower structure and black, white, and gray color scheme—the addition of a rooftop helipad and intimidating jail were impressive and helped to launch the new City theme. Since 2005 the City Police have made their mark with a large boat (7899), a Police Pontoon Plane (7723), and an impressive Police Truck (7743) that functions as a command center and surveillance unit. A new headquarters (7744) appeared in 2008, adding to the modern, fresh-white face of Police. Finished with plenty of blue transparent pieces, the station included an interrogation room, break room, and a water cooler.

Transportation

While 2005–2006 City focused more on the emergency services and construction toys, 2007 saw the release of more general transportation vehicles to complement the cityscape. These included a cement mixer (7990), a rubbish truck (7991), and a new gas station (7993) for the vehicles to refuel. In 2008 they launched a large cargo plane, a mail delivery van, and a large cargo truck with loading forklift. Unlike other City sub-themes, this one is not categorized by a color scheme, although green and white vehicles are common. More recently, LEGO added new leisure vehicles with a sporty red convertible (8402) and a surfer's Camper Van (7639) an updated version

Rather than being a city filled with crime and disaster, 2009's Camper (7639) exemplified LEGO City's leisurely pace and sense of fun. © Ruben Saldana

This mini-digger set (7246) was one of six new yellow construction sets released in 2005. © David Martin

This 2008 LEGO construction worker, in bright orange overalls, came with a cement mixer in set 5610. © Kent Quon

One of the latest Farm toys to be released in 2010 was this small Farmer set (7566), with a pig, dog, and feeding station. © Christopher Doyle

production and food sourcing, the Farm line gave children beyond DUPLO age the opportunity to explore a play theme not previously available to them; for parents and educators, it's a useful tool to explain real issues to their children, while offering violence-free play. The 2009 Farm (7637) was made up of a silo, a cow shed, and a hay barn and came with two cows, a dog, a cat, and a mouse. Other farm sets in-

FIFTY YEARS OF TOWN

Marking half a century of the modern LEGO brick and with it the Town theme, a special Golden Anniversary '50s-style town plan set was released in 2008 and was available until the end of 2009. The 1,947-piece set (10184) included a cinema, a gas station with garage and carwash, a town hall, and a town square with water fountain and gold brick statue. On the "50 Years-Town Plan" box was a photograph of Kjeld Kirk Kristiansen playing with the set, an homage to the photograph of him as a boy on the box of the original Town Plan. The attention to detail put into this set, from the movie theater posters and the gas pumps to the newspaper being read by one of the minifigures, made it a fitting tribute to the years of development and design that have gone into so many LEGO sets since 1958.

cluded a combine harvester (7636), a horse trailer set (7635), and the 2010 Pig Farm and Tractor set (7684).

Coast Guard

In 2008 a distinct coast guard range appeared to complement the Police and Fire sets. The minifigures were markedly different in orange and blue uniforms, and with their own life ring logo. Compared to previous water-based life-savers RES-Q, Coast Guard sets were more realistic and relevant to the everyday working situations of the profession. In the 2008 catalog they fronted the City section on a dramatic spread showing a wrecked vessel's crew being airlifted to safety. These Coast Guard sets were only available for one year, and included a four-wheel-drive car and jet scooter (7737), a large helicopter with life raft (7738), and the patrol tower which came with a large patrol boat, shark, and daredevil surfer (7739).

* * *

Focusing its efforts on the rejuvenation of the Town sets and the introduction of other narrative-driven play themes, it took a little longer for Space to get the "back-to-basics" treatment, resulting in a fairly quiet decade for the theme. Life on Mars were the first new sets to emerge, continuing with the aliens theme but reintroducing realistic-looking minifigure astronauts. Unlike the more violent cybernetic alien races of UFO and Insectoids, the organic alien life on Mars was not opposed to the presence of the human astronauts, and although there were distinct alien and human sets, they were all geared more toward exploration and excavation of the planet than destruction. The color scheme of this theme was not as distinct as previous space themes, due largely to the multicolored alien sets and the introduction of sand colors to reflect the red planet. Due to promotional sets available with Quaker Oats in North America and Kabaya Sweets in Japan, Life on Mars was the space sub-theme with the largest number of sets to be released since Classic Space. These smaller sets comprising predominantly of one minifigure and a small vehicle or spacecraft were accompanied by the full Life on Mars range released in 2001.

Avoiding repeating the minifigure robotic aliens from previous themes, designers opted for a different body shape for the aliens, with long arms articulated at the shoulder and elbow. The bent legs were joined together at the feet, and could not be moved. The aliens had larger heads with no top studs, and their faces were individually styled to give them different looks and mild gender distinctions. The Martians' skin was green, while their bodies came in a variety of colors. The human visitors were dressed in black, white, gray, blue, and silver spacesuits, with silver breathing apparatus. The four human spacewalkers included a redhead known as BB, a graying, bearded, bald astronaut called Mac, a technical assistant (dressed in blue) with blue-rimmed glasses, and a stubbly doctor with black frames.

The Martian base and launching station, Aero Tube Hangar (7317), was one of the theme's most popular sets. With its tube/pump system Martian minifigures could be fired down the tubes to their spacecrafts. This set was also popular because all the smaller Martian sets could be connected up to it, such as the Excavation Searcher (7316)—a scorpion-shaped robot vehicle—which came complete with a hangar to connect up to the base set.

After a six-year hiatus from the Space theme (with the exception of some Discovery Channel–licensed sets in 2003), a new group of minifigure astronauts suited up to head to Mars. Mars Mission (2007–2008), unlike Life on Mars, saw an alien race attacking the mission's astronauts who were trying to remove crystals for energy to ship back to Earth in their space shuttle. There were no welcoming colors and smiling faces for the bad-guy aliens of Mars Mission. Instead, identical green figures with glow-in-the-dark torsos fired down on the astronauts. Similar to the Life on Mars aliens, these figures were not shaped like minifigures and only their commanders (released in the second year of production) with black heads, yellow eyes,

---

MINIFIGURES IN SPACE

The release of Life on Mars was marketed to coincide with the real-life exploration of the planet. In 2001 NASA launched the robotic spacecraft Mars Odyssey to orbit the planet and search for evidence of volcanic activity and a history of liquid water. That same year, the LEGO Group sent 300 of the alien minifigures to the International Space Station from Russia, along with the Red Planet Protector (7313), which was used in the first toy-based experiment in space. The minifigures were later awarded as prizes to children of a Life on Mars LEGO building competition. Two years later, NASA launched the Mars Exploration Rovers *Spirit* and *Opportunity* complete with two important "astrobot" minifigures. Pictures of Biff Starling and Sandy Moondust were attached to the rover together with specially designed aluminum LEGO bricks and magnets to help determine the presence of liquid water, making minifigures the first "people" to land on Mars.

---

and larger appendages were fully articulated. Contrastingly, there were plenty of astronaut individuals living on Mars. While all Mars Mission astronauts wore a white uniform with orange torso design (including a planet logo similar to that used in Classic Space, Futuron, and Ice Planet 2002), their faces couldn't have been more different. There certainly wasn't time for shaving in space, with a large proportion of minifigures flaunting some stubble. There were no girls in space this time, but there were balaclavas, scared and angry faces, redheads, and sunglasses.

In terms of sets, Mars Mission clearly took its lead from Life on Mars—the tube/pump system was given a facelift in 2007's Eagle Command Base (7690) and the MT-31 Trik

This Life on Mars mono jet set (7310), released in 2001, came with the spectacled technical assistant. © David Martin

(7694) was very similar to Life on Mars's T3 Trike (7312). Despite the similarities, Mars Mission offered some imaginative new sets such as the drill turned mobile tank with moving drill (7649-1) and the aliens' mothership that came with a human missile launching base (7691-1). The clear color distinction between humans (orange, blue, white, and black) and the evil aliens (black, green, and red), combined with sleek designs and an inventive use of parts and mechanisms, was an effective way of reinstating the feel of Classic Space while modernizing it for a new generation of LEGO fans.

A classic theme was truly revived, however, when LEGO brought back the Space Police in 2009, not seen since the early 1990s. Unlike their predecessors who had been locking up human criminals from the thieving Blacktron and Spyrius factions, these Space Police were fighting badly behaved aliens such as members of the Space Biker Gang: fishy Slizer, reptilian Kranxx, "astropunk" Snake, and the Skull Twins, as well as goggle-eyed Squidman and four-armed Frenzy. They dressed in functional dark gray with belts and pockets and wore black helmets with black visors. There was also a female officer, and some minifigures came with alternative "scared" faces. The aliens themselves were of normal minifigure stature, with regular legs and arms. Their heads and clothing varied between individuals, who all seemed to come from different alien species, with great attention paid to details such as the Space

A classic sub-theme was reborn in the 2000s with the release of a new range of Space Police sets, including this Raid VPR (5981). © Christopher Doyle

Part of Space Police's success is due to the unusual alien minifigure designs, including Squidtron (left) and Squidman. © Christopher Doyle

New alien minifigures such as Rench (right) tried their best to make trouble for the new crime-fighters. © Christopher Doyle

Biker Gang's skull belts, Squidman's upturned eyes, and Frenzy's additional arms. There was also a white minifigure astronaut statue included in set 5974, commemorating the first LEGO astronaut in space.

The new Space Police range had moved on from the black, red, and green look of the 1990s to a fresh blue, gray, white, and black color scheme. They had an impressive base ship that could divide into five smaller vehicles, called the Galactic Enforcer (5974). It also came with four detachable prison pods and an alien craft ready to swoop in and free the prisoners. The alien crafts were styled with their criminal pilots in mind with jagged edges and dark colors, such as Snakes' Wrecker space truck (5972) in black and yellow with flaming boosters and spiky front bumper. And when the bad guys needed a tune-up, they headed to Squidman's Pitstop (5980) where there was a vehicle-lift and fuel pump alongside exploding barrels and a rocket launcher. In 2010 a new Space Police Central set (5985) gave the coppers a secure place to lock up all the bad guys.

The most recent Space Police sets combined the playability and colorful characters associated with action-figure toys, with inventive LEGO set designs, desirable

Space Police's aliens had their own colorful getaway vehicles, such as Squid-man's customized ram-raider, shown here without stickers applied, and available with Smash 'n' Grab (5982) © Christopher Doyle

accessories, and most importantly a sense of humor. The new minifigure faces, the unusual aliens, and the situations designers invented for them were more imaginative than any previous Space sub-theme, without being too prescriptive or dictatorial, giving children the freedom to develop their own storylines based around these innovative sets.

The contemporary and futuristic worlds of Town and Space were not the only evergreen themes to survive the introduction of experimental design and financial problems that plagued the 2000s. *Medieval Mischief and Mayhem* was the title of the LEGO Group's 2000 graphic novel based around the Knights' Kingdom sub-theme launched that same year. The comic introduced the Castle theme for the new millennium and the two warring factions—King Leo's Lion Knights and the Bulls, led by Cedric the Bull, as well as key characters from both sides. King Leo's crest was similar to the earlier Royal Knights'. A yellow lion face with a black mane sat in front of a yellow "x" over a blue background. Dressed regally in blue with a lion's crest on his torso and a gold crown was the white-bearded King Leo. His knights wore silver armor and black trousers with red tunics, apart from Princess Storm who stood out in gold corseted armor and red trousers. Their enemies were represented by the face of a brown bull complete with nose ring and glaring red eyes over a yellow background. In the U.K. catalog that year the Bulls were shown more as outlaws, fighting against the King—with no base of their own, they had a large cannon pointed straight at King Leo's Castle (6098). Cedric the Bull matched King Leo's gold crown with a black helmet finished off with bull horns, to match his black clothes emblazoned with the Bulls' logo. Cedric's various baddie cohorts are dressed similarly menacingly in black and brown—Gilbert the Bad was the one with the eye patch.

The return to European-style medieval knights gave LEGO designers the opportunity to update their older Castle designs in sets such as Catapult Crusher (6032), Guarded Treasure (6094), and the more civilized Royal Joust (6095). Gray bricks replaced the darker appearance of Royal Knights and Fright Knights, and the new castle was more of a modular structure—with interchangeable towers—built on a raised base plate. No new Knights' Kingdom sets from this range would appear after 2000, but the Knights' Kingdom name was revived in 2004 when LEGO re-branded it to appeal to a younger age group.

With the exception of the 2001 Harry Potter Hogwarts Castle, LEGO catalogs remained void of any new Castle play sets until 2004. By this time BIONICLE had been on the market for five years and was still selling well, especially the canister sets—small sets packaged in plastic boxes usually containing enough pieces to build an action figure—which along with BIONICLE's marketing strategy, clearly influenced the redesign of Knights' Kingdom. In 2004 six character sets were released, packaged similarly in plastic canisters with battlement-style lids. Made up largely of Technic bricks, these figures—consisting of four heroic knights, their king, and the evil Vladek—existed independently from the regular playsets. Targeting 6+ the LEGO sets, made up of castles and battle scenes, had a chunkier feel to them and included minifigures representative of the Technic models. TV advertising focused heavily on the fictional, magical world of the characters, as did the accompanying website, books, and trading cards. The "Hero" knights, who fought for King Mathias (and later King Jayko), were all from different provinces and had crests that reflected their personalities: a wolf, a hawk, a monkey, and a bear, which were visible on their shields. Their king and his castle bore the crest of a lion beneath a crown. The canister models and minifigures were dressed, for the most part, pretty similarly, so characters could be identified across the range. The four original knights were dressed in red, blue, green, or dark purple, while the king wore blue and gray attire finished off with gold. Their main enemy, Lord Vladek, and his Shadow Knights were recognized by the scorpion emblem on their shields and torsos, while his later ally, Dracus, leader of the Rogue Knights, sported an equally unnerving snake. Vladek looked suitably evil in black and red and his full-faced helmet covered up his scowl and glaring red eyes. Unlike previous LEGO Castle themes, the Knights' Kingdom (II) minifigures had bright colored swords and armor, something that caused controversy among the more traditional Castle fans. More Knights' Kingdom (II) sets were released than any other Castle sub-theme—and the Knights can be seen fending off flying scorpions in the Castle of Morcia (8781), trapped in a hanging cage in Scorpion Prison Cave (8876), and showing off their combat skills in Battle at the Pass (8813)—but after years of financial difficulties, and a short-lived Vikings sub-theme (2005), TLG reverted to more familiar terrain with another fantasy-led Castle range.

The centerpiece for 2007's "Castle"—the fantasy line—was King's Castle Siege (7094). Evidently influenced by a number of its Castle predecessors, one cannot help but notice the similarities between the simple four-walled structure with drawbridge and tall rear tower and the bright yellow set 375 released nearly thirty years before. In addition, the king's home bears the crest of a crown not that different from the original Castle set. The 2007 sets introduced us to this Crown King, his princess daughter, and his knights (often referred to as Crown Knights), as well as their skeletal enemies (both black and white and occasionally dressed in armor) and fire-breathing dragons led by the Evil Wizard with his one red eye, skull face logo, and creepy charms hanging from his belt. In 2008 new characters were added to the fantasy tapestry with the addition of dwarves and a green dragon as allies of the Crown King, and evil trolls to do the heavy duty work for the Evil Wizard. The line stands apart from previous Castle ranges for its more realistic use of gray and brown for building structures and vehicles, while maintaining a fantastical world with its characters. Although boats had featured in Castle before, this sub-theme included two large ships: Skeleton Ship Attack (7029) and Troll Warship (7048). In 2008 the LEGO Group released a special-edition set exclusively for its online shop, which saw the Crown Knights mingling with the locals. LEGO designers consulted Castle fans when designing Medieval Market Village (10193), the largest Castle set at the time, which included many special parts such as a roasted turkey, buildable LEGO chickens, and the first LEGO cow. They also produced role-playing costume products including swords, a crown, and an archery set.

The year 2010 saw the release of a new Castle theme to replace the fantasy sets mentioned above. Kingdoms took over as the official Castle sub-theme and saw a return to the medieval world originally associated with the Castle theme. Gone were the dragons, ninjas, and evil skeletons (although LEGO couldn't resist the inclusion of a wizard) replaced by a King, his Lion Kingdom (protected by Royal Lion Knights), and a clumsy Princess who kept getting captured by the Dragon Knights and their wizard. The impressive King's Castle (7946) was an amped-up version of the Crusader's castle (6080) from 1984 with its gray brickwork, turrets, battlements, and drawbridge. Other sets included the Dragon Knights' prison tower (7947) and a court jester minifigure set (7953).

The more recent Castle toys have evolved from the various permutations of sub-themes depicting LEGO life a both medieval and fantastical. From the introduction of bright green fire-breathers in 1993's Dragon Knights, to the impressive castles guarded by the earlier Black and Lion Knights, the influence of weaponry, structures, and color schemes can be seen in the detailed and colorful sets released more re-

LEGO Kingdoms introduced two new factions of knights—the Royal Lion Knights (left) and the Dragon Knights. © Christopher Doyle

According to LEGO.com, this wizard of the Dragon Kingdom spent his time brewing spells to help the Dragon Knights defeat their rivals. © Christopher Doyle

cently. A theme that began life in idea books and store displays and eventually found its way into children's hands as a bright yellow castle over thirty years ago has stood the test of time and looks set to continue to entertain LEGO fans for years to come.

*   *   *

Pirates did not manage to achieve the same continuous success as Castle, and by the end of 1997 all LEGO Pirates sets were no longer readily available. With the exception of a few re-released sets in 2001 and 2002, the theme lay dormant in minifigure scale throughout the 2000s. In 2003, TLG re-branded sets suitable for four year olds and upward as "4 Juniors." In 2004 the name was changed to simply "4+" and Pirates were chosen, alongside City and Spider-Man, to be given the 4+ treatment. Using regular-size LEGO bricks, the two key differences between 4+ sets and System sets were the figures themselves (4+ figures are larger and cannot be disassembled) and the complexity of the sets. The largest 4+ Pirates set—a new ship for Captain Redbeard (7075)—only consisted of 134 pieces, compared to the 925 pieces required to construct the Black Seas Barracuda. Rather than seeing pirates face off against angry natives or the military, 4+ took a new approach and introduced Captain Kragg (with a blue and black flag) to cause trouble for Redbeard and his crew. The majority of these 2004 Pirates sets were only available in Europe, and the line ended in 2005.

This 2009 LEGO Pirates Advent Calendar (6299) included Captain Brickbeard (top left), a female pirate, and a mermaid. © Ben Pillen

LEGO EXO-FORCE (2006–2008)

Among the LEGO-building community, mecha building—the construction of robotic mechanical machines controlled by humans—is a popular medium often referencing Japanese manga and anime. Combinations of LEGO bricks and Technic parts enable builders to design other-worldly creations with both organic and mechanical properties. The LEGO Group had touched on this kind of toy previously with Space themes such as 1994's Spyrius and 1997's Roboforce line, but EXO-FORCE was the first theme with a detailed storyline that centered on the idea of human-controlled mecha versus machines. Between November 2005 and March 2008, TLG released forty issues of the EXO-FORCE online comic, detailing the ongoing storyline that related to the waves of toys they released. These stories were embellished in a series of books for young readers as well as extended TV commercials.

Set on Sentai Mountain, EXO-FORCE referred to a group of elite human pilots chosen to protect their home, which was under attack from drone machines controlled by a rogue robot called Meca One. To arm themselves against the giant robot fighters, four EXO-FORCE members piloted their own uniquely designed mecha weapons. The comic followed the team as they battled the relentless robots, searched for new technology in the legendary Golden City, and eventually traveled to their enemy's jungle base to save their leader.

The first wave of toys released in 2006 included individual battle machines Grand Titan (7701) and Mobile Defence Tank (7706) powered by their EXO-FORCE pilots, as well as individual robot machines such as Thunder Fury (7702) and Sonic Phantom (7704). The largest sets for kids to get their hands on were Striking Venom (7707)—the robots' intimidating mobile battle station used to dig their way into the mountain and recharge their batteries—and Sentai Fortress, which at 1,499 pieces included Meca One's personal battle machine and EXO-FORCE'S blue Silent Strike. The 2007 toys were set in the Golden City and centered on the Fight for the Golden Tower (8107). The EXO-FORCE had a range of new mecha to play with and their robot enemies had also upgraded their machinery. In 2008 when the action moved to the jungle, there were new vehicles to pilot, but no base set where the EXO-FORCE leader, Sensei Keiken, was being held prisoner. The medium-size sets included the robots' Storm Lasher (8117), with its spinning turbine wings with blades to slash through the jungle, and the Hybrid Rescue Tank (8118), with moving treads, rotating blaster cannon, and detachable flying vessel.

One distinctive feature of the EXO-FORCE line was that particular models could be combined to produce super battle machines, referred to in the storylines. For example, Thunder Fury (7702) and Fire Vulture (7703) could be connected to create a larger robot machine known as Raging Storm. This extra construction value made the comic and other online material an integral part of the EXO-FORCE play experience and encouraged fans to collect the sets needed for these super builds, as well as to

Three of the EXO-FORCE team members (from left to right), Takeshi, Hikaru, and Ryo, show off their unique hairstyles and facial expressions. © Ruben Saldana

create their own. Additionally, the EXO-FORCE minifigures were some of the more unusual that LEGO has created. The robots themselves are mechanical drones available in gold (Meca One), silver (Devastator), and a rusty brown (Iron Drone), while the EXO-FORCE team members have distinctive faces with larger manga-style eyes and chunky hair pieces available in their cartoonish spiked styles and bright colors.

Due to the theme being discontinued in 2008, the final part of the EXO-FORCE storyline was never told, leaving some die-hard fans disappointed.

Aqua Raiders (2007)

After ten years of absence, the "Aquaraiders" name reappeared on toyshop shelves as Aqua Raiders, when the Aquazone sub-theme was reinvented as a stand-alone underwater theme. Set in the Bermuda Triangle, the new divers are the best of the best sent on a dangerous mission to uncover hidden treasures that lie deep at the bottom of the ocean using the latest technologies. According to the theme's backstory, as soon as the divers made their descent, they were attacked by sharks, eels, octopuses, lobsters, and a host of other unusual sea creatures.

These sets focused on predators of the deep rather than a conflict between two sets of deep-sea adventurers. Sets such as Tiger Shark Attack (7773) and Crab Crusher (7774) include pieces to build a large toothy fish and menacing crustacean that

This 2007 Aqua Raiders set included a mini-sub with the Raiders' logo and a giant anglerfish with glow-in-the-dark jaws. © Kent Quon

tower over the Aqua Raider's minifigures. The divers were not without their tools, though—there was the robot arm and drill on the exploration rover from Lobster Strike (7772), the harpoon cannon and aqua-missile from Tiger Shark Attack, and the mounted harpoons on top of Sub 76 in the Shipwreck (7776). The largest set by far was Aquabase Invasion (7775), which featured the Aqua Raiders underwater stronghold—a sizable base with mini-submarine launching ramp, harpoon turret, crane arm, and observation station—and a giant squid with articulated tentacles and a transparent belly to show off its last meal—a rather miserable skeleton.

The Aqua Raiders' base and fleet of underwater vessels were predominantly yellow and black, while their predators mainly had black and/or gray as a base color with red, green, or blue pieces added for more realistic decoration. The divers themselves, who rarely had smiles on their faces, wore black and blue zip-up wetsuits and blue snorkel-style goggles over their black helmets. Their ships and base as well as their uniforms featured the Aqua Raiders' logo—a blue forked trident.

Agents (2008–2009)

Although TLG retired the Alpha Team and their evil nemesis in 2005, they were not ready to leave the secret agent play theme. After much revision and a brand-new set of characters and storylines, they unleashed a new breed of action heroes with the Agents line in 2008. This time, the skilled team of special agents (with similar monikers, such as Chase, Fuse, Charge, and Trace) were fighting a more traditional villain—one who wanted money and enjoyed terrorizing LEGO City where part of the theme was set. His name was Dr. Inferno and he was helped by a band of willing henchmen including Gold Tooth, Fire Arm, Claw-Dette, Slime Face, and Spy Clops—detailed minifigures with various weapons in the place of limbs. The 2008 sets were all based around vignettes from an overarching storyline, which could be played out by amassing the entire collection. These included a secret swamp base with radio-controlled crocodiles (8632), a chase scene with the Agents' turbo car and Spy Clops' mecha-copter (8634), and a speedboat set with missile-wearing sharks (8633). The two largest sets were the Agents' impressive command center (8635)—which put the Alpha Team's equivalent to shame with five individual vehicles, crane, missiles, and light-up bricks that projected Dr. Inferno's image onto a screen—and the climax piece of the storyline, Volcano Base (8637), where Dr. Inferno himself controlled a giant laser cannon. The Agents' sets were mainly dark blue and gray with a hint of red, while Dr. Inferno's men drove orange and black vehicles to match the transparent-orange bricks of their base's volcano.

The sets of 2009 introduced two new Agents, the action moved to the City's streets, and the theme was now referred to as Agents 2.0. There was considerable use of Technic parts and more smooth surfaces with very few studs on display—as can be seen in the construction of Gold Tooth's bike (8967) and the slick Aerial Defence Unit (8971). The latter gives a subtle nod to Alpha Team with its magma drones—they have gear sticks for heads, like the Alpha Team TV robot, while the Agents themselves had some of the slickest "super-team" uniforms yet. The team looked snug in their blue, green, and silver suits with silver gloves, ID tags, and the "A" for Agents logo. Not to be outdone, Dr. Inferno's team wore orange or black zip-up jumpsuits with unusual features including a missing tooth (Gold Tooth), unibrow (Break Jaw), and slime dripping from their faces (Slime Face and Dr. D. Zaster). Agents did their bit to equalize the male/female minifigure ratio with four super ladies emerging from the theme in just two years—Agent Swift, Agent Trace, Claw-

The design team's use of a SNOT (studs not on top) style of building can clearly be seen on Agent Chase's car in Tubocar Chase (8634). © Ruben Saldana

Dette, and Dina-Mite. The adventure continued online with "missions" designed as computer games and more information about the various Agents' vehicles.

Power Miners (2009–2010)

Believing the underground-dwelling Rock Raiders were long forgotten in the tombs of LEGO past, some fans were surprised to see the launch of this new theme in 2009, with online forums jokingly referring to it as "Rock Raiders 2009" or "Power Raiders." The theme, while not set in a parallel alien galaxy, did feature a group of adventurous miners. This time they traveled into the earth to investigate some unusual "rumblings" where they encountered a new breed of rock monster and mysterious power crystals. The Power Miners' matching blue workers uniforms and the black, bright green, and transparent-orange vehicles had a more cohesive look than Rock Raiders, combining the heavy-duty appearance of mining equipment and the fun associated with LEGO sets. Sets ranged from small vehicles like the Stone Chopper (8956) to a large mining station with zip line and dynamite hurler (8709) and the impressive Titanium Command Rig (8964)—a mobile base that transformed into a vertical dual-geared spinning drill. There was a stronger focus on the Power Miners' adversaries, the Rock Monsters, in this range, with a monster being included in almost every set. The largest of the monsters was the Crystal King, a LEGO construction worthy of his own set where the gray and yellow monster grips a Power Miner in his claw (8962). There were two additional medium-size monsters and four small monsters roughly the same size as the Miners.

This onslaught of enemies was added to in 2010 with the release of sub-theme Power Miners: Core of the Underworld, which followed the miners on their 2009

In this display of set 8956, a Rock Monster makes easy work of lifting a worried Power Miner's excavation cycle. © Kent Quon

The Fire Blaster (8188) was one of the first Core of the Underworld sets, and included a water cannon to fire at the pesky Lava Monsters. © Christopher Doyle

comic-book adventure further into the Earth's core where they discovered the Lava Monsters. With transparent orange now the signature color of their foe, the Power Miners sets traded it in for a bright blue, and wore silver suits to protect them from the high temperatures in sets such as Lavatraz (8191)—a prison for the most powerful monster, Eruptorr—and EXO-FORCE style mecha, Magma Mech (8189). All the Power Miners sets made effective use of Technic parts to create structures, cranes, and claws capable of picking up the monster figures.

Atlantis (2010–2011)

After bidding farewell to the Aqua Raiders line after just one year, the LEGO Group brought flippers (of the lime-green variety) back into fashion with the exciting launch of Atlantis in 2010. Based around a crew's search for the mythical underwater city, the team's futuristic submarines and rovers were pitted against the strength of the local bad guys trying to steal their secrets.

The backstory of the Deep Sea Salvage Crew's mission had been detailed in the LEGO catalog and on the Atlantis mini-site online. The Crew, led by Captain Ace Speedman, were accompanied by Samantha Artesia Rhodes—the great granddaughter of a twentieth-century explorer who set out to find the Lost City of Atlantis after discovering a pyramid map off the Mexican coast in the early 1900s. With the knowledge of his adventure detailed in her great-grandfather's journal, it was Sam's

The Salvage Crew's impressive fleet of red vessels included the submarine
Neptune Carrier (8075), with flick-launching torpedos and a roving seabed vehicle.
© Christopher Doyle

job to complete his mission, with the help of her new brave friends. The team were
up against three distinct types of Atlantic Warriors—humanoid creatures with the
heads of sharks, squid, and manta rays, and their tridents for weapons.

The Salvage Crew had weapons, too, and intimidating-looking vessels such as
Seabed Scavenger (8059), with its chainsaw and pincer arms; Typhoon Turbo (8060),
whose dual turbine-style engines flipped round to reveal two deadly weapons; and
Neptune Carrier (8075—this product number was painted onto the side of the toy)—
as the largest vehicle in the fleet, she's fitted out with torpedos and a small roving
vehicle to take on ground attacks. The vessels were predominantly red with gray
and transparent green detailing, and continued to employ the SNOT (studs not on
top) method of building used in Aqua Raiders, Agents, and Power Miners, giving
the creations a contemporary feel. TLG also produced a number of large-scale non-

This 2010 Atlantis set, known as Gateway of the Squid (8061), shows the clever use of new parts employed by LEGO designers to produce menacing octopus and squid tentacles. © Christopher Doyle

brick, role-play toys including a water gun, a replica harpoon shooter, and a trident similar to those carried by the Atlantic Warriors. With the introduction of this dynamic deep-sea adventure range, it's likely the LEGO Group's relationship with the world beneath will continue for a while yet.

* * *

Not content to see its other non-character-led toys fall by the wayside, the company continued to develop and produce other lines. While some LEGO fans are drawn purely to the building play-themes that revolve around the construction of bases, buildings, and vehicles and the minifigures who inhabit them, others were brought to the toy through their love of cars, trains, sports, remote-controlled toys, engineering, robotics, and even competitive play. Understandably, TLG did not want to lose customers it had spent many years trying to win over, and as a result plowed ahead with introducing new toys to keep them happy in spite of the financial crisis. The consistent and, in some cases, increasing popularity of some of these lines is a testament to their individuality on the toy market; other less popular products or lines slowly disappeared as the company's portfolio was reassessed midway through the decade.

Racers (2001–2011)

Started up in 2001, LEGO Racers is one of the early-2000s themes to find its place in the market and bring new fans to LEGO. Prior to this year, car racing had featured as part of LEGO Town, evolving from simple minifigure cars of the early 1990s to its re-modeled face as LEGO Race in 2000 that included some unusual toy designs—Grip 'n' Go Challenge (6713) featured two cars with pincer arms grappling for control of a ball. A decade after officially defining Racers as a theme separate from Town, the toys had developed dramatically. Racers began life as a series of small sets (most with less than ten pieces) that focused more on car racing than construction. Each set included the pieces to build a small car with a non-minifigure driver (these characters, who went by names such as Warrior, Spiky, and Rip, had brightly colored features and expressive faces, with no movable arms or legs). The sets also included a packaged sandwich-shaped launcher to release the cars at high speed.

By the following year TLG had had a change of heart and decided to remarket Racers to appeal to an older age group—while the first year of Racers had been selling for four-to nine-year-olds, these Drome Racers were mainly for 7+. Extra detailing appeared not only in the use of minifigures as drivers, but also in the design of the various vehicles which now featured pull-back motors. Small cars increased in size from nine parts to nearly fifty, and there were much larger sets that pitted two vehicles against each other, e.g., Duel Racers (4587) and Zero Hurricane & Red Blizzard (4593). With story-led themes dominating the LEGO Group's output, even these race car sets had a context. Set in a futuristic 2015, the racing drivers (both heroes and villains) vied for the title of champion in a dangerous arena—the Drome run by Dromulus and his pet robot monkey. In 2002 nearly thirty Racers sets were released, and among these were remote-controlled cars Nitro Flash (4589) and, for slightly older children, the driver-less Race Buggy (8475), made almost completely from Technic parts. These remote-controlled cars could be transformed into more than one design, and the wheels were interchangeable with different Racers. The

RC unit allowed three different channels so three people could play with their cars together without interference.

The first Racers tracks were available in 2002 and consisted of an "off-road" track (4588) and a stunt track with a jump at the end onto a safety net (4589). Both sets relied on the pull-back motors of the cars, and did not allow for actual "racing" as both tracks were only one car wide. It wasn't until 2003 that the Multi-Challenge Race Track (8364) provided a complete electric race course that accommodated two cars. To fit minifigures into Racers cars, a new torso was created without any legs but with a steering wheel. Regular minifigure heads and helmets were then connected on to it. Technic pieces became an integral part of the Racers system, although smaller, more traditional racing cars were still being produced, such as Pro Stunt (8350) and Track Racer (8360).

Williams F1 (2002–2003), Ferrari F1 (2004–2010), and Lamborghini (2009–2011)

Before Ferrari designs became a staple on the LEGO racetrack, a Williams F1 car with BMW engine and Michelin tires was the first realistic F1 race car model TLG had produced (excluding Technic models). Known as the Williams F1 Team Racer (8461), this non-minifigure scale chassis was constructed from a base of LEGO bricks with a large number of Technic axles and connections to give it its streamlined and realistic appearance. For younger fans the Team Racer 1:27 (8374) with minifigure race driver was released in 2003.

In 2004 Ferrari replaced Williams as the licensed racing face of LEGO toys, and superstar driver Michael Schumacher became one of the first Formula One drivers (alongside teammate Rubens Barrichello) to be immortalized as a LEGO minifigure.

Ferrari had a long-standing relationship with the LEGO Group throughout the 2000s. This Ferrari 248 F1 was just one of the models available. © Owen J. Weber

The set (8398) featured the two drivers, who finished first and second in the 2004 Drivers' Championship, a podium with Ferrari flags, and a trophy for Schumacher to receive. Other Racers sets released that year focused heavily on the Ferrari brand, with a minifigure scale car (8362), pit stop set (8375), and a 1:10 scale car (8386). DU-PLO also got in on the Ferrari action with two sets—an F1 race car and a pit-stop set (4693 and 4694). The LEGO Group followed these up in 2005 with the Scuderia Ferrari Truck (8654)—an impressive transportation lorry with six minifigures and all the parts needed to put together the F1 car—and two Enzo Ferrari models in different scales. The LEGO Group continued its relationship with the car manufacturer and the development of the Racers Ferrari system. More recent additions include a finish line (8673), new pit stop set Ferrari F1 Team (8144), and a fleet of various scale cars modeled on real Ferrari cars such as the Ferrari 430 Spider, Ferrari 248 F1, Ferrari 599 GTB Fiorano, and the Ferrari FXX.

In 2009 TLG released the first Racers Lamborghini set—the Lamborghini Gallardo LP560-4 (8169) in the signature yellow. The 1:17 scale model set had a retractable top that could be folded into the back, and could be reconstructed to build either a coupe Gallardo or a spyder Gallardo. This was followed by the bright blue Lamborghini Gallardo LP560-4 Polizia (8214)—an authentic replica of the Gallardo police cars used by the Italian state police force during highway emergencies.

Power Racers (2005–2010), Tiny Turbos (2005–2011), and RC Racers (2004–2009)

With the exception of some Ferrari sets, the majority of LEGO Racers from 2005 onward were minifigure-less. Focusing more on the design and construction of the vehicles than the people racing them has enabled designers to alter the scale of Racers to suite children's play behaviour, and to build stable and robust remote-controlled vehicles as well as smaller mini-cars.

While the LEGO Group was never a likely manufacturer to corner the market on remote-controlled cars, its combination of construction first, drive second gave its simple RC vehicles more playing power than other prefabricated brands. Between 2004 and 2006 they released a few "outdoor RC" vehicles including Outdoor Challenger (8675), which was marketed as capable of racing in mud, rain, and on grass. More recently, Track Turbo RC (8183) became the first Racers car to include the LEGO Power Functions system.

In 2005 the company released the first Power Racers cars—these souped-up, pull-back, or slammer release cars such as Nitro Menace (8649), Buzz Saw (8648), and glow-in-the-dark Night Racer (8647) were the natural descendants of the Drome Racers, and were accompanied by new racing bikes with slammer-launch mechanisms, which when hit would release the bikes at high speed. TLG also unleashed its pod format on Racers (used to market small sets of Technic, BIONICLE and Knights' Kingdom sets) and began selling kits to build small vehicles (under sixty pieces) in

This 2010 Power Racers car (7971) included an Air Stomper to propel the car, and is one of the more recent Racers developments. © Christopher Doyle

A constructed 2010 Tiny Turbo (Blue Bullet, 8193), next to its included stickers and a few one-stud bricks that illustrate how small this car really is. © Christopher Doyle

plastic capsules with tire-style lids. These were sold alongside the larger pull-back motored Racers that had developed into less "sleek racing car," more "chunky-tired bumper car"—the word "CRASH" screamed out from the front of each box. Most sets were single-vehicle sets, and toward the end of the decade many came with launcher mechanisms to catapult them forward, as in Desert Hammer (8496), where two cars with pull-back motors and launchers took turns to leap through a ring with a swinging pendulum in a test of propulsion and timing, and the more recent Air Blasters that used compressed air and a pump to shoot the small cars across the room.

Even smaller cars, referred to as Tiny Turbos, were released from 2005 onward, some as small as twenty-four pieces. They were basic vehicles such as Yellow Sports Car (4947) and Blue Buggy (4949) that had more similarities with Matchbox cars than minifigure scale vehicles. In 2010 LEGO launched four sets with fold-out plastic boxes that transformed into sections of road, revealing different "race" scenarios that could all be connected together. Ramp Crash (8198) included a red pick-up truck heading straight for a crash with a cargo lorry, while Chopper Jump (8196) included a speeding gangster race car and a police helicopter.

World Racers (2010–present)

One of the latest themes to emerge from Billund's best designing brains is an attempt to re-bridge the gap between extreme racing and minifigures. World Racers was a story-based theme that saw two teams compete in a race around the world. Each team was made up or three members: the X-Treme Devils (Rex-Treme and his two brothers, Dex-Treme and Max-Treme) and the Backyard Blasters (Bart, Billy Bob, and Bubba). The competitors had different vehicles to complete the race by land or sea, and sets typically included one vehicle for each team, such as Blizzard's Peak (8863) with its ice-terrain vehicles and helicopter, Gator Swamp (8899) with boats, and Wreckage Road (8898) with more traditional race cars. Most vehicles had mounted weapons, to help the teams cause problems for each other along the way, and

In one of the smaller World Racers sets, Bart Blaster and Rex-Treme ride their bikes in Snake Canyon to determine who will take the trophy. © Ruben Saldana

sets typically included a checkered flag and trophy to be rewarded to the winning team of that leg of the race.

LEGO Sports (2000–2007)

Part of TLG's diversification strategy of the late 1990s and early 2000s was the introduction of sports-themed toys, with an initial emphasis on football. Table football sets, football game Subbuteo, and even pricey team strips had long been popular presents for young sports fans, but it wasn't until 2000 that the LEGO Group decided to take a slice of the market with the introduction of LEGO Sports.

Football (2000–2007)

The sports toys were branded and marketed differently from the majority of LEGO ranges, with French footballer Zinedine Zidane adorning the boxes of most of the 2000 football sets (the Real Madrid alumni player was the face of LEGO Sports for a while, and was immortalized as a LEGO minifigure wearing his blue Adidas France strip, available in set 3401). The majority of the range focused on the action of football and the players rather than building and therefore contained only a small number of pieces. To keep keen LEGO builders happy, there were mid-size sets such as Football Team Coaches (3404, 3405, 3406, 3407) that included a small vehicle for the team, and set 3408—a pitch entranceway for the players to run out onto the field. The sets that brought the themes to life, such as Championship Challenge

This 2002 Target Practice set (3424) was one of a number of LEGO football toys released to coincide with the 2002 World Cup. © Kent Quon

return of more realistic models, with the release of the 9 volt Santa Fe Super Chief (10020) followed by the Santa Fe Cars Set (10022) both in 2002, and the well-loved Burlington Northern Santa Fe Locomotive (10133) in 2005. The fact that they were targeted at the 10+ age range rather than 7+ (the age recommendation for 2004 High Speed Train sets 10157 and 10158) may have dramatically reduced their sales potential and pushed TLG to evaluate the future of Train a few years later. Fans were given the opportunity to stretch their design models with the "My Own Train" website, which let them create and order their own customized steam locomotive from a variety of sizes and colors.

By 2007 the company had discontinued the 9 volt trains, but not before replacing them with an entirely new system. LEGO Train sets were expensive, especially with the additional costs of extra track, carriages, and electronic components. In an effort to bring a new audience to LEGO Train and to make them more affordable, an infrared remote-controlled, battery-powered system was introduced under the "City" theme as mentioned earlier. Targeting ages five through twelve and six through twelve, these new trains, such as 2006's Passenger Train (7897), were more child-friendly in both their design and operation—especially when compared to the attention to detail of the 2007 adult fan-created Hobby Train Set (10183). The remote-controlled system allowed more than one person to control trains independently from each other, something that was not possible with the 9 volt trains, but the infrared system was not as reliable as radio control, and the 1.5 volt AA batteries required made the trains less powerful than the 9 or 12 volt motors, which can cause problems for trains going up steep inclines.

Although the remote-controlled train sets are still available, since 2009 there has been a shift toward the incorporation of LEGO Power Functions components to motorize trains. Power Functions, also used in Creator and Technic themes, is a

The Emerald Night, designed with the input of LEGO Train fans, was the first to incorporate the new Power Functions technology. © Paul Tichonczuk

cross-theme system that included a rechargeable lithium polymer battery box, an infrared receiver and remote control that allowed you to operate four different models simultaneously, and different sized motors to power your creations. These, combined with new plastic flexible train tracks that gave builders more control over the shape of their layout, made up the new Train system. The first Train set available that accommodated this technology was the Emerald Night (10194), released in 2009. Returning to where LEGO Train started with a steam engine, this was also the first train, and the first LEGO model, to incorporate large piston-powered wheels—the design was developed with input from some of the theme's biggest fans. The look and feel of the Emerald Night is in keeping with the realistic-looking trains from the late 1980s and '90s, but the cost, unfortunately, of the Power Functions system was significantly higher.

DUPLO

When DUPLO first came out in the 1970s, there were far less toys marketed toward tiny hands. Rattles, stacking toys, and the contents of the kitchen had long kept baby occupied. The interconnecting relationship between DUPLO and LEGO bricks was unprecedented in the industry—finally, a toy existed that children of all ages could really play together. DUPLO suffered a little from constant rebranding throughout the

1980s and 1990s, as it attempted to compete with the growing sector of infant play. One positive move in 2001, which was clearly in the interest of the DUPLO range, was the licensing of popular BBC animated children's program *Bob the Builder*. With the show's construction theme, its characters were a perfect fit for DUPLO and the toys proved just that by winning industry awards and placing in the British Toy and Hobby Association's Top 50 Toys for 2001. Shockingly, despite years of

Over its eight-year life as a DUPLO licensed toy, there were twenty-eight Bob the Builder sets made, many of which included this DUPLO Bob figure.
© Kent Quon

brand recognition, in 2002 all the infant toys produced by TLG were branded with the name "LEGO Explore," with different color-coded packaging highlighting the different age recommendations for the products. As the LEGO Group fought to get its house in order, "Explore" didn't make the cut and was phased out after less than two years. The year 2004 saw the re-emergence of the DUPLO and Baby brands, and the introduction of LEGO QUATRO. The dimensions of QUATRO bricks were two times larger than DUPLO bricks and two times smaller than the large Baby stacking cubes, serving as a bridge between the two. The original DUPLO rabbit was given a facelift while the elephant logo was taken over by QUATRO, and Baby products featured a new teddy bear logo instead. Since 2005 the LEGO Group has moved away from products suitable for babies. Although some of its licensed products and DUPLO toys are recommended for ages as young as eighteen months old, there have not been any new Baby or QUATRO releases since 2006. Other than Bob the Builder, which ran between 2001–2009, new licenses taken on for the infant market included Little Robots (2003), Dora the Explorer (2004), Ferrari (2004), Thomas & Friends (2005–2009), and Disney Pixar's Toy Story (2010) and Cars (2010).

The majority of non-licensed DUPLO were marketed as part of the "LEGO Ville" range, and varied almost as much as their LEGO Town/City counterparts with construction sites, fire trucks, horse stables, zoos, and police stations, some of which were available with light and sound components. The LEGO Group also marketed some basic "Easy to Build" sets under its "Preschool" products which were composed of regular LEGO bricks.

4+

When Jack Stone failed to capture the imagination of LEGO builders, it was replaced swiftly by a new line called 4 Juniors. A kid-friendly, bright yellow logo featured on the boxes of the new sets, but in every other way they looked the same as the LEGO City sets, which targeted the 5+ age group. The new designs, such as 2003's Police Motorcycle (4651) and Dump Truck (4653), were toned down, and more realistic in comparison with the Jack Stone sets. They included the same action-figure types, with the Jack Stone figure also appearing, despite his name not being mentioned. The LEGO Group's set selections seemed more cohesive with the City toys, and they included two building sets in 2003—a garage called Quick Fix Station (4655) and a fire house (4657). The structures in each, while still made primarily of larger pieces, were aesthetically superior to the Jack Stone sets, but still required significantly less construction than the regular sets.

The following year, 4 Juniors was rebranded as 4+ with the release of a police car and boat, digger, and crane. More significant, however, were the new 4+ Pirates sets. LEGO Pirates, one of the most iconic themes, was treated to some Jack Stone–style swashbucklers complete with eye patches, hooks, and peg legs. The emergence of the Pirates meant parents could buy another LEGO theme for their younger children that provided new characters and imaginative play. Given that there had been no new LEGO Pirates sets since 1997, some fans were disappointed by these 2004 sets. The larger scale aside, the sets provided minimum construction value and included lots of large pieces only suitable for small children, which some felt went against the company's core principles. That same year, the 4+ brand featured in the licensed Spider-Man 2 range with two sets targeting younger fans. These were Doc Ock's Crime Spree (4858) and Doc Ock's Café Attack (4860). Some fans felt the LEGO Group was underestimating young builders with the simplicity of the sets and that the minifigure scale with its distinctive, interchangeable figures had more charm and appeal than the larger 4+ style of building. While parents may have welcomed the diversity of the 4+ range, the fans did not, and by 2005, 4+ was no more.

Technic

To maximize Technic sales, and perhaps to introduce even more fans to the range, the newly acquired *Star Wars* license resulted in a Droid Developer Kit for the MIND-STORMS robotics line, and then Technic Star Wars toys such as 2000's Battle Droid (8001) and Destroyer Droid (8002). By 2001, with the release of the first BIONICLE toys, the landscape for Technic had become very confused. With products ranging from expert building sets and licensed builds to story-based characters, competitive action toys, and even pump-start racing cars, it was no longer clear where LEGO toys left off and Technic toys began. The spin-off brand that had initially been an expert version of traditional LEGO bricks had lost its identity.

Decisions were made to cut BIONICLE loose from the Technic name, end the Slizer and RoboRiders themes, produce no more Technic Star Wars, and rebrand racing car toys as LEGO Racers (although they were made almost entirely from Technic parts). This dramatic action meant only three "Technic" sets appeared on shelves in 2002—a helicopter (8429), a motorbike (8430), and a crane truck (8431)—not far from the toy lineup that had started it all in 1977.

For the next eight years, Technic remained true to the fundamental vehicle-building ideals that made it such a success story for TLG in the first place. When designing a Technic toy, LEGO employees have three guiding principles they build by: "authenticity" (creating a model that replicates a full-scale version so that children can easily identify it and understand its purpose), "functionality" (defining the key functions of the model and how to achieve them), and "challenging building" (utilizing the many and varied LEGO parts to create a model to challenge older kids). Steadily, each year, the number of new Technic sets continued to rise with new designs for old ideas, providing building fans with new challenges, such as 2005's Mobile Crane (8421) and 2006's Tow Truck (8285). In 2007 Technic became one of the first lines to incorporate the Power Functions RC motor system, an integral part of popular recent releases such as Motorised Bulldozer (8275). While recent Technic products

2009's Mini Bulldozer (8259) was a small Technic set suitable for introducing younger builders to the Technic system. © Ben Pillen

This close-up of 2008's Cherry Picker (8292) set shows how far Technic designers go to create realistic models of real-life vehicles. © Hamid (Katanaz)

are fundamentally the same as the original 1977 creations, the impact Technic-style building and parts has had on TLG is far-reaching. Not only did BIONICLE go on to be one of the LEGO Group's most successful product lines, but other non-Technic themes now incorporate the impressive array of beams and connectors that over thirty years of Technic products have helped to create.

Advanced Building

A more accurate style of building is something AFOLs wanted to see LEGO toys return to when they were surveyed in 2006. It was clear fans wanted more everyday buildings such as houses, shops, and offices in minifigure scale with greater architectural details. And thus the Modular House series was born. The first was the charming Café Corner (10182); with a recommended building age of 16+ this was truly a design for the grown-ups. Using many building techniques usually associated with fan building, designers even consulted with fans after prototypes were produced, using their input to improve the design.

The Market Street set (10190) released the same year was actually designed by LEGO fans using the Modular House theme on the LEGO Factory service launched by LEGO in 2005. LEGO Factory, now called LEGO Design byME, enabled fans to use LEGO program Digital Designer to invent and purchase their own LEGO designs (see below for more on Design byME). Market Street, created by Dutch AFOL Eric Brok, was aimed at children ten and older, inviting younger LEGO fans to use the online design tools to create their own modular floors, and at a lower price point than Café Corner, encouraging more people to consider buying other Modular House sets.

With the majority of these sets including more than 2,000 pieces, the announcement of any future releases is based on the success of the previous designs. And while many fans may have marveled at the modular green grocer (10185), fire house

From left to right, the Modular Houses pictured are Market Street (10190), Fire Brigade (10197), Green Grocer (10185), and Café Corner (10182). © Ben Pillen

This Jedi Starfighter and Vulture Droid set (7256) was released in 2005 to coincide with the release of *Episode III: Revenge of the Sith.* © David Martin

they could also get their hands on their favorite Star Wars characters—in minifigure form, of course.

The first fourteen products from 1999 set the bar for what was to follow. While TLG focused predominantly on releasing sets related to the new film—the dramatic pod racing scene (7131 and 7171) and Darth Maul's Sith Infiltrator (7151)—there were also some ships from the original trilogy including the TIE Fighter and Y-wing set (7150) and the X-wing Fighter (7140).

This marketing pattern was repeated throughout the 2000s, as TLG continued to introduce interpretations of ships and scenes from the original movies while simultaneously releasing sets to coincide with the new movies released in 2002 and 2005. As designers developed a distinct style for the Star Wars sets, they evaluated past models from the first few waves and reinterpreted them, adding detail and new building methods. Results of this can be seen in 2006's X-wing Fighter and 2007's Ultimate Millennium Falcon (10179), a collector's upgrade from set 7190 (although this set is slightly larger, and intended for display purposes). More characters and locales from the *Star Wars* universe were featured, such as the Ewoks (7139), Jabba the Hutt (made from an assembly of prefabricated green pieces), and the Wookiee (7258).

2007's Millennium Falcon was part of the Ultimate Collector's series of sets and was built using over 5,000 LEGO elements. © Hamid (Katanaz)

Distinctively, LEGO Star Wars sets are action-based, made up largely of ships and vehicles. Compared to other themes—licensed ones, in particular—Star Wars is noticeably void of chunky base plates and building structures, with a weighty focus on accurately capturing the many memorable scenes and spacecraft so beloved by Star Wars fans. Perhaps one of the sets most apt at this is 2008's Death Star (10188). While the Ultimate Collector Series Death Star II (10143), a new battle station under construction during Return of the Jedi, focused on re-creating the half-built look of the structure, the new Death Star provided a detailed sneak peek inside the many rooms of the huge orb—and with twenty-five minifigures, you could re-create the final battle between Luke Skywalker and Darth Vader, rescue Princess Leia from the cells, and hang out with R2-D2 and C-3PO.

The last Star Wars film was released in 2005, but despite this the LEGO theme has continued to grow in popularity. The Star Wars universe is always expanding through novels, comic books, and video games and while TLG has produced some "expanded universe" sets, in 2008 it took a pronounced leap beyond the original films when designs were derived from the animated film Star Wars: The Clone Wars, a movie that introduced the TV series of the same name that began airing on Car-

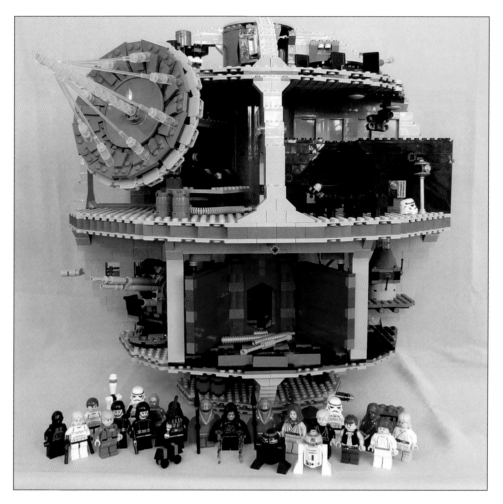

This Death Star set (10188) is highly prized by LEGO Star Wars fans for its multi-scene depictions, details, and playability. © Hamid (Katanaz)

toon Network in 2008. This TV series, designed to introduce new, younger fans to the franchise, specifically targeted children, making LEGO Star Wars even more enticing to young eyes. With these most recent sets, the designers did not bite the adult hands that had fed them since 1999—while some sets were targeted toward less experienced building fingers, the designs were every bit as inventive, dynamic, and exciting as those based on the six movies. Lucas Licensing, who approves the models, are more than happy for designers to take some liberties with a ship's inside details and their playability, as long as the external shell is accurate and faithful to the franchise.

Following in the footsteps of *LEGO Island* and *LEGO Racers*, 2005 saw the release of *LEGO Star Wars: The Video Game*. The multi-platform game developed by Traveller's Tales covered action from the three new movies in the saga and was promoted

In 2010 LEGO released another version of Luke's Landspeeder (first seen in 1999, and pictured earlier)—the design and detailing of this more recent set shows how the theme had developed and progressed. © Christopher Doyle

for younger players. Despite the often violent nature of the film material, designers attempted to inject humor and lightness into the dark context of the game. This popularity was followed up with a second game covering the action of the original trilogy in 2006 and a compilation of the two games in 2007. In 2010 it was announced that a new game—*LEGO Star Wars III: The Clone Wars*—was due for a release in 2011, incorporating the new characters and storylines introduced by the *Clone Wars* TV program.

This lineup of *Clone Wars* characters, including Cad Bain (center) and Shahan Alama (second from right), featured in 2010's Speeder set (8182). © Christopher Doyle

In a 2009 *New York Times* article, LEGO executive Soren Torp Laursen explained that the LEGO Group's answer to the competition faced from more violence-oriented games has been to include non-explicit, humoristic violence. For example, when a minifigure is killed or dies in a LEGO game, it dissolves into a pile of bricks and then springs back to life, similar to cartoon characters' multiple "deaths." Laursen also said that there were many toy licenses TLG has turned down over the years because they represent a level of violence not suitable for the company, conflicting with the trust placed in the brand by parents. This fun approach to the dark territory of the *Star Wars* saga was a huge hit with the fans, and according to market researcher NPD Group, was the thirteenth best-selling game of 2005. This humor can also be seen in the short animated film *LEGO Star Wars: The Quest for R2-D2*, released in 2009 to mark ten years of the theme.

Mickey Mouse (2000)

Despite Disney and the LEGO Group both being market leaders targeting children of the same age, it wasn't until 1999 that a business relationship was started between the two corporations. This occured when TLG acquired the rights to produce Winnie the Pooh DUPLO sets based on the 1970s–1980s animated films produced by Disney. Then, in 2000, the Disney name appeared on LEGO sets for the first time with the release of LEGO Mickey Mouse—based around the iconic character and his friends. While the sets included regular-size LEGO bricks and were marketed toward four- to nine-year-olds, they were not construction-based and featured Belville and FABULAND parts not otherwise seen in regular LEGO sets. The central focus were the FABULAND-scale figures of Mickey, Minnie, and Pluto that came with Minnie's Birthday Party (4165), Mickey's Garage (4166), and Mickey's Mansion (4267). Mickey and Minnie could also be found as baby versions of themselves the same year with the LEGO Baby Mickey range. Although LEGO only produced these Disney sets for one year, its professional relationship with the company has continued, and can be seen most recently in LEGO and DUPLO Toy Story, LEGO Prince of Persia, and DUPLO Cars.

Harry Potter (2001–2011)

In the midst of the popularity of the *Harry Potter* books (published between 1997 and 2007) and the same year the first film was released, the LEGO Group obtained the license from Warner Bros. to re-create some of the movie's iconic moments in trademark LEGO bricks. Over the theme's run, sets have been produced in a timely fashion to coordinate with the release of the film series. Some of the most distinguished sets included two incarnations of the Hogwarts Express (4708 and 4758), four interpretations of Hogwarts Castle (4709, 4757, 5378, and 4842), the most recent of which, released after a three-year hiatus from the theme, was made up of 1,290 parts and included eleven minifigures. Between 2001 and 2002, *Harry Potter* minifigures had the customary yellow heads and hands; they were later changed to more natural skin tones in 2003. Other interesting sets included the giant Hagrid's infamous hut (4707, 4754, and 4738), school sport Quidditch practice (4726), and triple-decker people-carrier, the Knight Bus (4755).

In the face of financial loss in 2004, TLG announced that there would be a stronger focus on core products rather than movie-related platforms such as *Harry Potter*, and although the company was quick to point out they would still be producing the theme, the number of new sets gradually decreased—in 2007, only one new set appeared to mark the release of the fifth film. Evidently, though, this was not the last fans would see of LEGO Harry Potter. The year 2010 marked the release of *LEGO Harry Potter: Year 1–4*; a multi-platform game combining puzzle-solving and exploration of the *Harry Potter* universe with a light-hearted LEGO twist. Six new Harry Potter sets, many based on previous sets, were also released to launch the game.

Galidor (2002)

When asked what the worst selling LEGO theme was in a 2006 interview with Gizmodo.com, a LEGO spokesperson said, "A few years back, we strayed too far from our core product line when we entered into an action figure line called Galidor." Unfortunately, the one-year obscurity of Galidor was a fairly large investment for TLG and the production of unusual nonstandard LEGO parts and packaging were one of many bad management decisions that led to significant financial losses in 2003 and 2004.

The toys were based on characters from a Fox Kids TV show (*Galidor: Defenders of the Outer Dimension*) that aired for twenty-six episodes in 2002 before being canceled. The show was about Nick, a fifteen-year-old boy who finds an alien map and a dimensional transport vehicle and travels with his best friend to Galidor, a realm in the Outer Dimension that is under attack from sinister forces. The toys were buildable action figures of the main characters and Nick's transport module, each made from a small number of pieces not compatible with LEGO, Technic, or BIONICLE sets—one of the reason for fans' dislike of the range. As the LEGO Group told Gizmodo: "With no traditional LEGO construction elements, it proved to be unfamiliar to LEGO fans who expect a certain kind of play experience from the LEGO brand." There was also a video game that tied in with the toys, which unfortunately didn't fare too well either.

Discovery Channel (2003)

Sandwiched between the 2001 Life on Mars sets and 2007's Mars Mission was another Space-centered flash-in-the-pan license. Six sets were released, inspired by the 2003 Mars Exploration Rover Mission, covered by the Discovery Channel. The non-minifigure scale sets included a model replica of the space shuttle *Discovery* (7470), the International Space Station (7467), and one of the Mars exploration rovers (7471), made largely of Technic parts. While not as playful as other lines, the Discov-

SpongeBob SquarePants LEGO toys, based on the popular cartoon series of the same name, focused on the titular sea sponge and his band of underwater friends. The sets centered on recognized locations from the show such as restaurants the Krusty Krab (3825) and Chum Bucket (4981) and SpongeBob's pineapple house (3834), as well as a Build-A-Bob set (3826) to make a larger-scale LEGO SpongeBob. The minifigure version of the famous yellow sea creature was created using shorter legs and a separate outer layer that slipped over the minifigure torso to create SpongeBob's square head.

Batman (2006)

After the success of Warner Bros. *Batman* reboot movie *Batman Begins* in 2005, the LEGO Group, on license from DC Comics, produced a series of Batman sets. Although these were not directly connected to any of the films featuring the comic book hero, there are some noticeable similarities between the design of specific sets and particular movies. The original yellow and black Batman logo was used, and no photographic images of Batman from other media were included on the packaging. Sets are known for their use of black bricks with all vehicles and most structures appearing in the Dark Knight's favored color. One of the most complex and popular

The Joker's ice cream truck, as found in set 7888, with its colorful sticker details and secret missile weapon. © Ruben Saldana

Robin from set 7885 and Nightwing from Arkham Asylum set 7785 were just some of the colorful minifigures introduced by LEGO Batman. © Ruben Saldana

sets was the Batcave (7783) with three vehicles, spiral staircase, information screen, and a number of clever mechanisms; it also included villains Mr. Freeze and the Penguin. High-octane vehicles such as the Batmobile, the Batwing, and the Bat Tank added to the range. The 2008 sets, released the same year as popular Batman film *The Dark Knight* and *LEGO Batman: The Videogame*, were more playful and colorful than their predecessors. Robin's bright red and green scuba jet (7885) was attacked in this set by the Penguin and two of his penguin soldiers, while Batman's Tumbler (7888) has to face a disguised ice cream truck owned by the Joker. Despite Batman's continuing popularity and the 2008 game selling over four million copies worldwide, the 2006 sets were the last new LEGO Batman toys to be released.

Speed Racer (2008)

The LEGO Group released four Speed Racer toys to coincide with the 2008 release of the film of the same name, based on the original Japanese manga and anime, *Mach Go Go Go*. The story focuses on the eponymous hero who wants to be a racing driver, despite his father's objections. Taking the film's depiction of the story and characters, the LEGO toys included three sets with two competing drivers in each. There was also Grand Prix Race (8161) with its futuristic commentator box, big-screen

TV, and three racing cars, including Speed Racer's Mach 6, as well as a monkey (more commonly seen in LEGO Pirates sets) standing in for pet chimp Chim-Chim.

Indiana Jones (2008–2009)

When Indiana Jones appeared in LEGO form for the first time in 2008, some fans may have had a sense of déjà vu. It's fair to say that LEGO Indy and his wilderness escapades closely resembled those of popular Adventurers character Johnny Thunder. But while the two heroes both donned a fedora, enjoyed wearing khaki colors and often had company in the form of a pretty lady and wise older gentleman, the sets they appeared in were very different. The LEGO Group secured the rights to produce construction toys of Indiana Jones's movie adventures from LucasFilm, who also own *Star Wars*.

While it would've been easy for TLG to simply capitalize on the publicity machine of the new film, *Kingdom of the Crystal Skull*, with play sets devoted only to that movie as they had done with *Star Wars*, the LEGO Group released four sets based on two of the three original Indy movies earlier in 2008, and then six sets designed around the fourth installment became available to coincide with the film's May release that same year. These original sets were some of the most popular (especially with adult fans) as they captured iconic movie scenes such as Dr. Jones's brush with death and a giant rolling boulder in the temple scene from *Raiders of the Lost Ark* (7623), and the motorcycle chase with his father riding in the side car in *Last Crusade* (7620). LEGO designers also paid homage to the second film *Temple of Doom* with the infamous mining car chase sequence (7199), which came with cult leader and

2008's Race for the Stolen Treasure (7622) saw LEGO Indiana Jones re-creating the famous treasure chase sequence from *Raiders of the Lost Ark*, complete with minifigure-scale Indy whip. © Owen J. Weber

villain Mola Ram. The *Crystal Skull* sets drew heavily on the vehicle sequences from the movie such as airport set Peril in Peru (7628), the Jungle Cutter (7626), and the river chase scene (7625).

From Willie Scott dressed up in her two-piece sacrificial outfit from *Temple of Doom* to Venetian vacation Indy in that unusual gray suit from *Last Crusade*, the range of character minifigures was not disappointing and TLG captured Indy's various allies and nemeses with its usual creativity, also including weapons emulating those used in the films despite the company's anti-war toys approach to play.

Boosted by the release of two LEGO Indiana Jones video games (*The Original Adventures* and *The Adventure Continues*), the range proved to be popular with fans. In a 2008 press release, TLG cited LEGO Indiana Jones as one of the reasons for its financial growth in the first half of 2007, despite a global economic crisis and predictions of a stagnant toy market, stating that it had sold extremely well specifically in North America. But despite being a cinematic classic, and ideal play theme, it's clear that the success of the sets was in large part due to the promotional tie-in to the movie and games. Unlike Star Wars, which has a dedicated universal fan base constantly being supplied with new media in the form of magazines, books, events, and new TV show *The Clone Wars*, Indiana Jones was only really introduced to LEGO toys' core audience through *The Crystal Skull*. While the theme is currently out of production, rumors of a fifth Indiana Jones film mean the LEGO theme could return in the future, similarly to the recent reprieve of LEGO Harry Potter.

Ben 10: Alien Force (2010)

In 2009 the LEGO Group announced that they would be discontinuing the successful BIONICLE line that focused almost exclusively on buildable figures. In a letter addressed to BIONICLE fans, released in November of that year, the company revealed that while the last BIONICLE sets would be released in January 2010, a new flexible building figure would be available in the summer of that year, as well as another line targeting a younger audience through an "established third-party property." This second new line was Ben 10: Alien Force, and in January 2010 six new buildable figures from that range were released for the 5+ age range.

Ben 10: Alien Force was an animated cartoon series that aired on the Cartoon Network between 2008 and 2010. The titular character was a fifteen year-old boy who had an alien wristwatch device that allowed him to transform into different alien forms, each with their own special abilities and powers. In *Alien Force* he must use these powers to track down his missing grandpa and fight off evil alien enemies. The original six LEGO sets included a small number of pieces (the largest set had twenty-two) that connected similarly to BIONICLE toys to produce one of these alien forms. Through the LEGO Ben 10: Alien Force website, TLG encouraged combination building—using two or more sets to produce a larger alien hybrid—and produced instructions to create new imaginative designs.

To defeat evil aliens and villains, Ben transforms into a range of powerful creatures, such as ChromaStone (an alien hero made from crystal). © Christopher Doyle

With many BIONICLE fans unhappy about the cancelation of that line, the response to this new theme from the older LEGO community has not been particularly positive, with comparisons being made to the unsuccessful 2002 Galidor range, and comments highlighting the move away from the traditional building ethos of LEGO toys toward action-figure style play. In 2010 the Cartoon Network began airing *Ben 10: Evolution*, providing more story material for the LEGO Group if they want it.

Toy Story (2010) and Cars (2010)

Although LEGO toys never featured in the original *Toy Story* or *Toy Story 2*, mini figures and DUPLO people did feature, albeit subtly, in the third installment released in June 2010. This change is no coincidence, as TLG recently became the only company with a license to produce construction toys based on the movie and its characters. Arguably, by taking on a brand that is already well established and producing toys based on films that have an existing history of success, the company will hopefully avoid the short-lived nature of themes such as Spider-Man and Avatar or no success at all, as with Galidor. Notably, with this license, LEGO realigned themselves with Disney, who now own Pixar (the studio responsible for the *Toy Story* films), and with this association comes additional sales outlets and opportunities.

Set 7590 captured the memorable climax from the first *Toy Story* film with a pull-back RC. © Christopher Doyle

The 2010 sets re-created the colorful *Toy Story* characters and settings faithfully, while maintaining elements of construction and interactivity. Sets capturing moments from the first two movies and the latest installment were released. Nostalgic sets featuring RC (7590), Evil Emperor Zurg (7593), and the Army Men (7595) were clever LEGO toy takes on beloved characters from the 1990s films. The largest set, Woody's Roundup! (7594), with its boardwalk catapult, booby-trapped mine, and jail cell, offered real play value. Sets connected to the 2010 movie were

Iconic animated characters Sheriff Woody and Buzz Lightyear as LEGO minifigures.
© Christopher Doyle

all larger, focusing on key scenes such as the opening train chase sequence (7597) or the frightening climax in the trash compactor (7596). Unfortunately, other sets such as Construct-a-Buzz (7592) included a number of prebuilt pieces that restricted building and offered few alternatives to the action figure they were designed to create.

The Toy Story world is one children already know, with characters they are familiar with, and designers dramatically altered one of their own staple components—the minifigure—to give children the Woody and Buzz characters. Unlike with LEGO Harry Potter, where Harry and friends received regular minifigure heads with identifying facial features to tell them apart, Toy Story minifigures have different leg lengths and head shapes to create more accurate depictions of the famous toys. A new horse was also created to capture Woody's lanky steed, Bullseye.

Toy Story 3 also appeared in a few DUPLO sets that were more simplified versions of the LEGO sets. The year 2010 also saw a new addition to the DUPLO playroom. Disney Pixar's *Cars* film was released in 2006 with a sequel in 2011; the *Cars* characters appeared in the DUPLO format in 2010 and in the LEGO format in 2011. The four 2010 DUPLO Cars sets included Flo's V-8 Café (5815), where the cars go to fill up their tanks and have fun, and Mack's Road Trip! (5816), which included highway signs and a cactus.

Prince of Persia (2010)

The new relationship with Disney was not restricted to animated films, however, and when theaters played host to Disney's *Prince of Persia: The Sands of Time* in May 2010, toy shops were busy stocking shelves with its new tie-in LEGO theme. *Prince of Persia,* based on a 2003 video game of the same name, is a fantasy adventure film set in sixth-century Iran. The story's protagonist, Dastan, and heir to the throne, teams up with a princess to stop an evil ruler unleashing a deadly sandstorm. History, desert landscapes, a brave prince, and the Disney label made this film an ideal project to team up with. While the film's PG-13/12A cinema rating in the United States and United Kingdom respectively may have deterred parents from purchasing the sets for their younger children over *Toy Story* toys, for example, the LEGO Group did not shy away from the film's violent moments with set names like Desert Attack (7569), the Fight for the Dagger (7571), and Battle of Alamut (7573). The Iranian-inspired structures and colors added to the theme's historical context, as did the minifigures themselves with headdresses and robes to match the desert climate—Dastan even featured topless with muscles painted onto his torso. Sand and noble warriors were areas the LEGO Group has some experience in (e.g., Adventurers, Indiana Jones, Castle), but they added to the colorful tapestry with fitting weapons, camels, scorpions, and ostriches, which minifigures could ride!

*   *   *

The LEGO Group's turnaround between 2001 and 2010 was remarkable. In 2004 many cynics thought it was high time the small Danish firm owned up to the fact that it just couldn't handle itself on the world stage dominated by big multinationals like Hasbro and Mattel. Business minds saw the collapse of TLG coming, and weren't surprised when those deficits were announced. What might have made them sit up and take notice, however, was the immediacy with which Kjeld Kirk Kristiansen found someone to take his job, the certainty with which Jørgen Vig Knudstorp began making essential changes, and the way the world responded to the new face of the LEGO Group—with even more enthusiasm than before.

Smart moves in uncertain financial times under its new Shared Vision strategy enabled LEGO to brace itself much better than other companies for the economic hit of global recession. Having sold properties and a 70 percent share in the LEGO-LAND parks when the market was strong was something it would have struggled to do a few years later. The decision to regain control of outsourced production was made at the right time, saving LEGO from the PR debacle experienced by other brands such as Mattel, Marvel, and RC2 Corp in 2007 when a number of Chinese-made toys were found to contain excessive amounts of lead. The LEGO Group was seen as a trusted, reliable brand that made its own toys rather than palming off the responsibility to a third party. The chance to restructure and reassess before the financial problems hit the rest of the world meant TLG had already tightened its belt and plugged its leaks, hence why they were able to post an increase in profit and sales for 2009 and the first half of 2010. And while other companies were making job cuts in 2008, the LEGO Group was taking on more workers, with the average number of full-time employees rising from 4,199 in 2007 to 5,388—almost as many as worked for the company before the 2004 changes began.

But as far as Jørgen Vig Knudstorp was concerned, the LEGO Group has a long way to go before it can rest on its laurels. In 2009 he said, "If I'm a little bit blunt, I'd say we are a traditional toy manufacturer with a strong base in Europe that's really starting to drive its exports to the U.S. That would hurt some feelings in the company but that's the truth. I'm talking about how little we sell in Asia or South America and about expanding in the U.S." But expanding production and distribution to reach more children in more countries is just part of the challenge TLG faces if it wants to keep up with the competition. A toy manufacturer is only as good as the products it makes, but in today's digital age, creating a good-quality toy is just part of a package deal. It's plain to see a huge portion of the budget of any company goes on promoting the brand, reaching the consumers, and keeping one step ahead of the market, and this is no more obvious than in the toy industry, as brands try to connect with kids and parents to make sure their products are the must-have toys on every wish list. Television and the Internet are key tools involved in this connection process, and in this the LEGO Group is leading the way, determined not to miss out on the business opportunities these tools represent. "This company was founded on wooden toys, then moved to plastics after the Second World War," Knudstorp said. "I think we missed out a bit on transistors and microchips and computers when they emerged. But we're not going to miss out on digitalization. I'm committed to bringing this business into the twenty-first century by globalizing it and bringing in digital technologies." Knudstorp's commitment, combined with LEGO products, and the company's new lease on life, makes TLG a force to be reckoned with and a future contender for the title of largest toy manufacturer in the world. Why not dream big? After all, that's what LEGO bricks are all about.

Ole Kirk Christiansen knew that for a company to survive hard times it has to be able to adapt. The many setbacks he faced in his efforts as a carpenter and as a toy manufacturer seem insignificant compared to the hurdles the LEGO Group has overcome since, and those it might face in the future, but in a sense they are very much the same. They taught him that just because someone says it won't work, or it won't sell, it doesn't mean it won't; that trends and crazes don't always last; that a toy can always be improved upon; that a family business can't survive with the help of family alone; and that success does not happen overnight. Like all wonderful things, it must be built, one brick at a time.

CHAPTER 6

Building Outside the Box

ne of the LEGO Group's fundamental aims from the start was to educate children through play and to inspire creativity in young minds. Now sold in over 130 countries, LEGO bricks have long been a toy and a system of play that is commonplace in many a toy box and enjoyed by children across the globe; not only that but the brand has stood the test of time, still producing town-based sets that encourage the same play experience they did over 50 years ago. LEGO bricks were one of the few classic toys BBC TV series *James May's Toy Stories* decided to feature in 2009—the result of the program was an entire house made from LEGO bricks, with LEGO furniture, staircase, and toilet that presenter James May spent the night in. The LEGO Group remains one of the few toy brands to still appeal as much (if not more) today than it did when it was first conceived. And it is one of the few toys to be used as an artists' medium, an educative tool, and to bring together a global community—this one bound by its passion for LEGO. This world beyond the brick is what is explored here.

Designs by You

The LEGO Group has always encouraged its customers to think outside of the box, literally. As early as 1950, after the introduction of Automatic Binding Bricks, the company included black and white pamphlets with photographs of possible models children could build from the bricks. This evolved into catalogs that doubled up as building books with tips and ideas, and from those into the Idea Books of the 1960s and 1970s. The 1960 Idea Book (238), released in several European languages, was filled with photographs of children and adults playing and building with LEGO bricks. Some designs to spark the imagination of consumers included houses, boats, planes, animals, and even replicas of real buildings such as the Empire State Building and the SAS Building in Copenhagen. More recently the Creator sets encouraged unbridled building restricted only by the number of bricks in your collection. Over the years, TLG has also experimented with other types of building and shown that there is more fun to be had than what its printed instructions offer.

Originally released in the 1950s as LEGO *Mosaik*, these sets were simply large base plates, which served as a background for a picture made up of lots of small bricks. This "2D" method of building was not particularly popular in comparison with the playable models children could also build with LEGO bricks and was discontinued after a short time. The idea has been revisited by the LEGO Group a number of times, especially with the Dacta sets (now known as LEGO Education). In 2000, however, LEGO Mosaic reappeared on a grander scale, inspired by large-scale models adult hobbyists were creating with the aid of digitizing photo software. Between 2000 and 2005, the LEGO website was home to the Brick-o-Lizer, which allowed you to upload a photograph, and order the parts and instructions required to build it as an image using 1 × 1 tiles. Although the tiles were only available in black, white, and three shades of gray, it was the first opportunity LEGO customers had to purchase parts to build precisely what they wanted. With a toy that is as varied as your imagination, this principle was soon developed into LEGO Factory (now known as Design byME), the latest way to transform LEGO elements into something that appeals to you.

The year 2005 saw the launch of LEGO Digital Designer—a free program on LEGOfactory.com that allowed consumers to design their own LEGO models, upload these designs to the website to share with fellow fans, and design a custom box for their set. The website proved hugely popular, with 77,000 designs uploaded before LEGO announced customers would be able to buy their designs. And this is what has added to the system's success. While there is much fun and creativity to be had in simply designing a house, vehicle, or fantasy world using the software, the real pleasure was that you could order them directly from LEGO via the website; as soon as 48 hours later, a box would arrive with all the pieces needed to assemble it.

Design byME has been embraced by the LEGO community and vice versa. In 2005 three micro-scale Factory sets were released that had been designed by LEGO fans and then three more sets in 2008. The initial Factory designs were the result of a competition that saw some 8,000 entrants vying for the chance to have their design sold all over the world. The winning designers received royalties, depending on the success of their creations. In addition, many fans bought each other's designs directly from the website. Some notable Factory products include Amusement Park (5525) with pirate ship, ski slope, and robot ride, and Star Justice (10191)—a LEGO fan's take on Space with a planet rover, two mini-spaceships, and a command base. The set also included four astronauts dressed in white and the cleverly conceived Star Justice droids. The Design byME website gives fans the opportunity to be as creative as they choose and to enjoy the models others have created. The site also hosts competitions with LEGO sets as prizes for builders to come up with the best designs (for example, a Halloween-themed model).

The LEGO Group's play sets are carefully designed to achieve a certain price point resulting in small, medium, and large sets to cater to a varied market of different consumers. The limits of the LEGO mind don't account for the cost of individual LEGO parts and minifigures, meaning many of the models fans build with their extensive collections or design on their computers are just too expensive to produce and sell to customers, so it's unlikely that Design byME or large buckets of bricks will eclipse the sales of the company's play theme sets just yet. At least, with the 2010 release of online game *LEGO Universe* (see below), players can build with no limits and see their models exist in a world, albeit a virtual one.

Expand the Brand

Through the Internet, television, advertising, food packaging, and even in their learning environments, children's lives are saturated by products and the brands behind them more than ever before. While the simplicity of LEGO is what makes it sell, and has been the key element to its early success and the recent turnaround of the company, bringing in revenue is the main objective of any business, even the LEGO Group. To compete with emerging licensed markets, where children are prompted to desire toys based on their favorite TV show, and bombarded with advertising, LEGO has diversified, producing items often completely unrelated to the construction principles of the toy. This brand, which over the years has included books, apparel, video games, and even advent calendars, seeks to create brand awareness and loyalty. If a child loves LEGO toys, it makes good business sense to make LEGO watches, LEGO clothes, and LEGO bedside lamps so that parents needn't look elsewhere when they want to buy something that isn't a LEGO set for their child's birthday. Here we explore some of these varied products, and take an in-depth look at the emergence of LEGO video games, one of the company's biggest spin-off success stories.

Books

From as early as the 1960s, the LEGO Group was producing non-toy products for fans to spend their extra pocket money on. The earliest Idea Books were a cheap way for the company to advertise its products, promote the LEGO brand, and generate extra revenue. Since those days, various books have been produced by the LEGO Group and its licensed publishing partners (Dorling Kindersley, Scholastic, and Ameet) to help bring the LEGO world and its characters to consumers in dif-

More than a just a minifigure, these keychain minifigures also double as torches. © Ruben Saldana

LEGO watches, made up of special link elements, usually include a LEGO minifigure, such as this Space Police watch. © Sarah Herman

ferent ways. This has resulted in a variety of publications including large hardcover photographic history books and sticker collections (e.g., *LEGO Star Wars The Visual Dictionary, The LEGO Book, Minifigure Ultimate Sticker Collection*), LEGO Atlantis activity books with minifigures, the *BIONICLE Chronicles* and *Adventures* series, annuals, a collector's guide, and Scholastic Readers set in LEGO City. For BIONICLE, the books were an integral part of the play theme, similar to Hasbro's Transformers and the comics associated with them. Obviously, one can be enjoyed without the other, but for children who wanted to fully understand the mythology and world surrounding the toys they were playing with, these books provided an accessible way to achieve that.

Apparel

While various LEGO clothing items have appeared over the years, children's clothes are now produced almost exclusively by long-standing licensed partner Kabooki (some T-shirts are made by other companies). LEGO Wear is a clothing line for children aged up to twelve years, sold across Europe with sales offices in Germany, Denmark, Sweden, and Portugal. While the clothes do not all feature LEGO characters or theme references (there are, of course, LEGO Star Wars–themed clothes for boys ages three to twelve), they all say LEGO Wear on them, and many items include the LEGO logo. There is an emphasis on clothes "made for play" and Kabooki even produces LEGO ski pants and jackets. LEGO shoes are available from Swiss manufacturer Ross Company who make LEGO, DUPLO, BIONICLE, and CLIKITS shoes. Unfortunately, the "studs" on the rubber components of the shoes are not compatible with real LEGO bricks. TLG has also manufactured watches associated with different themes such as Star Wars, Space Police, and Power Miners made up from LEGO links elements and a few studs to add your own finishing touches. With backpacks, sunglasses, and even fancy-dress costumes, it's now possible for kids to be dressed in LEGO products from head to toe.

Household Items

Various licensed partners work with the LEGO Group to produce gadgets, gizmos, and gifts that reflect LEGO's values, which stand out as unique products not always on toyshop shelves. From giant LEGO brick storage boxes to salt and pepper shakers, ice cube trays, MP3 players, digital cameras, lamps, and pens built from minifigure heads, TLG has invited innovative ideas from manufacturers all over the world. But as with its own toys, the company doesn't want a regular bedside lamp with the LEGO logo stuck on the side—it wants a unique product that is obviously a part of the LEGO portfolio—the result? A giant minifigure hanging from a swing (which doubles as a handle), with lights inside its chest that illuminate its white torso. TLG wants its licensed partners to understand the brick, its abilities, and how the functional and play values of LEGO toys can be incorporated into different items.

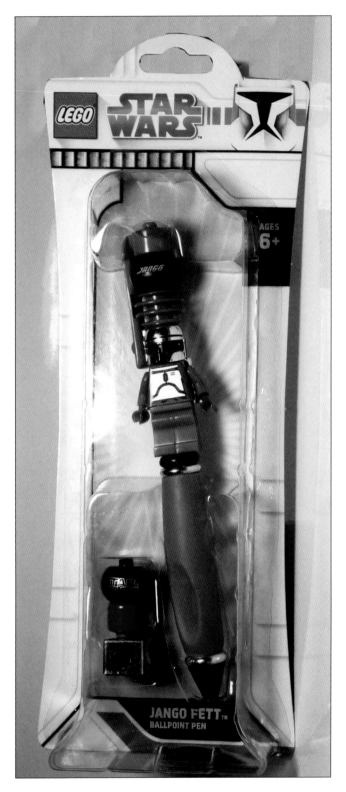

A LEGO Star Wars
Jango Fett minifigure
makes up the mid-
section of this pen.
© Christopher Doyle

They say you shouldn't play with your food, but it's hard not to when you have these minifigure-head salt and pepper shakers. © Ruben Saldana

Some spend years meeting with TLG, discussing different ideas, and perfecting designs and measurements before products are manufactured.

Board Games

Long before the first LEGO bricks were molded in Billund, Ole Kirk Christiansen's toy company produced a board game called *Monypoli* (not to be confused with the family staple, *Monopoly*). Christiansen's 1947 game had a road safety theme—an important education issue for the company which they would later hope to encourage with the Town Plan system, and a popular motif that was offered by many European toy manufacturers. After the popularity of LEGO bricks took off, the LEGO Group did not choose to focus on producing its own games (although one noticeable exception is the inclusion of a board game with the sets for 2003 theme Orient Expedition); instead, it has licensed out the rights to produce LEGO board games to other publishers who produced a diverse range including:

Lego Creator—This popular game, released in 1999 and published by Rose Art Industries, stuck to the fundamental principle of what LEGO play is all about. The game saw players select a model card and then move around a board collecting LEGO pieces to build the model it dictated. The first player to build their model correctly was the winner. This game even went on to win an Årets Spil (Danish Game of the Year Award) for Best Children's Game in 2001.

Lego Dominoes—University Games' 2006 offering took a fairly traditional approach to the use of LEGO bricks in a board game format. Containing 56 bricks and 28 plates, players matched and stacked the colored bricks to move across the board, choosing whether to try and block their opponent's route or race to the finish line.

But something changed for the LEGO Group when they decided that board games were a market they wanted to re-enter in 2009. It's likely this was related to the rise in sales of board games during the recession. In a U.K. *Times* article published in December 2008, market researcher Mintel said that retailers had reported stronger sales of more traditional toys over "must-have" craze items, especially in the run-up to Christmas. Popular board games such as *Monopoly*, *Trivial Pursuit*, and *Operation* saw a noticeable increase in sales, with John Lewis's department stores revealing they had sold 23 times more games of *Scrabble* than the previous year. The LEGO Group had long been considered a traditional, quality toy, and while moving into the board game market could be seen as a risky move for a toy retailer during a global recession, TLG recognized that a family-friendly group game that incorporated LEGO toys' building principles, branded with the LEGO name, had the potential to be a big seller.

Unlike earlier LEGO board games that had revolved around traditional game play with a LEGO element, these new games were referred to as the world's first collection of games that were meant to be built, played, and changed. The "building" required players to put together a unique LEGO die, playing pieces, and even build the board itself. The initial ten games released in 2009 included *Monster 4*, a four-in-a-row game set in a spooky LEGO graveyard; *Race 3000*, where players move racing car pieces around the LEGO track, dodging obstacles to try and reach the finish line first; maze game *Minotaurus* and *Creationary*—a twist on family favorite *Pictionary* where players draw clues to elicit guesses from their team. Similar to the 1999 Warren Company LEGO game *Constructionary*, in *Creationary* players must choose a card from one of four categories: vehicles, buildings, nature, or things, and then build the object written on the card while the other players guess what they are building. Almost all of the games were recommended for children age eight and up, with some games suitable for those as young as six. These ages are not unusual in terms of the board game market—*Monopoly* is sold at the 8+ market and *Operation* to 6+. But given the appeal of LEGO toys to adults, and the older age recommendations of some of its toys, TLG's initial approach was more heavily targeted toward younger fans. Julie Stern, the assistant brand relations manager for the LEGO Group, explained to BoardgameNews.com that this approach was intentional and that while TLG was introducing its line to its strongest audience, more complex games could be on the horizon. In spite of this, the eight games released in 2010 were still appealing to this younger market. The charmingly named *Shave a Sheep* game, which sees players trying to rid their LEGO sheep of its wool before the other players, while steering clear of a LEGO wolf, is considered suitable for children as young as two.

Initially the new games were only available in the U.K. and in German-speaking European countries, but with sales figures higher than expected (LEGO achieved a 10 percent share of the board games market in both countries), the decision was made to launch the games in the United States and Canada in 2010. The U.K.'s LEGO-buying market, being similar to that of the United States but on a much smaller scale, provided the ideal testing ground to see how LEGO games would go down with buyers.

Video Games: LEGO Play Reinvented

While computer games and consoles had featured on wish lists for some years, especially since the release of Nintendo's Game Boy in 1990, the end of the century saw a move toward technologically enhanced toys that provided more interactive play. In 1997 Bandai's Tamagotchi—hand-held electronic devices that hatch as pets in need of attention and care—received the Innovative Toy of the Year Award from the British Association of Toy Retailers, and in 1999, Tiger Electronics took the Toy of the Year Award for the second year running with the hugely successful Furby. First-generation Furbies were furry, owl-like sensory robots, which, through infrared ports and electric motors, were able to communicate with each other, develop their English, communication skills, and move various parts of their bodies.

With children expecting more and more from their toys and with their young minds developing computer literacy levels unseen in previous generations, the LEGO Group made the decision to put its name on a number of video games, beginning in 1997 with *LEGO Island*. Created and published by Mindscape in an agreement with TLG, *LEGO Island* was an action-adventure game for PCs. Set on a small island, there were a number of playable characters each with customizable abilities. Although there was no ultimate objective to the game—it was possible to explore the environment and customize the island—there were a number of missions that could be completed, the central one being returning the Brickster (a known LEGO criminal) to prison after the events of the game led to his escape. The various locales that featured in the game such as the police station, the Octan gas station, the bank, and the race track were modeled on LEGO sets that were available at that time.

Despite this being the LEGO Group's first foray into the world of video games, *LEGO Island* was a huge success. It was the only game targeting children to appear in PC Data's top ten best-selling software games of the year in 1997. On top of impressive sales figures, *LEGO Island* was honored by the critical gaming community when the Academy of Interactive Arts and Sciences awarded it the Interactive Achievement Award for Family Game of 1997—this award has since been won by gaming blockbusters *Guitar Hero*, *Rock Band*, and *LittleBigPlanet*. Critics commented that the game managed to retain the quirky style and humor of LEGO toys while providing a stimulating, customizable environment that was easy for younger children to use. Arguably it was the success of *LEGO Island* (a game not based on any existing range of LEGO products, or a licensed brand), that paved the way for the future of video games at the company, including two *Island* sequels, *Star Wars,* and *Indiana Jones.* The *Island* games even spawned their own LEGO building theme— Island Xtreme Stunts (released 2002–2003), featuring characters and scenarios from the games.

Between 1997 and 2009, TLG released thirty-five original LEGO games, making the name a recognized staple in child-friendly software. While the company did develop some games themselves, such as *LEGO Stunt Rally* and *LEGO Rock Raiders*, it became apparent that greater success would be achieved through the outsourcing of game development to experienced established production houses. The LEGO Group put its ideas and characters in the hands of companies such as British developer Silicon Dreams Studios, known largely for their football games; Traveller's Tales (owned by Warner Bros. since 2007), who are responsible for the majority of recent LEGO video game successes; and NetDevil—the Colorado-based company who took on the mammoth task of creating a massive multi-player online game for the LEGO Group.

LEGO Island's success was followed by a number of popular games. Here are just some of the more memorable ones.

LEGO Racers

Although not as successful in terms of sales and critical reception as *Island*, 1999's *Racers* was the first LEGO game to be available for both the PC and games consoles such as Game Boy Color, Nintendo 64, and PlayStation. Racing games series such as *Super Mario Kart* and *Gran Turismo* were some of the most popular console games of the 1990s, so the LEGO Group's venture into racing games (there was also a *Racers 2* released in 2001) was very reflective of the popular market at the time. *Racers* saw players drive around a circuit in a series of rounds—scoring high led to a new race circuit being "unlocked." With twenty-four race tracks in total and a number of power weapons and shortcuts available, *Racers* matched up to other similar go-kart games, but was lacking in terms of multi-player capabilities. Popular features of the game that made it particularly LEGO-esque were its sense of humor (before racing, players had to obtain a driver's license with the obligatory bad photograph) and creativity (gamers customized their own drivers and built their own race cars from various LEGO-themed pieces). The game preceded the launch of the new-look LEGO car racing toys, which also became known as LEGO Racers in 2001, with the same branding as the game.

Rock Raiders, Alpha Team, and *BIONICLE*

While *LEGO Racers* was a game first and a toy second (incidentally, the LEGO Racers line has continued long after the game's availability), a number of games that followed it were produced as part of a supporting media package created to help sell a new line of LEGO toys. Unfortunately, the originality and gaming nuance evident in the production of *LEGO Island* was clearly lacking from some of these new releases, and as a result they failed to have much impact on the gaming community beyond LEGO fans. These included mining theme Rock Raiders' tie-in—a mission-based real-time strategy game that saw players completing missions such as searching for equipment or rescuing fellow Raiders to obtain energy crystals. *Alpha Team* was also one of the primary outlets for its toy theme's storyline. Developed by Oscar-winning special effects company Digital Domain, it saw the player take on the role of Agent Dash who must save the other members of the team and stop the evil Ogel from using his mind-controlling orbs. Another theme that received the video game treatment a number of times is Technic spin-off BIONICLE. With its built-in storyline and complex mythology, BIONICLE was ripe material for game developers, but the 2000s' offerings of *LEGO BIONICLE* (also known as *Tales of the Tohunga*), *Matoran Adventures*, and *BIONICLE: The Game* were not particularly well-received either. Many gaming reviews pointed to the fact that unless you were a hard-core BIONICLE fan, the game wasn't that enjoyable. The latest BIONICLE game *BIONICLE Heroes* released in 2006/2007 fared slightly better, its release overshadowed by the long-awaited arrival of PlayStation 3 and Wii consoles the same week. The game was the first of the BIONICLE series to be developed by *LEGO Star Wars* developer Traveller's Tales (see below) and thus many comparisons were drawn between the two games, BIONICLE seen as the lesser of the two for its lack of originality and LEGO qualities, as well as its repetitiveness.

LEGO Star Wars

By 2005 the LEGO Group had had varied success with different game releases. It wasn't until 2005, with the release of *LEGO Star Wars: The Video Game* that the true potential in this medium was realized. PR Newswire reported total worldwide sales figures for the game at 6.7 million copies in 2009, and this figure was overtaken by the game's sequel *LEGO Star Wars: The Original Trilogy* (2006) with 8.2 million units sold. With *Star Wars*' enormous fan presence and the LEGO toys' unmatched success as a licensed product, the marriage of LEGO, *Star Wars*, and games consoles was one that all involved had good reason to feel confident in, but it was the execution of the development and the unique feel of the overall product that caused a buzz in the gaming world. Despite being targeted toward children, its combination of accessible puzzles, challenges, destructible scenery, and the well-loved *Star Wars* mythology, characters, familiar locales, and music made it a popular game with adults, too, who could also appreciate the comical spin put on such an iconic movie series, especially in the cut-scenes created especially for the game.

The sequel (the action of which focused on the original three films produced) sought to improve on the camera movement, and levels played out completely from inside a vehicle, to create a more enjoyable play experience. The game featured over fifty playable characters and was praised for its "cute" and "priceless" retelling of classic *Star Wars* film scenes. It was featured in *Time* magazine's top 10 video games of 2006 and received a BAFTA at the British Academy Video Game Awards for Best Gameplay that same year. The LEGO Group continued this success with a compilation edition of both games called *LEGO Star Wars: The Complete Saga* in 2007, which was included in Guinness World Records' top 50 games of all time at number 23. With these games remaining some of the most successful ever made under the LEGO name, and with other new titles selling well, 2011 saw the release of a new *Star Wars* game based around the televised *Star Wars: The Clone Wars* animated series (for which there are already a number of LEGO sets).

LEGO Indiana Jones

With the phenomenal success of the Star Wars games, Traveller's Tales, which was bought by Warner Bros. in 2007, began production on two games to coincide with the 2008 release of the fourth Indiana Jones film. The first, *Indiana Jones: The Original Adventures* (2008) saw players re-creating famous scenes from the first three Indiana Jones films, and, similar to the Star Wars games, humor was injected into the characters and story—now a LEGO games trademark that has reinvigorated the licensed gaming market. Much of the fundamental game play was similar to that of the *Star Wars* movies (e.g., there was still the two-player drop-in/drop-out functionality, only this game had split-screen capabilities) but with minor changes—rather than collecting canisters containing parts of vehicles, for example, the Indy characters collect parts of ancient artifacts. Some additions were made, however, such as characters being able to interact more with objects in the environment, and build and ride new vehicles. The 2009 sequel *The Adventure Continues*, released after the fourth film installment, had a level and object creator, and split-screen capabilities for two-player mode, meaning players' avatars could move farther from each other to explore the environment. The game received less favorable reviews than *Original Adventures*, probably due to the fans' lack of affinity with the new film, on which the majority of the game was based.

LEGO Batman: The Videogame

Following Indy that same year was another release from TT Games that also included a well-known adventurer. The LEGO Batman toys of 2006–2008 were modeled on a traditional comic book image of Batman and included many of the famed characters from the stories (Robin, the Joker, the Riddler, Scarecrow, and Poison Ivy, to name a few). While Warner Bros. was the publisher on the video game, released as the toy line was wound down, it did not model the game or the characters on any of the existing Batman films, choosing instead the more cartoonish and old-fashioned style of the LEGO toys and an original story as the basis for the game. Similar to the

Indiana Jones games, *Batman* included more combat challenges. With three groups of escaped criminals to lock back up, the player (as Batman or sidekick Robin) could experience each level from the villains' point of view, and try and carry out their criminal acts. Less LEGO building is required than in other LEGO games, but characters are customizable with a number of different suits available for specific abilities. The game was received well and praised for the less restrictive nature of the Batman license, providing more characters, locations, and freedom for creativity than with other LEGO games. According to an article in *X360 Magazine*, ten months after its release the game had sold 4.15 million copies worldwide, an impressive figure considering it was without the backing of a film release, and competed with the Indiana Jones game released previously in the year.

LEGO Rock Band

Traveller's Tales' unique video games seemed an odd partner for Harmonix Music Systems—the original developer of the *Guitar Hero* and *Rock Band* music games— but sure enough, in 2009 the companies who had brought the world *LEGO Star Wars* and *The Beatles: Rock Band* joined forces to produce *LEGO Rock Band*. Similar to other Rock Band games, this version allowed up to four players to use instruments to re-create the sounds of guitar, bass guitar, drums, and vocalist on a number of popular songs, chosen for their family-friendly content, to earn points in the form of LEGO bricks. This child-proofed game also includes an easy setting where players do not have to hit the right notes, instead striking any note to achieve points; a feature to help those who can't reach the drum pedal; and a no-fail setting so that rather than a song prematurely ending for poor playing, LEGO bricks are removed from the overall score. Though much of the environment was re-created in LEGO brick form, compared to previous LEGO games, *Rock Band* does not feature much building—a familiar aspect is the customization of avatars, and their Rock Den using accessories awarded to players for completing gigs. While the game fared reasonably well with the critics, particularly the Xbox 360 and Playstation 3 versions, and received a nomination for Best Family Game from the Academy for Interactive Arts and Sciences (it lost out to *The Beatles: Rock Band*), overall most felt the LEGO element was a secondary selling point, with customers paying more attention to the song list when selecting a music game rather than theme.

LEGO Harry Potter

In March 2010 TT Games announced they had signed a six-year deal with the LEGO Group to allow them to continue producing LEGO-based video games until 2016. Since Warner Bros. bought the game developer in 2007, its output has been almost exclusively film-related, and most of those titles have been LEGO games. *Harry Potter*, being a Warner Bros. film property, had previously been licensed out to LEGO for the production of the Harry Potter theme which was first available in 2001. While new *Harry Potter* films have been released since 2007 (when only one Harry Potter set was released), 2010 marked a return to the theme for LEGO in the form of TT Games' *LEGO Harry Potter: Years 1–4*. Some new sets were also produced to coincide with the game's release.

With the final two Harry Potter films not yet released at the time of the game's launch, the storyline, for those who had not read the books, was not spoiled by the LEGO offering—this game only revealed plot details from the first four films. Similar to previous LEGO games, there was a strong focus on exploration and adventure, rather than combat. Characters used their powers of sorcery to fight off evil, and players cast spells and made potions to progress in the game. Jumping on where *LEGO Star Wars* left off, there were over 100 playable characters in the game. Early trailers for *LEGO Harry Potter* saw classic brown LEGO boats carrying the students across the water to their new school, a wall of LEGO bricks revealing Diagon Alley, and all the light-hearted touches fans have come to expect from LEGO games. *LEGO Harry Potter: Years 5–7* followed in late 2011 after the final film had debuted that summer.

LEGO Universe

Perhaps Ole Kirk Christiansen would have been skeptical if asked if he saw a bright future for LEGO video games when the idea was first revealed to the public in 1997. In one sense, the games produced today are a world away from stacking small plastic bricks to build a house, and in another sense the similarities are quite apparent. Many children are submerged in a technological world from a young age, even in their own home, and LEGO video games, with their interactive play and family-friendly gaming style are an obvious contemporary extension of the toys Ole Kirk originally created. Arguably, the LEGO Group's original vision attempted to be inclusive of as many children as possible, boys and girls, toddlers and teenagers, rich and poor—these video games are products that require access to a computer or gaming console, making them less inclusive than the core LEGO product line.

Speaking to *Business Management* magazine, CEO and President of the LEGO Group Jørgen Vig Knudstorp said even he had his doubts about the success of the format. "I have to admit that we had our fears that the video games could cannibalize the physical play experience. With boys of that age there's a strong synergy between the gaming experience we offer and the physical play experienced. We have learned that just as children still want to read books and not just watch movies they still want to have that physical LEGO building experience that cannot be replaced by digital play." Given that the release of LEGO games has, if anything, boosted sales of the Star Wars and Indiana Jones toys, it was time for the LEGO Group to find a more social way to connect LEGO builders, in a new interactive play format.

The company's latest venture aimed to pull together the success of its unique style of family-friendly games and the growing online LEGO community. *LEGO Uni-*

verse, released in 2010, is a massive multi-player online game (MMO), set in an alternate universe populated by LEGO minifigures recognizable from a number of existing LEGO themes. Players join forces online to help defeat a dark force trying to rid this LEGO world of imagination. MMOs and online game servers are popular ways for gamers to interact and share their gaming experience with real people, rather than playing against a computer. On entering *Universe*, the first creation players build is a customized minifigure to represent them in the game. This avatar is their own personal hero with whom they build, interact, and play with other LEGO fans. As well as being able to construct virtual LEGO designs of their own using different building methods, there are various challenges and tasks embedded in the game such as player vs. player skill competitions, smashable LEGO models that release in-world rewards, and personal achievements that can see your name appear on a number of *Universe* leader boards. The game also fosters a strong sense of community, and though players can compete against each other, marketing materials focus more heavily on the importance of teamwork building and challenges within the game, rather than individual success. The game has chat capabilities so LEGO fans can communicate in real-time with each other, no matter where in the world they live. Children and adult fans from different parts of the world who may only meet up

This MOC titled "Inception" by Alex Eylar uses clever building techniques to create this gravity-defying scene from the 2010 film of the same name. © Alex Eylar

once a year at a LEGO event, or not at all, are now able to enjoy their LEGO hobby together in this virtual environment.

While most MMOs such as Blizzard's *World of Warcraft* are targeted more toward teenagers and adults, *LEGO Universe* has been developed with a minimum age recommendation of eight years old, making it one of the most kid-friendly MMOs available. To ensure it remains suitable for children, there are strict monitory controls in place to give parents peace of mind. For example, there are rules regarding player names and creations—every time a LEGO creation is built in *Universe*, before it is visible to other players, it is sent to a server where it is moderated, transformed into a single-game play object, and returned to the game. There are also parental controls, such as time limits on play and zoning restrictions to enable parents to feel comfortable allowing young children to engage in this online environment.

For the Love of LEGO: Meet the Fan Community

Search the word "LEGO" on any photo-sharing website and hundreds of thousands of results will appear. The majority of pictures people have taken the time to upload are not snaps from their latest trip to LEGOLAND or LEGO Star Wars birthday presents, but MOCs (My Own Creation)—impressively crafted LEGO creations dreamed up from their own imaginations. From photos of minifigure armies and impressive Battle Bugs to dioramas from Star Wars and stone-work castles, pirate ships, and contemporary buildings, there is a dazzling array of LEGO delights sure to impress even the most skilled builder. Under the majority of these photos are comments left by other similarly inclined hobbyists. Many of these LEGO fans have LEGO minifigures as their social networking profile photographs, and sometimes a username to match.

Welcome to the LEGO fan community. Ask many adult LEGO fans (AFOLs) about their experiences before the emergence of unofficial Internet sites and forums dedicated to LEGO building and many will tell you they were a closeted fan, believing they were one of a few adults in the world still building with LEGO toys. Then they found like-minded people online in other countries, in other states or counties, and some in their own city or town.

In 1997 Boston couple Todd Lehman and Suzanne Rich set up Lugnet.com (Lugnet is an abbreviation of LEGO Users Groups Network). As a computer programmer who used to freelance for the LEGO Group as a conceptual artist, Lehman told the *Los Angeles Times* in 2001 that he figured it was just a matter of time before a dedicated LEGO fan produced a site like this, given the intelligence and enthusiasm of the community. Lugnet, despite its simplistic design, is still one of the largest online LEGO-oriented communities. The site provides users with a series of forums—general topics, LEGO themes, a marketplace for selling LEGO toys, and local boards for specific countries and locations. Users post pictures of their MOCs and access a parts database to find which sets contain pieces they need to build their next project. A quick browse of Lugnet's LUGMap reveals nearly 100 registered LEGO groups around the world, most of which have their own websites dedicated to news and forums relevant to that localized area. Lugnet is not the only site to offer AFOLs this kind of experience—there are now a number of similar sites in a variety of languages, some focusing on a particular LEGO building theme. Beyond the forums, there are enthusiastic LEGO bloggers highlighting their favorite new MOCs and builders, reporting news, and discussing new LEGO products. One such blog is The Brothers Brick.

Started in 2005, The Brothers Brick (TBB) serves the online community through its reportage of LEGO news and by posting MOC photographs that have caught the attention of the blog's contributors. Important news does take precedent, but the spotlight focus on exciting MOCs and their creators—offering links to the builders' own websites or Flickr.com accounts—is what really makes the blog such a success. Many fans view it regularly, and post comments to get involved in the discussion of a particular model or news story. The Brothers Brick is well-known in North America, where the team regularly sponsor events and attend conventions. In 2009 the site received nearly 1.5 million unique visitors, with users coming from 207 different countries and regions, no small achievement for a blog run voluntarily by passionate fans.

Although the LEGO Group go to all that effort of creating varied and interesting sets for its customers to build, there's a large sector of LEGO fans that can't wait to get their hands on those shiny, perfectly designed boxes so they can rip them open and use the parts inside to build something completely original. These creations are MOCs. They exist in the minds, bedrooms, and LEGO rooms (yes, some fans do have these) of creative LEGO fans everywhere. The Brothers Brick defines MOC as "My Own Creation. Any LEGO creation designed and built by a LEGO fan without instructions. Generally pronounced 'mock.'" For a MOC builder there are no limitations, with the exception of their disposable income and the pieces that TLG creates (and even these are sometimes modified by fans).

While building MOCs is as old as the LEGO brick itself, the idea of sharing them with like-minded fans on an international scale is a relatively new phenomenon. Before social networking and photo-sharing sites had really taken off, LEGO Certified Professional Sean Kenney wanted a place where others could show off their LEGO creations like he did on his own blog, and so he created MOCpages.com, one of the first sites dedicated to sharing LEGO creations. The community welcomes anyone who loves LEGO bricks, including children, adult hobbyists, artists and engineers who use the bricks as a medium, and LEGO employees, although the site is not officially endorsed by the LEGO Group.

While MOC builders do buy LEGO sets to add to their collection, often they are looking to buy particular bricks or minifigures rather than the specialized parts or base plates that increase the cost of the set. To facilitate this demand for specific bricks and encourage builders to buy directly from the LEGO Group rather than sec-

This beautiful whaling ship, named 66.5°N, was built by AFOL Jordan Schwartz.
© Jordan Schwartz

ond-hand sellers, the company created the "Pick a Brick" system. First introduced into LEGO retail outlets in 2002, this shopping experience saw customers paying to fill a cup or bag with any number of pieces they wanted from a shelving unit full of parts. Pick A Brick is also available online at LEGO.com, where it is possible to browse through nearly 1,500 different LEGO elements costing as little as ten cents for a 1 × 1 brick. And it's not just bricks; you can give your existing minifigures a makeover with new clothes, hats, heads, and hairpieces. Unfortunately, not every LEGO element is available, and there is not an on-demand service provided. While it's possible for TLG to monitor the popularity of most staple pieces, or colors, making them readily available, they do not unnecessarily produce large amounts of pink bricks, for example, just in case one MOC builder decides to build a candy-colored fairy castle. This, however, is where second-hand brick selling plays its part.

Websites such as Bricklink.com bring buyers and sellers together. Want to pick up an original 1984 Black Falcons' Knights Castle? Need fifty black monkey tails to decorate your latest Wizard of Oz MOC? Then Bricklink is the place to start looking. While some sellers are just getting rid of their old collection, online retailers usually offer more competitive prices, meaning vintage sets and unusual parts are available, and everything is generally cheaper, keeping buyers coming back for more and more bricks.

Some individuals have gone a little bit further than simply selling parts, and have taken it upon themselves to modify minifigures and create accessories not currently available from LEGO themselves. One such seller is Will Chapman, whose custom

BRICKFILMS

For some, simply building with LEGO bricks is not enough. With the increased availability of home video cameras and editing software in the 1980s and '90s, amateur filmmakers began creating their own stop-motion animations using a variety of materials. LEGO toys, being an easy-to-build-and-dismantle material with its own minifigure scale and smiley-face characters, made the perfect subject for these short animations. Creating a simple LEGO film, or "brickfilm," as they have become known, involves making a scene entirely or in part from LEGO bricks, recording the still image, and then altering the environment (such as moving a minifigure one step forward) before recording again to create movement when the shots are edited together. As fans began sharing their videos on websites like YouTube, so the appreciation for brickfilms began to grow—this LEGO building off-shoot now has its own dedicated community websites such as BricksinMotion.com and Brickfilms.com. Here, filmmakers and fans share their movies, ideas and tips, enter contests, and even recruit others to work with them on projects. LEGO films are often shown at fan conventions and there are even brickfilm festivals and awards highlighting the very best of what's on offer. The LEGO Group has even shot its own brickfilms such as 2002's *LEGO Star Wars: The Han Solo Affair* and *LEGO Indiana Jones: Raiders of the Lost Brick* to promote its toy lines and dedicated an entire theme to the hobby. The Steven Spielberg Moviemaker set was the first toy in the 2000–2002 Studios theme. Endorsed by the Oscar-winning director, this kit included a camera and computer software to edit a LEGO film, as well as various LEGO parts to re-create an iconic movie movement. The theme may have been short-lived but the LEGO Group's recognition of this popular medium introduced many fans to the idea of using LEGO to make short films, and provided basic tools for young, budding brickfilm-makers.

toy business Brick Arms is a huge success story. Based in the United States, it is one of the largest manufacturers of LEGO-compatible weaponry and customized minifigures. Chapman initially went into business to make World War II LEGO weapons for his son; now his custom products are sold across the United States and in Canada, Australia, the U.K., Sweden, and the Netherlands. For an average of $1.15 you can arm your minifigures with a sword or gun modeled on real and fantasy weapons. While the LEGO Group has produced weapons in the past, it is wary of focusing too much on toys that encourage violent play, meaning Brick Arms is one of a few manufacturers offering LEGO fans alternatives to traditional minifigure attire and accessories.

Nowhere is the AFOL community more evident than at a LEGO convention. Similar to the fandoms of other toys and products collected by adults, LEGO fans of all ages can benefit from the dedication of the older members of the community to organize and run various unofficial events. With LEGO toys' international popularity and family-friendly appeal, there are events hosted by LEGO communities all over the world. From small model shows and displays to convention halls packed with builders from a host of different countries, and lines of excitable fans, the LEGO convention is a sight to behold. And why would fans of a toy travel all over the world to hang out in a windowless convention hall? As *Brick Journal* editor Joe Meno put

Some LEGO events take up entire convention centers or halls (such as BrickCon, pictured) and are filled with AFOLs and members of the public eager to see the impressive creations on display. © Jordan Schwartz

it so simply, "Being with like-minded people is the primary thing. The other thing would be learning from each other."

At the larger events, which are often stretched over a long weekend, convention halls will be sectioned off into different table areas for builders to display their MOCs in an appropriate context. Most builders will have built and disassembled their creations at home in preparation for the event, but occasionally new builds appear at the convention spurred on by the creativity of their surroundings. Some AFOLs build big, re-creating landmark buildings or impressive sculptures, some choose the other end of the spectrum, building in micro-scale—whole cities covering a table-top—while the vast majority build in minifigure scale, resulting in a room populated with more little yellow faces than you would've thought possible.

Building is the main reason most of these fans pay the exhibitor's fee and spend four days in a large room with lots of little bricks. And while there is not much ego on display, most events give out prizes for the best builds in a number of categories, so a friendly competitive spirit encourages fans to show the best of their latest creations. Men quite clearly outnumber women at these events, but the atmosphere is far from boisterous. Builders wander the floor observing the creativity and building techniques of others, reuniting with friends they know well from the online community but rarely see in person. And while there is a slight club atmosphere, new builders as well as younger fans are welcomed into the fold with open arms—especially considering some of the most prolific and popular builders are still teenagers.

Some of the most attended and well-known conventions as of 2010 include:

LEGO World—Every autumn, the LEGO community descends on the small Dutch riverside city of Zwolle for what, as the name may suggest, is one of the world's largest LEGO events. It boasts giant LEGO buildings, world-record-breaking attempts, a petting zoo, laser show, and a LEGO World party with live music and performances; this truly is a celebration of the LEGO brand and LEGO toys suitable for all ages.

Brickworld—With one of the largest LEGO-buying populations in the world, and only one LEGOLAND to call their own (until LEGOLAND Florida opened in 2011), it's no surprise that the United States is home to a fair few LEGO conventions. Repeatedly hailed as the largest LEGO fan event in North America, this June gathering of builders, hosted in Chicago, draws big names from across the world to come and share their work. Founded by AFOLs in 2007, the popular public event, which receives a fair amount of media attention, has helped to overcome the stigma attached to the idea of adults playing with LEGO.

BrickCon—Formerly known as North-West BrickCon, this convention and public exhibition has been held every year in Seattle since 2002. Growing steadily in attendance each year, some 375 builders contributed to the displays in 2009, while 9,300 members of the public paid to come along and enjoy their hard work. There are plenty of community builds, contests, seminars, and presentations to keep all the attendees busy throughout the weekend.

Brickvention—First held in 2006 in Melbourne, this was Australia's first LEGO convention. The inaugural year saw some 35 registered LEGO fans and 150 members of the public attend—this figure jumped dramatically to 1,000 in 2009, encouraging the event to occupy a larger space in 2010. The convention is usually held in January.

BrickFair—A large two-day event held in August every year in Washington, D.C. with predominantly American, Canadian, and British attendees. BrickFairs past have included a theater room playing brickfilms all weekend long, as well as interactive models and a large Stay & Play area to keep little hands busy.

BrickFest—Originally held in Virginia, this Portland, Oregon-based event has been held every year since 2000 (with the exception of 2010), drawing public crowds of up to 4,000. Past highlights have included an appearance by Kjeld Kirk Kristiansen in 2005, and author Allan Bedford signing copies of his popular book *The Unofficial LEGO Builder's Guide* in 2006. The organizers also hosted a new event in 2011 called BricKids.

U.K. LEGO events—Currently, there are no dedicated U.K. LEGO conventions on the same scale as the above events. The U.K. forum for AFOLs, The Brickish Association, regularly posts photographs and information about events involving LEGO models and builders. Often these include LEGO Train displays at transport museums, or exhibitions at other educational centers. There is also the Petersfield LEGO Show—2010 was its seventh year—and Brickish regularly hosts its own member events.

*　*　*

The AFOL movement witnessed both online and at public events is growing steadily and as technology develops easier and more accessible ways for LEGO lovers to communicate and share information, so the community will expand. While sales of LEGO products to adults for adults are relatively low when compared to the amount of money spent buying LEGO toys for children, the AFOL community's presence and buying power is significant. To make sure the company is well-connected to the community, there is the LEGO Ambassador Program—comprising (in 2010) of forty ambassadors in twenty-two countries around the world. Ambassadors are volunteer positions held by AFOLs who are voted in by LEGO User Groups, lasting for one year. Their role is to work with the LEGO Community team to give a voice to the fans and to actively engage with the community online and at events. Due to the growth in fan events and AFOL groups, especially in North America, the LEGO

No matter their size or subject matter, AFOLs take MOC building to the extreme, as can be seen with Jordan Schwartz's "Rapunzel's Tower."
© Jordan Schwartz

Alex Eylar's "Relativity" build proves that if you can imagine it, it can be built—even if it doesn't look possible. © Alex Eylar

Group's Community team includes a Community Relations Coordinator to act as a go-between, acting as a point of contact within the LEGO Group for the fans and attending events across the country as the embodied voice of TLG. Whether they want more realistic Train designs, less Big Ugly Rock Pieces (BURPs), or more pink bricks, LEGO fans now have many ways to let the suits and designers in Billund know.

For the younger LEGO fans, however, the LEGO Club is still one of the most popular ways to connect to the brand and to the community. The earliest official LEGO Clubs were created in Canada in 1966 and Sweden in 1967. Soon clubs were popping up all over the LEGO map and many of them had their own official newsletters and magazines to keep in touch with their fans. Titles varied from country to country—while U.K. fans read *Bricks 'n Pieces*, fans in the United States received *Brick Kicks* then *LEGO Mania Magazine*, and Germany's kids could subscribe to *World Club Magazine*. These were gradually phased out and replaced by *LEGO Magazine* and then *LEGO Club Magazine* in 2008. There is also a junior version of the current magazine for children under seven. The magazine is free and is the face of the LEGO Club around the world. For those who want more, there is a constantly evolving website dedicated to the Club, which provides fans with news, building tips, events

BUILDING TIPS

Building with LEGO bricks is child's play—suitable for all ages (given the right type of brick) and all skill levels, especially if you follow the LEGO Group's carefully created, universally understood directions. But for those who want to create something truly outside of the box, then a little more imagination is required. Approaching MOC building, especially as an adult who may not have played with LEGO in many years, can be a daunting challenge, but as any LEGO convention reveals, it's always a fun one. Here, *BrickJournal* contributor and prolific MOC builder Jordan Schwartz presents his top tips for making the most out of making whatever you want.

- The first step in creating a MOC is being inspired. Anything can be an inspiration. Part of the fun of the medium is thinking of a subject in your head and seeing it in person when you are finished building it—a positively rewarding experience!
- From a quick doodle to a complicated blueprint, sketching your ideas on paper can help you visualize your dream LEGO build.
- If you plan on building something for accuracy or realism, do research first. Photographs and other three-dimensional models can be excellent references. Bear in mind, though, it is almost impossible to perfectly match a LEGO creation to its real-life counterpart so there's no shame in changing a few details to more easily realize the subject in LEGO bricks.
- Sorting, although time-consuming and often difficult, can help the building process go smoothly. It is common to sort by color or element type, but if you know your collection and previous MOCs themselves well enough, keeping the broken MOCs in separate containers can help you pinpoint the locations of specific elements.
- Just because your planned MOC is small doesn't mean you will complete it in a short period of time. Oftentimes, the smaller MOCs require the most detail and can take just as long to complete as something larger. When beginning a project for fun, don't set a deadline for yourself.
- If you are not happy with the way something looks, change it! There are over 20,000 different LEGO elements out there so there's always another way to create the look you're trying to achieve.
- Get feedback. A MOC is never finished, and by showing your model to friends, or posting a photograph online, other LEGO fans may suggest ways you could improve certain techniques or features to make it even better.

- Don't restrict yourself to building in one theme. Although we all have our preferences—from space to castle and everything in between—try your hand at something new. You will notice that techniques you thought only worked for one theme serve a different purpose altogether for another.
- Most importantly, build often. The more you build, the better you get.

information, and most importantly an uploading and viewing gallery to show off their latest models, and with 2.7 million members worldwide at the last count, they have to be doing something right.

LEGO.com is a growing force and one of the most visited toy manufacturer websites in the world. Through registering with My LEGO Network, fans of all ages can connect, trade their LEGO toys, and display their latest creations. According to a 2008 survey conducted by Nielsen, 25 percent (98,000 people) of LEGO.com's U.K.

BRICKJOURNAL

Kids might have the *LEGO Club Magazine* to read all the latest LEGO news in, but they're not the only LEGO fans appreciating the written word. While not exclusive to AFOLs, *BrickJournal* started out as a digital-only magazine in 2005 and has since become available in stores across North America. While it's not an official LEGO publication, TLG provided seed funding for the publication's first year in print, and are supportive in providing materials and interview access for the magazine. Each issue focuses on different aspects of the LEGO world, including news, new products, features, and LEGO builders (professionals and amateurs), with in-depth features on LEGOLAND parks, the LEGO Group's history, specific themes, and conventions. Despite the abundance of online LEGO fan material, Editor Joe Meno doesn't feel threatened. "Websites and blogs haven't really affected the sales of *BrickJournal*," he said. "This is mainly because the magazine is a different format—it's not something that is constantly changing. *BrickJournal* comes out as a publication that people can stop and take their time to read. The articles we write have different content from the websites, too." But he's also quick to recognize the importance of the online community. "There has been a lot of expansion in the community recently—the growth of community conventions is evidence of that. The web is behind a lot of this, as it's easy to search online about building. The increase in events has also created a higher number of places for community people to meet."

audience were under twelve years old, making it the fourth most visited website for that age group in Britain. This popularity can be put down to the combination of the online shop, the LEGO Club, and the vast number of games, comics, and interactive elements across nearly 90,000 separate pages. The website is also widely accessed by teachers who can access and download teaching materials for children as young as eighteen months.

As much as LEGO really is all fun and games, it's also an educational tool that prides itself on its long-standing relationship with educators and school organizations. The Educational Products Department (renamed Dacta in 1989, and now known as LEGO Education) was established in 1980 to collaborate with education experts to design LEGO "toys" that could benefit a learning environment. Over the years, these toys have included oversize softer bricks (9020), tiled letters, numbers, and mosaic sets (9530 and 9531), as well as sets to encourage children to learn about real life through play (available with either larger doll-like play figures or minifigures), large sets filled with LEGO brick elements, and larger kits for older children to learn about structures, machines, and mechanisms and robotics. Many of the products available to schools are similar to those the students might have played with at home such as LEGO MINDSTORMS, but the accompanying teaching materials show how LEGO products can be used to educate children both socially and scientifically in an engaging and interactive way.

LEGO for a Living

For many LEGO fans, young and old, being paid to design models and build with LEGO bricks is the ultimate dream. For a lucky few, this dream is their reality and their job is that of a LEGO builder. Walking around the Miniland areas at LEGOLAND parks and marveling at the intricate replicas of iconic landmarks, it doesn't take a LEGO expert to deduce that an enormous amount of time and skill is devoted to creating and maintaining these giant models. As with any job, however, there is a hierarchy of roles in the LEGO model designing/building department and not all of them require the creative input and freedom aspiring model makers may take for granted. Bottom-of-the-ladder roles such as LEGO copy builders see employees (predominantly at a large facility in the Czech Republic) assembling exact replicas of the same LEGO model en masse in a factory-style production. These LEGO creations, which are often sets available to buy, are shipped all over the world for display use in LEGO stores and other toy retailers to promote certain products. At the other end of the career spectrum are the highly coveted positions of model designers who create the sets that go into production and are purchased around the world. Other Master Builders work for LEGOLAND parks or at model shops in the Czech Republic, Denmark, and the United States creating models to be displayed in LEGO stores and at other LEGO events. Master Builders, who previously had to build half-scale prototypes for their giant creations, are now assisted by advanced computer

Artist Nathan Sawaya poses with one of his works—a LEGO mosaic self-portrait.
© Brickartist.com

software that allows them to perfect the model virtually before sitting down with a big pile of bricks. For some models, one builder may be directing and managing a group who interpret their blueprints, and will also oversee the final quality control of the model shop's output.

While the maintenance and development of new installations at LEGO-LAND parks is essential for the continued success of these entertainment centers, as a branch of the company's marketing department much of the work carried out by Master Builders is dictated by the product lines that need to be promoted, and for the few builders who don't work at a LEGOLAND location, their job focuses on building specific promotional models for use at in-store events, toy fairs, and corporate functions. Often new LEGO model builders are recruited through Master Builder contests, where after various interview stages, prospective employee finalists are set a series of building challenges, competing against each other under the clock.

Not everyone finds work building with LEGO bricks through this official avenue, however. For a lucky few expert builders and artists, there is the honor of being named a LEGO Certified Professional. These individuals, while not LEGO employees are officially recognized by TLG as "trusted business partners." They may not be paid a salary by the LEGO Group, but are able to use their title to increase their business profile and legally use the LEGO name when referring to their work. Not only that, but for an annual enrollment fee these professionals can buy bulk amounts of LEGO bricks at a discounted rate. Currently there are eleven people certified by the LEGO Group, and their work ranges from BrickWorld creator Adam Reed Tucker's skyscrapers and Nicolas Foo's charming gifts to Beth Weis's education enrichment program and Nathan Sawaya's extraordinary LEGO art. These individuals show how, with the right business mind and enthusiasm for the medium, making a LEGO living is possible.

New York–based Nathan Sawaya started sculpting in LEGO bricks as a way to unwind from his high-pressure job as a corporate attorney, but after his work caught the public's imagination and his website, Brickartist.com, crashed under the strain of too many hits, he realized it was time to quit law and get building professionally. "New York corporate attorneys work over 80 hours a week," he said. "These days I'm working more hours, but having more fun." As a freelance artist, Sawaya's "fun" is derived from building unusual large-scale sculptures, which have been seen on television and in museums around the world. "I love all of my pieces," he explained. "If asked to pick a favorite, I say 'the next one!' I think my sculpture *Yellow* has become a small part of pop culture. It really seems to resonate with people. I have found it everywhere—on book covers, on album covers, even on a jacket as part of a clothing line." Some artists would struggle with the restrictions that building with LEGO bricks creates for an artist, with only specific colors and shapes to work with, but Sawaya says it's all a matter of perspective. "I appreciate the cleanliness of the medium, the right angles, the distinct lines. Up close, the shape of the brick is dis-

Many of Sawaya's large LEGO
sculptures seem to defy the laws of
nature, physics, and LEGO building.
© Brickartist.com

tinctive, but from a distance, those right angles and distinct lines change to curves." And even as a child, Sawaya was fully aware of the LEGO brick's creative potential. "With some other toys, if you lost a piece, then the whole toy couldn't be played with, but not with LEGO bricks. If you lost one LEGO brick, you just had to be creative and find some other way to build it."

Unfortunately, the title of Certified Professional is not given out easily by the LEGO Group. In order to receive certification from TLG, an individual must demonstrate a certain degree of building proficiency and enthusiasm for the LEGO brand and its building system, as well as have a professional approach toward other LEGO

Nathan Sawaya's *Yellow*, 2006 © Brickartist.com

A LEGO lamp, shaped like a giant minifigure, clutches the real deal in its hand—the LEGO world now encompasses so much more than simple building blocks. © Ruben Saldana

fans and the public. Sawaya's creations are certainly not easy to build, but if you have the bricks at your disposal, there's no harm in trying. Here he reveals how to build like a professional.

When designing a large-scale LEGO build, how do you go about calculating how many bricks you're going to need?

You don't need to. Don't worry about how many bricks you need—just start building. If you run out of bricks, just buy more. How could you know how many bricks you will need? It is much more fun just to create and see what happens. Does a painter calculate how many tubes of paint he will need before he starts painting? Well, maybe he does, but it seems like a waste of time. I sketch out my ideas ahead of time, so there is definitely a blueprint in place. But of course, changes happen throughout the process. That is the natural part of creating.

How do you get your mind around creating spheres and curves using such angular objects?

It is all rectangles. Just use them in a stair-step method in order to create curves. But do practice your spheres. If you ever apply for a job at the LEGO Group, at one point during the interview process they give you a pile of bricks and ask you to build a sphere. Then, after a few minutes, they take whatever you've built and roll it across the room. If it rolls like a ball, congrats, you can move on to the next part of the interview. If it just sits there, then you have likely built a box and it's time for you to go home.

How do you know when a build is complete and when to stop adding to it?

It's up to the artist. I know that a sculpture is done when it looks just like I want it to. Not a brick more, not a brick less.

What's your secret shortcut or cheat for creating a specific effect with LEGO bricks?

Ha! I'm not telling.

Have you ever dropped or destroyed a build accidentally?

Accidents happen, but of course the great thing about LEGO is that anything can be rebuilt again. I had a sculpture of a giraffe at the Turtle Bay museum in Redding, California. A young boy liked the giraffe sculpture so much that he wanted to give it a hug and he tackled the sculpture and took it to the ground. The museum let me know that I would be receiving a box of giraffe parts. But in the end, I was able to rebuild the sculpture.

What tools or essential items should every serious LEGO builder have?

A hammer and a chisel. Oh, and patience.

From the inception of the LEGO System of Play, the small plastic brick was more than just another construction block. It was conceived as part of a bigger plan—a toy that existed beyond the box it was bought in, a toy with endless possibilities.

That bigger plan now extends to a whole range of media, platforms, and intentions. Whether being used to teach kids about robotics, featured in an online computer game played by children around the world, or as an artist's paint box, the possibilities really are endless.

"The LEGO Group has been very good at diversifying, especially now," said *Brick-Journal* editor Joe Meno. "Keeping relevant has become something that they've gotten pretty proficient in. With LEGO Mindstorms and *LEGO Universe* they are pushing the building experience to places outside the playroom and that is the exact right thing to do. The LEGO Group's identity is in building, so coming up with more mediums to build in would be the best way to move forward." And move forward they shall, because it would be pretty difficult to ignore the 400 million children and adults who play and build with LEGO toys every year. "The LEGO Group also has to continue to work with the LEGO building community," Meno insisted. "Some of the best things built in LEGO [bricks] don't come from the company!" With fans building more and more sophisticated designs, and the growing communication between the fan community and TLG, the company will be pushed to produce better products and keep up to date with technological advancements if they want to see that number grow in the future. But Meno's pretty sure nothing's going to rival the brand any time soon, because underneath all the websites, video games, giant fan conventions, and the marketing machine that runs it all, its simplicity is its worst-kept secret. "The LEGO brick is a simple building system that is scalable to the ambition of the builder," he explained. "There is nothing else like it anywhere. It encourages creativity on a basic level—place a pile of bricks on the floor of a waiting room, and watch what happens. People will play and build."

Bibliography

Books

Bedford, Allan. *The Unofficial LEGO Builder's Guide.* San Francisco: No Starch Press, 2005.

Brown, Kenneth. *The British Toy Business: A History Since 1700.* London: Hambledon Continuum, 1996.

Clark, Eric. *The Real Toy Story: Inside the Ruthless Battle for America's Youngest Consumer.* Free Press, New York: Free 2007.

Fantasia Verlag GmbH. *LEGO Collector: Collector's Guide.* Fantasia Verlag GmbH, 2008.

Fleming, Dan. *Powerplay: Toys as Popular Culture.* Manchester, UK: Manchester University Press, 1996.

Fraser, Antonia. *History of Toys.* London: Spring Books, 1972.

Hanlon, Bill. *Plastic Toys: Dimestore Dreams of the '40s and '50s.* Atglen, PA: Schiffer Publishing, 1993.

Istok, Gerhard R. *The Unofficial LEGO Sets/Parts Collectors Guide 1949–1980s, Version 3.* Gerhard R. Istok, 2009.

Lundahl, Jenny. *The LEGO Brick in the Borderzone Between Forms of Protection.* Göteborg University, 2005.

May, James and Harrison, Ian. *James May's Toy Stories.* London: Conway, 2009.

McClary, Andrew. *Toys with Nine Lives: A Social History of American Toys.* North Haven, CT: Books, 1997.

McKee, Jacob H. *Getting Started with LEGO Trains.* San Francisco: No Starch Press, 2003.

Miller, G. Wayne. *Toy Wars: The Epic Struggle Between G.I. Joe, Barbie, and the Companies That Make Them.* Avon, MA: Adams Media Corp, 1999.

Schoenhaus, Ted and Stern, Sydney Ladensohn. *Toyland: The High-Stakes Game of the Toy Industry.* New York: Contemporary Books, 1991.

Walsh, Tim. *Timeless Toys: Classic Toys and the Playmakers Who Created Them.* Riverside, NJ: Andrews McMeel Publishing, 2005.

Wiencek, Henry. *The World of LEGO Toys.* New York: Harry N. Abrams, 1987.

Websites

http://bioniclestory.com

http://boardgamenews.com

http://brickartist.com

http://brickfilms.com

http://brickset.com

http://business.timesonline.co.uk/tol/business/industry_sectors/consumer_-goods/article5826790.ece

http://gizmodo.com

http://eurobricks.com/forum

http://isodomos.com/technica/technica.html

http://masscustomization.blogs.com/mass_customization_open_i/2005/08/lego_-factory_ch.html

http://news.bbc.co.uk/2/hi/business/4417585.stm

http://pc.ign.com/articles/497/497303p2.html

http://peeron.com

http://ps2.ign.com/articles/692/692888p1.html

http://thetyee.ca/ArtsAndCulture/2009/08/04/LEGOVideo

http://toynewsi.com/news.php?catid=176&itemid=14102

http://women.timesonline.co.uk/tol/life_and_style/women/the_way_we_live/article5372678.ece

http://www.architoys.net/toys/toylist1.html

http://www.azcentral.com/arizonarepublic/arizonaliving/articles/2008/07/26/20080726legos0726.html

http://www.bailii.org/uk/cases/UKPC/1988/3.html

http://www.bme.eu.com/article/Childs-play

http://www.brettspiel.co.uk/2009/07/lego-board-games-interview-with-cephas.html

http://www.brickarms.com

http://www.brickfetish.com

http://www.brickjournal.com

http://www.bricklink.com

http://www.bricksinmotion.com

http://www.brothers-brick.com

http://www.btha.co.uk

http://www.bzpower.com/story.php?ID=4419

http://www.dailymail.co.uk/home/moslive/article-1234465/When-Lego-lost-head–toy-story-got-happy-ending.html

http://www.dailymail.co.uk/home/moslive/article-1234465/When-Lego-lost-head–toy-story-got-happy-ending.html

http://www.europeanceo.com/news/home/ceo-profiles/article940.html

http://www.firstlegoleague.org

http://www.forbes.com/2008/08/12/lego-earnings-results-markets-equity-cx_je_0812markets21.html

http://www.guardian.co.uk/lifeandstyle/2009/mar/26/lego-billund-denmark

http://www.guardian.co.uk/lifeandstyle/2009/mar/26/lego-billund-denmark

http://www.hilarypagetoys.com

http://www.historia.com.pt/legos/clones/texts/kiddicraft.htm

http://www.independent.co.uk/life-style/gadgets-and-tech/news/warner-bros-to-carry-on-making-LEGO-video-games-until-2016-1916339.html

http://www.lego.com

http://www.legoland.com

http://www.licensemag.com

http://www.lugnet.com

http://www.minifig.co.uk/default.asp?id=10

http://www.miniland.nl/Miniland/Miniland%20home.htm

http://www.misbi.com

http://www.mocpages.com

http://www.nowgamer.com/features/356/building-an-empire

http://www.nytimes.com/2009/09/06/business/global/06lego.html?pagewanted=3&_r=2

http://www.readwriteweb.com/archives/most_popular_websites_for_kids.php

http://www.strategy-business.com/article/07306?pg=6

http://www.telegraph.co.uk/news/worldnews/1555834/LEGOs-grown-up-fans-build-global-fellowship.html

http://www.time.com/time/world/article/0,8599,1707379,00.html

http://www.toyretailersassociation.co.uk

http://www.wired.com/geekdad/2009/06/LEGO-for-a-living-conversation-with-a-master-builder

http://www.worldbricks.com

http://www3.sympatico.ca/richard.smallbone/postwar3.html

Photo Credits

Thank you to all the people who so kindly contributed their wonderful photos to this book.

Alex Eylar
Alex Howe
Andrew Martin
Ben Pillen (www.flickr.com/benlego)
Bjørn Richter
Chas Saunter
Christopher Doyle (www.reasonablyclever.com)
David Martin
Eileen Sandá (http://www.flickr.com/eileensanda/)
Fatima Pires Santos
Geraldine and Vivienne Page
Hamid (Katanaz)
Harlen Chen (www.flickr.com/photos/tomichen)
Ian Greig
Jens Nygaard Knudsen
Jeremy Tilston
Jordan Schwartz
Kent Quon
Maxx Kroes

Miwaza
Otto-vintagetoys
Owen J. Weber
Paul Tichonczuk (http://tracer.ca)
Pieter Stok
Richard Ashworth
Richard Wyatt
Ruben Saldana
StreetFly JZ
Thorskegga Thorn
www.brickartist.com
www.hilarypagetoys.com

Index